THE AGE OF TRANSLATION

The Age of Translation is the first English translation of Antoine Berman's commentary on Walter Benjamin's seminal essay 'The Task of the Translator'. Chantal Wright's translation includes an introduction which positions the text in relation to current developments in translation studies, and provides prefatory explanations before each section as a guide to Walter Benjamin's ideas. These include influential concepts such as the 'afterlife' of literary works, the 'kinship' of languages, and the metaphysical notion of 'pure language'. *The Age of Translation* is a vital read for students and scholars in the fields of translation studies, literary studies, cultural studies and philosophy.

Chantal Wright is Associate Professor at the University of Warwick. She is the author of *Literary Translation* (Routledge, 2016).

THE AGE OF TRANSLATION

A Commentary on
Walter Benjamin's
'The Task of the Translator'

L'Âge de la traduction: <<La tâche
du traducteur>> de Walter
Benjamin, un commentaire

Antoine Berman, Isabelle Berman and
Valentina Sommella

TRANSLATED AND WITH AN INTRODUCTION BY CHANTAL WRIGHT

Routledge
Taylor & Francis Group

LONDON AND NEW YORK

This translation published 2018
by Routledge
2 Park Square, Milton Park, Abingdon, Oxon OX14 4RN

and by Routledge
711 Third Avenue, New York, NY 10017

Routledge is an imprint of the Taylor & Francis Group, an informa business

Original edition © 2008 Presses Universitaires de Vincennes, Saint-Denis
English language translation © 2018 Chantal Wright

Original edition published by Presses Universitaires de Vincennes 2008 in French as
L'Âge de la traduction: <<La tâche du traducteur>> de Walter Benjamin, un commentaire

British Library Cataloguing-in-Publication Data
A catalogue record for this book is available from the British Library

Library of Congress Cataloging-in-Publication Data
A catalog record has been requested for this title

ISBN: 978-1-138-88630-8 (hbk)
ISBN: 978-1-138-88631-5 (pbk)
ISBN: 978-1-315-71493-6 (ebk)

Typeset in Bembo
by Out of House Publishing

Confrontation pensante de deux langues, le commentaire ne peut se traduire. Ceci est peut-être digne de réflexion.

Commentary, a thinking confrontation between two languages, cannot be translated. We might do well to ponder this.

Antoine Berman

CONTENTS

ACKNOWLEDGEMENTS

My sincere thanks go to Isabelle Berman, Valentina Sommella and the Presses Universitaires de Vincennes, and in particular to Zoulikha Bendahmane, for granting the rights to the English-language translation of Antoine Berman's text. I would also like to thank Fernando Concha Correa, Corinne Prigent and David McCallam, Johannes Haubold, and Joe Peschio, for answering questions relating to Spanish, French, Ancient Greek and Russian respectively. My thanks to Jean Boase-Beier for kindly sharing a pre-publication copy of her essay on Walter Benjamin, and to Paul Michael Lützeler for identifying the text on translation by Hermann Broch that Antoine Berman mentions in his commentary. I would also like to thank Lawrence Venuti, Karen Van Dyck, Maureen Freely and Cecilia Rossi for conversations and encouragement at various stages along the way. With much gratitude to my editor Michelle Bolduc for her insightful comments on the manuscript and to Laura Sandford, Hannah Rowe and Louisa Semlyen at Routledge. My thanks also to Tina Lupton and Heiko Henkel for their generosity in enabling a highly unofficial translation residency at the Black Diamond in Copenhagen in 2017. Finally, to Dan Vyleta, thank you for enthusiastically puzzling over Benjamin's syntax with me and for understanding the value of this commentary. *Ja, und mit dem Hölderlin hätten wir noch ein Hühnchen zu rupfen.*

TRANSLATOR'S INTRODUCTION

This is an introduction to a translation of a commentary on an introduction. It is an introduction to an English translation of a French commentary written about a German text that itself is an introduction of sorts, since it prefaces the German author's own translation of a French text, Baudelaire's *Les Fleurs du mal*. From the start, then, we find ourselves in a hall of mirrors.

In 1984–5, French translation theorist Antoine Berman (1942–1991) gave a series of lectures at the *Collège international de philosophie* in Paris that, in the sum of their parts, formed a commentary on German philosopher and cultural theorist Walter Benjamin's essay 'Die Aufgabe des Übersetzers' (1923), an essay most commonly known to the English reader as 'The Task of the Translator'. Paul de Man (1986) and Jacques Derrida (1985) also lectured and wrote, respectively, about 'The Task of the Translator', but Berman's book-length commentary constitutes the most extensive engagement with Benjamin's short (thirteen-page) yet incredibly dense 'prologue', a text that Berman describes as *the* twentieth-century text on translation, but a text that is often ignored or dismissed on the grounds of its obscurity.

Like much of Antoine Berman's work, his commentary was published posthumously, in 2008. Berman's wife Isabelle Berman, with the collaboration of Valentina Sommella, created the manuscript on the basis of the cahiers that Berman kept in preparation for his lectures. Isabelle Berman also had access to recordings of the lectures, to which she listened at the end of the process of editing Antoine Berman's notebooks. She writes about the editorial process in the editor's note which follows this introduction, addressing the tension between the written and the oral modes that arises from the cahiers' function as a preparatory aid to the lecture process. Like Isabelle Berman, I have retained the term 'cahier' to describe the text's subdivisions, rather than using the conventional 'chapter', in an *hommage* to Berman's notebooks.

Walter Benjamin's essay was first published in 1923 as a preface – Berman settles on the word 'prologue' as the most apt nomenclature for the text – to his German translations of Baudelaire's collection of poems *Les Fleurs du mal* (this collection was first published in French in 1857). In his first, introductory cahier, Berman notes the complete absence of any mention of Benjamin's Baudelaire translation in 'The Task of the Translator':

> Normally, when a translation prologue aims to have a more general or theoretical reach, it focuses on the translation that it is introducing. This is almost a law of the genre: consider Humboldt with Aeschylus' *Agamemnon*, George with *Die Blumen des Bösen*, Bonnefoy with Shakespeare's *Hamlet*, Meschonnic with *Le Chant des Chants* … Always, without exception, when translators preface their work, they discuss the translations they have created. We find nothing of the sort in Benjamin, and because this is too out of the ordinary not to have been deliberate, it indicates a desire to produce a *different* kind of discourse on translation.
>
> *(Berman 2008:35)*

Berman goes on to argue that the paradox inherent in this prologue that fails to focus on the translations of Baudelaire it precedes is indicative of a wider gulf between discourse on translation and the experience or practice thereof. The paradox of the prologue is joined by a paradox in the prologue's title: the translator is so little discussed in Benjamin's text, Berman argues, that his prologue could just as well have borne the title 'The Task of Translation' (Berman 2008:36). Taking these two paradoxes as his starting point, Berman sets out to comment on Benjamin's text and on the only French translation in existence at the time of his lecture series. 'La tâche du traducteur' was the work of philosopher and historian Maurice de Gandillac (1906–2006), the man who introduced Benjamin's texts into France. Berman worked from Gandillac's own 1971 revision of a first, 1959 attempt at translating Benjamin's text. As part of the commentary, Berman offers re-translations of selected passages from Benjamin's text and suggests ways in which Gandillac's translation might be altered but also discusses how this translation influenced his own thinking on Benjamin's text.

★★★

In her translator's introduction to Berman's final work *Towards a Translation Criticism: John Donne* (1995/2009), Françoise Massardier-Kenney states that she wishes to 'make accessible to a wide number of readers the entirety of a text that is crucial to our understanding of what translation is' and to avoid the 'simplification of [Berman's] ideas' that has tended to come about because of the unavailability of his work in English translation (2009:xi). There was something of this in my own desire to translate *L'Âge de la Traduction* but, if I am very honest, I was primarily motivated by the thought that reading and translating Berman's commentary would offer an unparalleled intensity of engagement with Benjamin's text – for myself, and subsequently for the interested reader of my translation. Furthermore, the translation project offered the opportunity to work trilingually, to spend a period of time living between German, French and English; an opportunity, revelatory of a hubristic assumption on my part perhaps, to glimpse the 'pure language' that Benjamin argues is gestured towards when we translate the natural languages we use every day. Reading Benjamin's text through Berman's eyes, and through Berman's and Gandillac's translations, the tension between the materiality of language – the letter – and the reader's struggle for meaning – for content or what Benjamin calls 'substance' – would become a constant companion. In fact, Benjamin's text feels calculated to produce this tension, marked as it is by syntactic and lexical idiosyncrasy, by re-definitions of terms and by slippery signifiers. To use Berman's terminology, Benjamin's text both refuses and demands translation; this is the paradox that prompts Berman's commentary, which has its own slippages and idiosyncrasies. Now, when its translation has very much been 'abandoned' rather than finished, I feel the weight and the truth of two statements from Berman's commentary. The first is that of the original text's indifference to the act of translation, which is

> one of the most painful experiences a translator can have: to see the text with which he or she has been in the most intimate contact – an intimacy that one might call infinite, an intimacy that one might call the most intimate of intimacies that one can possibly have with a text – withdraw from the translator disdainfully, as though it has not been translated. *What appears to have taken place has not taken place.*
>
> *(Berman 2008:68)*

From beginning to end, I have spent some four years – with periods of greater and lesser intensity – working on this translation and yet at its close I could begin all over again, such is the text's complexity but also its self-containedness, its *accomplissement*.

The second statement from the commentary whose truth strikes me is that 'The Task of the Translator' is 'not quotable, nor can it be summarised' (2008:31) and that commentary is therefore the most appropriate – indeed the only – way of approaching Benjamin's text. Key terms and concepts from this text – 'afterlife'; the transparency of true translation – have become part of Anglophone literary and translation studies' conceptual vocabulary, but they reach us firstly through translation (an 'untrustworthy' medium, to borrow the term that Berman uses to emphasise the contingency of the translated letter in relation to the letter of the original (2008:19)) and secondly, these terms and concepts have been decontextualised, thus contravening Berman's assertion that 'none of its statements can be separated from the rest without them immediately becoming gratuitous and baseless' (ibid.). One cannot summarise Benjamin's text, nor can Berman's commentary on it be summarised, and the two texts are indeed fundamentally 'untouched' by my translational endeavours. Such is the situation at the close of translating this text.

★★★

Translating not one but two theorists of translation, both with very firm views on what translation is and is not, is an obvious invitation to anxiety, particularly since the discursive gap between the theory and the practice of translation greatly pre-occupied Benjamin – it characterised his own experience with Baudelaire – and is discussed at length by Berman in his opening cahier. How would the relationship between theory and practice play out in my own translation? In Berman's essay 'La traduction comme épreuve de l'étranger' (1985), translated into English by translation practitioner and theorist Lawrence Venuti as 'Translation and the Trials of the Foreign' (2000), Berman offers a 'negative analytic' of twelve tendencies in translation that deform the literary text. These tendencies range from clarification to the destruction of linguistic patternings. Each time I struggled with Berman's *s'accomplir* and *accomplissement*, for example, terms that he employs to translate Benjamin's *Erfüllung* [fulfilment, realisation, completion] but also to talk more generally about something that language and the literary text can do, a property that they can possess or work toward, his list of deforming tendencies was not far from my thoughts. The following examples from the second and third cahiers show that I have translated these two terms variously as 'fulfilment', 'realisation' and 'complete', nominalising the verb in the second and third examples given below, and opting for an adjective instead of a noun in the final example.

in its state of fulfilment [*Dans son accomplissement*], a literary text never concerns itself with a receiver. (Cahier 2)

In a poem, language is in a self-contained state of fulfilment [*s'accomplit purement en lui-même*]. (Cahier 2)

This relationship has produced a text which, in its textuality, is wholly translatable, because its goal is realisation [*sa visée est de s'accomplir*] within a language *where no particularising element is retained*. (Cahier 2)

There is a shift here from a perpetual temporality to an elevated temporality, that is to say to a different temporal 'sphere', a sphere where it is always the text that changes – it becomes, if not complete, at least the *promise of fulfilment* [*sinon accomplissement, du moins* annonce de l'accomplissement]. (Cahier 3)

Clearly the chain of *accomplissement* is disrupted in the English translation and new signifying relationships arise as a result, some consciously created and some not. But I have examined my translator's conscience and found it (almost) clear. It is clear, in part, thanks to the work of analysing the translator's unconscious begun by Antoine Berman back in the 1980s, work that was implicitly continued by Lawrence Venuti in his monographs *The Translator's Invisibility* (1995) and *The Scandals of Translation* (1998) and much more explicitly in the thought-provoking essay 'The Difference that Translation Makes: The Translator's Unconscious' (2002). These contributions have produced a greater awareness of the unconscious, culturally sanctioned drive to normativity in translation that often involves a failure to pay attention to such networks. Benefitting from this awareness, I have consciously endeavoured to be sensitive to Antoine Berman's use of *s'accomplir* and its associated forms, and to the other networks within his text; and thus any disruptions of these networks reflect conscious choices embraced on grounds of one of the myriad other factors (rhythm, voice, intelligibility) that a translator must consider. And there is a further sense in which my conscience is clear, tied up with the fact that Antoine Berman fails to sufficiently credit the translator with the ability to (re)establish networks in the target text.

> Commentary on a translated text [...] can only be a movement through meaning, whereas by its very nature, commentary is *commentary-on-the-letter*. In a translated text, the relationship between meaning and the letter is such that it allows only for analysis of the former, not for commentary on the latter. Since the text of a translation is not the 'letter', there can be no commentary *stricto sensu* on a translation.
>
> *(Berman 2008:19)*

This is ultimately an essentialist approach that pre-dates more recent thinking on how we might read and write translations (cf. Venuti 2008; Boase-Beier 2006, 2011), on how the translator's trace in a text is always there to be uncovered (cf. Hermans 2014), and indeed on how the translator establishes networks in the target text that are independent of or intermingle with those in the source (cf. Scott 2012a and 2012b). The letter of a translation is of course not the more fixed letter of the original; it can have rivals or complements in the letter of other translations of the same source text, but that is not to say that one cannot read the letter of a given translation as a wilfully constructed letter in its own right, as a 'writing-down' of a particular reading. If I have 'deformed' aspects of Berman's text therefore, I hope that I have nonetheless shaped an English-language text that has its own literary qualities and that reflects in its emphases a particular reading of Berman's text.

Berman also categorically states that the translation of commentary is an impossible task or at least that it cannot be undertaken 'without [the commentary] being profoundly altered' (Berman 2008:66). While it is true that translating a commentary that reflects on a German text in French – necessarily using the alignment and non-alignment of those two languages to think about what Benjamin's text might be saying – requires a degree of intervention and explanation to make it accessible to the English reader, it is also true that something interesting happens with the addition of a third language which Berman perhaps did not anticipate. The third language adds an extra layer that complicates matters but also creates additional space: 'gibt zu denken', 'gives [*pause for*] thought' as Heidegger says (1961:2), and as he is cited by Berman in Cahier 3.

I discuss examples of this interlingual complexity in my introductions to the cahiers. The German verb *verlangen*, for example, which Benjamin uses to describe the relationship of the literary text to translation, can be translated as either 'demand' or 'desire' – the literary text 'demands' translation, but within this demand there is also an element of desire. *Verlangen* is rendered by Berman using the French verb *désirer*, a verb that privileges the element of desire. English is unable to reconcile desire and demand within a single verb, but this interlingual play of signifiers in German and French brings the issue sharply into focus for the translator. Other examples include the German noun *Bedeutung* (*la signification*; meaning, significance and/or signification) and the verb *meinen* (*viser* and/or *voulu-dire*; mean, intend, want to say). Reading 'The Task of the Translator' in Berman and Gandillac's translations has enriched my engagement with Benjamin's text and highlighted conceptual nodes such as these. It has also given me the opportunity to mark tensions by translating some passages in deliberate counterpoint to Gandillac and Berman (whose translations are always translated into English in a literal form for the reader's reference). In the lexical – and at times syntactic – tensions between this literal translation of the French and my English translation, the English words can find a trace of the tensions inhabiting the original.

Where Berman's commentary – as distinct from Benjamin's essay – is concerned, what also helped make my translation a possible rather than an impossible task was that the firm views expressed by Berman elsewhere are offset by a refreshingly human and humane attitude to translation that is surely informed by his own experience of the practice. Yes, Berman says, Benjamin is difficult: 'It may well be that his texts cannot be completely "understood"' (Berman 2008:28). Yes, there are mistakes in Gandillac's translation – 'défaillances', a term that Berman borrows from a French translation of Freud and which I have translated as 'defaults' (ibid.:78); but there are mistakes in every translation, and particularly in first translations as Berman argues in an articulation of his now discredited 're-translation hypothesis' which suggests that subsequent translations always improve upon their predecessors. I have found 'défaillances' in some of Berman's re-translations of passages from Benjamin; Steven Rendall has a note on the 'défaillances' in Harry Zohn's English translation of Benjamin's text (Rendall 2000); doubtless readers will spot 'défaillances' in my translation of Berman's commentary and of Benjamin's text. Such mistakes demonstrate the complexity of these texts and the humanity of the translational endeavour. The same humanity can be found in the oral qualities of Berman's commentary. The cahiers, a preparatory aid for a performance given in a lecture theatre, contain a record of Berman's voice, a voice that is by turns regal, erudite, teasing and playful.

★★★

If Berman's views on translation are firm, Benjamin's are no less so.

> True translation is translucent, it does not cover the original text, does not block its light, but allows pure language to fall on the original all the more fully, as though strengthened by its own medium. Above all this requires literality in the transposition of syntax and precisely this literality establishes the word, not the sentence, as the primordial unit of the translator.
>
> *(Benjamin 1991:18)*

Benjamin holds up the notorious syntactic fusion found in Hölderlin's translation of Sophocles – the translation that ultimately 'enclose[d Hölderlin] in silence' (Benjamin 1991:21) – as *the* model for emulation. Such fusion or harmony between languages is achieved via literality in translation. If I have, in places, disregarded Berman's 'negative analytic', I have roundly ignored Benjamin's call for syntactic fusion. My translation of Berman's commentary does not fuse the syntax of English and French, nor do my partial translations of Benjamin's text fuse the syntax of German and English. It is impossible and even undesirable to escape Benjamin's syntax entirely, however, since it is both constitutive and characteristic of his thought. But it remains a central irony of my endeavour that translating Benjamin's text, a text that accords meaning a much lower status than the 'letter' – the physiognomy or materiality of signs – nonetheless involves a desperate struggle to impose some sort of meaning on it, to penetrate its opacity. It might be possible to offer a truly 'Benjaminian' translation of 'The Task of the Translator', but to do so one first has to form an opinion on what it is that Benjamin is proposing. We owe it to Benjamin to try to understand him, even if it should turn out that understanding is beside the point. Moreover, any desire to straightforwardly 'apply' Benjamin's thought to the practice of translation (of his own text or any other text) may itself be misguided. Berman describes Benjamin as 'a great translation *thinker* who is not a great translator' (Berman 2008:34); certainly what he proposes is nothing so bound as a method, nor is it necessarily a truth that can be either embraced or refuted.

But simply because Benjamin's ideas cannot be applied (and are therefore not a method) and do not attempt to account for some aspect of the translation process (and are therefore not a theory), does not mean that they have no relevance for translators. Berman's distinction between translation theory and reflection upon translation (2008:35, 161) is relevant here: Benjamin's text is the latter. It poses very serious questions about translation and literature that are fresh and radical and remain unacknowledged and unanswered today. Whereas language philosophy and cultural studies have embraced Benjamin's thought, Translation Studies have tended to underappreciate him, perhaps precisely because of the lack of applicability of 'The Task of the Translator'. Translators ultimately work in a marketplace and pursue a very practical kind of reading that results in a target text. There is suspicion of mysticism, of approaches that do not result in readable texts, and of theoreticians' pronouncements on the translational act.

And Benjamin's text *is* mystical, or at least mysterious. It centres on the singular nature and temporality of the work of art, on translatability as a property of a certain kind of text, and on translation as an act with metaphysical implications. It goes against the grain of twentieth-century linguistics' focus on the communicative properties of language, displays little interest in the reader who would come to dominate literary theory later in Benjamin's century, nor is it interested in the political and historical readings of literature that would be promoted by critical theory. There is no discussion whatsoever of translation's role as an ideological tool or cultural agent, even if Benjamin's championing of syntactic fusion is a version of the foreignisation that lies at the root of later ideological approaches to translation. Benjamin's essay is both radical and reactionary, and many of the ideas that it dismisses or challenges continue to dominate the contemporary theory and practice of literary translation today.

'The Task of the Translator' encourages the translator to step away from the commission in hand and to think about the question of why we translate – a powerful and important question, and one that all too often unthinkingly receives the standard humanistic answer: to make texts available to the 'ignorant' reader; to promote literary exchange. This is a valid answer, but not the only one, perhaps not even the main answer. Benjamin's text asks us to ponder why *else* we translate. It also encourages us to reflect on the nature of language and literature, the relationship between literariness and translatability and between the 'self-same' (Venuti's translation of the French adjective 'propre', cf. Berman 2000) and the foreign, about language as an aspect of human-ness, an aspect that also connects us to the divine. Benjamin's notion of syntactic fusion, of two languages moving into one, may seem absurd within the framework of the marketplace; it is also profound. It reflects an understanding that difference is ultimately located in the way languages sequence and order thought via grammar. From a contemporary, post-cognitive-turn perspective, a translation that attempts such fusion could be framed as an attempt at restructuring the brain. On so many levels, Benjamin thus asks us to think differently.

Benjamin the prose stylist – as distinct from Benjamin the philosopher of translation – is certainly a cognitive challenge for the translator. Benjamin pushes German syntax to the limit, using endless clauses but adhering only idiosyncratically to the language's robust rules for comma usage and favouring unconventional prepositions and collocations; 'information' is ordered eclectically and thought is always elliptical. Berman discusses the logic of the digressions in Benjamin's text in Cahier 4. Although Benjamin's sentences are, technically speaking, grammatically coherent, one finds oneself uncertainly seeking the referents of pronouns in earlier sentences; the reading experience is thus far from linear.

Benjamin's syntactic complexity is compounded by the opacity of his conceptual terminology. As Berman points out:

> All Benjamin's texts are written at a level where the language is magical, which is to say unmediated by reason or illumination. They deal with concepts first by rendering them opaque, by withdrawing them from the communal sphere of use. In a second step, they render them more discursive, or more illuminating. Benjamin borrows almost all of his categories from tradition, but works them over in such a manner that they become almost undecodable or hermetic.
>
> *(Berman 2008:29)*

German, which has a comparatively small lexis and can flexibly combine morphemes, lends itself to such a manoeuvre. In German, units of philosophical language generally also have everyday meanings, whereas English tends to shift to a distinct register and separate lexis for philosophical and scientific discussion. This is part of the reason why Strachey's translations of Freud, for instance, famously created a new, more scientific terminology for psychoanalysis that is not present to the same degree in Freud's German writings. A similar danger is present when translating Benjamin, whose vocabulary is both utterly conventional and deeply strange – that is, magical.

The *Aufgabe* in the prologue's title is one such example of Benjamin's magical language, and Berman discusses this in Cahier 1 (2008:39–41). Derived from the verb *aufgeben*, which means 'to give in' (in the sense of handing something in or submitting something), but also 'to give up' (in the sense of 'abandon' or 'renounce'), in everyday life *die Aufgabe* means 'task' in the sense of 'chore', 'duty', 'responsibility' or 'small job', and can be combined with the noun *Haus* [house] to create the word for 'homework' – *die Hausaufgabe*, a task to be completed at home. Berman points out that *Aufgabe* acquired a new meaning with the Romantics, and particularly in Novalis, and that this meaning relates to *Auflösung*, which can mean 'dissolution' or 'dissipation', philosophically but also prosaically so, for example dissolving a powder in liquid. The noun *Lösung* which is present in *Auflösung* means 'solution' or 'answer'. *Aufgabe* is therefore not just a task but a surrender or a submission, a giving up of oneself, and the implication in Benjamin's title is that the translator's task is also a process of submitting, of dedicating oneself to a particular kind of translating, a translating that concerns 'the "dissolution" of a primordial "dissonance" in the sphere of language' (Berman 2008:40). The English and French languages are ill-equipped to deal with this magical melding of the philosophical and the everyday, but it is here that the commentary does its work, complementing and supporting the translation. As Berman argues, citing Granoff and Rey, when translation is faced with untranslatable terms in the original text, it has to be accompanied by – or give way to – commentary (2008:73). As for this introduction, the time has (almost) come for commentary to give way to translation.

Chantal Wright
Stratford-upon-Avon, January 2018

Some textual notes on the translation of Antoine Berman's commentary

The circumstances under which the manuscript of Berman's commentary was produced mean that the French source text for my English translation inevitably has omissions and errors which, nonetheless, bear important witness to the text's origins as an oral performance piece that was delivered in a public seminar and left unedited at the time of Antoine Berman's death. Many texts and writers are mentioned or cited in the French source text without bibliographical references. These missing references have been added to my English translation wherever possible, but I have not always been able to locate citations that may have occurred anywhere in the totality of a writer's oeuvre and were potentially misremembered or paraphrased, as was the case with some of the citations that I was able to identity after much sleuthing. Berman's writing is characterised by the use of italics for what I will call Bermanisms – self-coined phrases that acquire their own textual gravity and are often also hyphenated, for example *pulsion-de-traduire* [*urge-to-translate*] (2008:34); *lecteur-de-traductions* [*reader-of-translations*] (ibid.:31) – and for the emphasis of key words, phrases and ideas, for example *Ce qui paraissait avoir eu lieu n'a pas eu lieu* [*What appears to have taken place has not taken place.*] (2008:68). Berman's use of French *guillemets* [« »] is also florid. Since so many references were absent from the French commentary, it was not always possible to differentiate between the use of *guillemets* for (unreferenced) citations and their use for emphasis. I have exercised my judgement and not rendered the *guillemets* with the equivalent inverted commas or quotation marks on occasions where these appeared unnecessary or excessive. If this constitutes what Berman dismisses as *peignage* [combing] (ibid.:171), so be it. The Berman of my English translation is still, I believe, sufficiently idiosyncratic.

The handful of citations from Ancient Greek were rendered with missing or incorrect diacritics in the French source text. These citations appear uncorrected in the body of the English translation; corrected versions are given in the accompanying notes. I am grateful to Johannes Haubold of the Department of Classics and Ancient History at Durham University for these corrections.

Antoine Berman worked from Walter Benjamin's German text and a revised version of Maurice de Gandillac's French translation thereof, the version published in *Œuvres I, Mythe et violence* (1971). The revisions in the 1971 edition were Gandillac's own. Gandillac's was the only existing French translation at the time Berman gave his seminars in 1984–5. It was first published in 1959 in the single volume *Œuvres choisies* and still forms part of the first volume of Gallimard's most recent three-volume edition of Benjamin's works, *Œuvres I* (2000), but in a version edited by Rainer Rochlitz. A further French translation, by Martine Broda, was published in 1990 (in *Po&sie* 55, pp.150–158).

Since the excerpts from Gandillac's translation and those fragments that Berman either translated anew into French or offered in a revised version of Gandillac's translation are key for the *sens* of Berman's commentary, I have retained them, in French, in this English translation. I have provided literal English translations and additional explanation where necessary to aid the English reader's understanding of discussion of the French translation(s), bearing in mind the need to address Berman's assertion that 'commentary, a thinking confrontation between two languages, cannot be translated' (Berman 2008:66) – or at least not without profoundly altering the nature of the text. This English translation of a French-language commentary on a German text (and on an existing French translation of that German text) is necessarily a complex endeavour that requires of its readers a willingness to engage with the multilingual and to enter into a space that uses languages (*les langues*) to reflect on language (*le langage*) as an entity that has both a material and a spiritual aspect. This is very much in keeping with the preoccupations of 'The Task of the Translator'. Nonetheless, I have prefaced each cahier with an introduction that highlights key areas of linguistic and conceptual difficulty in the particular passage from Benjamin's text under discussion and reflects upon insights gained from Berman's French translation.

When I embarked upon this project, I had originally contemplated bringing discussion of the four existing English translations of Benjamin's essay into Berman's commentary, to echo Berman's use and re-translation of Gandillac's version as a means of thinking about Benjamin's text. I soon abandoned this idea, for various reasons, some to do with time and space, but more properly because I felt that this was a translation of Berman's engagement with Benjamin rather than an investigation of how Benjamin has been represented and interpreted in the English-speaking world. I was also concerned that the density of the text is already such that an extensive commentary on the commentary might render the text unreadable. Engagement with these four translations is important and will find expression in another forum, hopefully accompanied by a complete re-translation of Benjamin's prologue, a text which, as is the case with the greater part of Benjamin's work and indeed much philosophical writing in German, has not yet found a female translator.

The French source text uses footnotes for both bibliographical references and authorial asides. This English translation uses the Harvard citation system; bibliographical references have therefore migrated into the body of the text. Berman's remaining digressive footnotes have become end-of-chapter notes. My own notes have been placed in square brackets in order to distinguish them from Berman's and those of his editors.

All translations from Walter Benjamin's texts and correspondence in this commentary are my own. I have worked from the standard German edition of Walter Benjamin's writings, the *Gesammelte Schriften*, which is edited by Rolf Tiedemann and Hermann Schweppenhäuser, and published by Suhrkamp Verlag (1991); and from the two-volume edition of Benjamin's correspondence, *Briefe*, which was edited by Gershom Scholem and Theodor W. Adorno, and published by Suhrkamp Verlag (1978 but copyrighted in 1966).

The most complete collection of Walter Benjamin's writings in English translation is the four-volume *Selected Writings*, which is edited by Marcus Bullock and Michael W. Jennings, with texts translated by a number of translators, and published by Harvard University Press (1996–2003). The standard edition of Walter Benjamin's correspondence in English translation is *The Correspondence of Walter Benjamin 1910–1940*, translated by Manfred R. Jacobson and Evelyn M. Jacobson with contributions from other translators, and published by The University of Chicago Press (1994). The Jacobsons' translation is based on the same German edition of the correspondence from which I have worked. There are four existing English translations of 'The Task of the Translator', by Harry Zohn (1968), Hynd and Valk (1968), Steven Rendall (1997/2012), and J.A. Underwood (2009) respectively. Zohn's translation was first published in the collection *Illuminations* (1968) and can now be found in the first and second editions of *The Translation Studies Reader* (2000 and 2004). Hynd and Valk's translation, first published in the journal *Delos*, is included in the anthology *Translation – Theory and Practice: A Historical Reader*. Rendall's translation was first published in the journal *TTR* (1997) and is now included in a revised version in the third edition of *The Translation Studies Reader* (2012). Underwood's translation features in a Penguin anthology of Benjamin's texts entitled *One-Way Street and Other Writings* (2009). Engagement with multiple translations of a text enhances appreciation of that text irrespective of whether one has access to the text in its source language or not. My own understanding of Benjamin's text in German has been immeasurably enhanced by my reading of Gandillac's and Berman's respective translations, and by the four existing English translations.

Texts by Walter Benjamin discussed in *The Age of Translation*

For ease of reference, texts by Walter Benjamin cited in Antoine Berman's commentary are listed below, in the order in which they appear in Berman's discussion. For each title, the following bibliographical details are given: the most commonly used English title(s) of the text; the German title and its date of composition or publication (these dates are taken from the Harvard University Press edition of the *Selected Writings*); the names of the text's translator(s) with the first date of publication of their English translation(s). Many of these translations are included in the Harvard University Press four-volume edition. Full bibliographical references for the German texts are given at the end of the individual chapters in which these texts are cited.

'The Task of the Translator' or 'The Translator's Task' ['Die Aufgabe des Übersetzers', 1923]; translations by Harry Zohn (1968), Hynd and Valk (1968), Steven Rendall (1997/2012), J.A. Underwood (2009).

One-Way Street [*Einbahnstrasse*, 1928]; translations by Edmund Jephcott (1978), J.A. Underwood (2009).

'On Language as such and on the Language of Man' ['Über Sprache überhaupt und über die Sprache des Menschen', written in 1916, unpublished in Benjamin's lifetime]; translation by Edmund Jephcott (1978).

'On the Mimetic Faculty' ['Über das mimetische Vermögen', written in 1933, unpublished in Benjamin's lifetime]; translation by Edmund Jephcott (1978).

'Doctrine of the Similar' ['Lehre vom Ähnlichen', written in 1933, unpublished in Benjamin's lifetime]; translation by Michael Jennings, on the basis of prior versions by Knut Tarnowski and Edmund Jephcott (1999 [1979]).

'On The Programme of the Coming Philosophy' ['Über das Programm der kommenden Philosophie', written in 1918, unpublished in Benjamin's lifetime]; translation by Mark Ritter (1983–4).

Goethe's Elective Affinities [*Goethes Wahlverwandschaften*, published in 1924–5]; translation by Stanley Corngold (1996).

Berlin Childhood around 1900 [*Berliner Kindheit um Neunzehnhundert,* written in 1932–4 and revised in 1938, unpublished in Benjamin's lifetime]; translation by Howard Eiland (2002).

'Two Poems by Friedrich Hölderlin' ['Zwei Gedichte von Friedrich Hölderlin', written in 1914–15, unpublished in Benjamin's lifetime]; translation by Stanley Corngold (1996).

'Metaphysics of Youth' ['Metaphysik der Jugend', written in 1913–14, unpublished in Benjamin's lifetime]; translation by Rodney Livingstone (1996).

The Origin of German Tragic Drama [*Ursprung des deutschen Trauerspiels*, 1928]; translation by John Osborne (1977).

'Fate and Character', also known as 'Destiny and Character' ['Schicksal und Charakter', 1921]; translation by Edmund Jephcott (1978).

The Concept of Criticism in German Romanticism [*Der Begriff der Kunstkritik in der deutschen Romantik*, 1920]; translation by David Lachtermann, Howard Eiland and Ian Balfour (1996).

'Critique of Violence', also known as 'On the Critique of Violence' ['Zur Kritik der Gewalt', 1921]; translations by Edmund Jephcott (1978), J.A. Underwood (2009).

'Theses on the Philosophy of History', also referred to as 'On the Concept of History' ['Über den Begriff der Geschichte', written in 1940, unpublished in Benjamin's lifetime]; translation by Harry Zohn (1968).

Charles Baudelaire, A Lyric Poet in the Era of High Capitalism [*Charles Baudelaire: Ein Lyriker im Zeitalter des Hochkapitalismus*, first published in its current three-part format in 1974]. Of the three texts collected under this title in the *Gesammelte Schriften*, only one was published in Benjamin's lifetime. 'On Some Motifs in Baudelaire' ['Über einige Motive bei Baudelaire', written in 1939, published in 1940]; translation by Harry Zohn (1968); 'The Paris of the Second Empire in Baudelaire' ['Das Paris des Second Empire bei Baudelaire', written in 1938, unpublished in Benjamin's lifetime]; translation by Harry Zohn (1973); 'Central Park' ['Zentralpark', written 1938–9, unpublished in Benjamin's lifetime]; translation by Edmund Jephcott and Howard Eiland (2003).

Bibliography

Benjamin, W., 1978. *Briefe I und II. Herausgegeben und mit Anmerkungen versehen von Gershom Scholem und Theodor Wolfgang Adorno.* Frankfurt am Main: Suhrkamp.

Benjamin, W., 1991 [1923]. Die Aufgabe des Übersetzers. In: R. Tiedemann and H. Schweppenhäuser, eds. 1991. *Gesammelte Schriften.* IV.I. Frankfurt am Main: Suhrkamp. pp.9–21.

Benjamin, W., 2012 [1994]. *The Correspondence of Walter Benjamin 1910–1940. Edited and Annotated by Gershom Scholem and Theodor W. Adorno.* Translated from German by M.R. Jacobson and Evelyn M. Jacobson. Chicago: University of Chicago Press.

Benjamin, W., 2000 [1923]. La tâche du traducteur. In: W. Benjamin. *Oeuvres I.* Translated from German by M. de Gandillac, R. Rochlitz and P. Rusch. Paris: Gallimard. pp.244–262.

Berman, A., 1985. La traduction comme épreuve de l'étranger. *Texte*, 4, pp.67–81.

Berman, A., 2000 [1985]. Translation and the Trials of the Foreign. Translated from French by L. Venuti. In: L. Venuti, ed. 2000. *The Translation Studies Reader.* 1st ed. New York: Routledge. pp.284–297.

Berman, A., 2008. *L'Âge de la traduction.* Paris: Presses Universitaires de Vincennes.

Boase-Beier, J., 2006. *Stylistic Approaches to Translation.* Manchester: St. Jerome.

Boase-Beier, J., 2011. *A Critical Introduction to Translation Studies.* London: Continuum.

Broda, M., trans. 1990. La tâche du traducteur. *Po&sie*, 55, pp.150–158.

Bullock, M. and Jennings M.W., eds. 1996. *Walter Benjamin. Selected Writings. Volume One. 1913–1926.* Cambridge, Mass.: The Belknap Press.

De Man, P., 1986. *The Resistance to Theory.* Minneapolis: University of Minnesota Press.

Derrida, J., 1985. Des Tours de Babel. In: J.F. Graham, ed. *Difference in Translation.* Ithaca, NY: Cornell University Press. pp.165–207.

Eiland, H. and Jennings, M.W., eds. 2002. *Walter Benjamin. Selected Writings. Volume Three. 1935–1938.* Cambridge, Mass.: The Belknap Press.

Eiland, H. and Jennings, M.W., eds. 2003. *Walter Benjamin. Selected Writings. Volume Four. 1938–1940.* Cambridge, Mass.: The Belknap Press.

Gandillac, M. de, trans. 1959. La tâche du traducteur. In: *Œuvres choisies.* Paris: Juillard. pp.57–74.

Gandillac, M. de, trans. 1971. La tâche du traducteur. In: *Œuvres I, Mythe et violence.* Paris: Denoël/Les Lettres Nouvelles. pp.261–275.

Gandillac, M. de and Rochlitz, R., trans. 2000. La tâche du traducteur. In: *Œuvres I.* Paris: Gallimard. pp.244–262.

Heidegger, M., 1961. *Was heisst Denken?* Tübingen: Max Niemeyer Verlag.

Hermans, T., 2014. Positioning Translators: Voices, Views and Values in Translation, *Language and Literature,* 23(3), pp.285–301.

Hynd, J. and Valk, E.M., trans. 2006 [1968]. The Task of the Translator. In: D. Weissbort and A. Eysteinsson, eds. 2006. *Translation – Theory and Practice.* Oxford: Oxford University Press. pp.298–307.

Jennings, M.W., Eiland, H. and Smith, G., eds. 1999. *Walter Benjamin. Selected Writings. Volume Two. 1927–1934.* Cambridge, Mass.: The Belknap Press.

Massardier-Kenney, F., 2009. Translator's Introduction. In: A. Berman, 2009 [1995]. *Toward a Translation Criticism: John Donne.* Kent, Ohio: Kent State University Press.

Rendall, S., trans. 1997. The Translator's Task. *TTR,* 102, pp.151–165.

Rendall, S., 2000. A Note on Harry Zohn's Translation. In: L. Venuti, ed. 2000. *The Translation Studies Reader.* 1st ed. New York: Routledge. pp.9–11.

Rendall, S., trans. 2012. The Translator's Task. In: L. Venuti, ed. 2012. *The Translation Studies Reader.* 3rd ed. New York: Routledge. pp.75–83.

Scott, C., 2012a. *Translating the Perception of Text.* London: Legenda.

Scott, C., 2012b. *Literary Translation and the Rediscovery of Reading.* Cambridge: Cambridge University Press.

Underwood, J.A., trans. 2009. The Task of the Translator. In: W. Benjamin, 2009. *One-Way Street and Other Writings.* London: Penguin. pp.29–45.

Venuti, L., 1998. *The Scandals of Translation.* New York: Routledge.

Venuti, L., 2012 [2002]. The Difference that Translation Makes: The Translator's Unconscious. In: L. Venuti, 2012. *Translation Changes Everything.* New York: Routledge. pp.32–56.

Venuti, L., 2008 [1995]. *The Translator's Invisibility.* New York: Routledge.

Zohn, H., trans. 1968. The Task of the Translator. In: H. Arendt, ed. *Illuminations.* New York: Harcourt Inc. pp.69–82.

Zohn, H., trans. 2000 [1968]. The Task of the Translator. In: L. Venuti, ed. 2000. *The Translation Studies Reader.* 1st ed. New York: Routledge. pp.15–25.

FRENCH EDITOR'S NOTE

From the foundation of the *Collège international de philosophie*, Antoine Berman gave a number of seminars within the framework of his role as programme director.

This is the first time that one of Antoine's seminars has been published without him having edited it or prepared it for publication. He had intended his Benjamin seminar to become a book (the existence in his cahiers of several different written versions of the opening point to this), but he put it to one side. As this is the first attempt at a publication of this nature – one without the author's help – some explanatory preliminaries are necessary. From the outset, publishing the text as a 'documentary record' did not seem desirable. Nor could there be any question of rewriting or *peignage*. The approach would consist of reading and rereading the drafts as many times as necessary, passively so to speak, until they revealed themselves, until the writing asserted itself in its incredible density, all the while remaining anchored, on its surface, by recurrent terms, by threads, by necessary repetitions.

The publication of this manuscript has established, if not principles, then at least a basis for future publications of unedited seminar series.

From the beginning we had at our disposal the cahiers in which Antoine prepared his seminars, and recordings – generously made available by Wladimir Granoff – of almost all of the sessions. Was the written or the oral the right place to begin? Should the written and the oral be tackled together? Michel Deguy advised me to start from the written text, which I then did. But the question of the oral nature of this written text remained. The writing in the cahiers, seemingly written in haste and intended for oral delivery, did not really produce an oral text. A handful of direct addresses to the audience, the occasional summary of an earlier session and a few colloquial expressions were not really indicative of this. The written form imposed itself. But orality resonated within it, 'without any strain, silently even', in the form of a desire for orality.

Over the years, the manuscript progressed slowly. Several friends contributed their help. Valentina Sommella knocked at my door one day from Naples. Thanks to our late-stage joint effort and her *joie de vivre* and intelligence, *L'Âge de la Traduction* took the final step towards publication and reached those who were waiting to read it.

Valentina and I only listened to the recordings of the seminar series in the final stages. We expected that they would mirror the written text. And they did, yet over time we came to realise how radically different they were.

This is how the idea of giving people access to both 'texts' came about: this book is the first part of this project; making the recordings available will be the second part.

The order in which Antoine Berman's work has been published does not follow the order in which it was written; it has a different temporal logic. This commentary has been enriched by the reading of his final work on John Donne, which has a similar critical aim.

A few additional notes. The title *L'Âge de la Traduction* is taken from the text. Antoine Berman only used sub-headings in the first part of the seminar; he may well have added more but we left things as they were in order to respect the ever more demanding rhythm of the commentary. We also decided to divide the body of the text into 'cahiers' rather than into 'seminar sessions' or 'chapters'. The most recent editions of the works cited have been added to the footnotes and are placed in parentheses.

I would like to thank the *Centre national du livre* for its financial support.

I would like to thank Claire Miquel, and also Marie-Geneviève Freyssenet, Jonas Tophoven and Marc Berdet for their help.

My thanks also go to the founding members of the *Association Antoine Berman: les tâches de la traduction* and in particular, where this text is concerned, to Jean-Michel Rey, who shepherded this text to its readers.

I should also point out that there is a re-translation of 'La tâche du traducteur' by Martine Broda; this was published in *Po&sie* 55 (1991). Martine Broda attended Antoine's seminar and draws on it in her translation.

Isabelle Berman
Paris, August 2008

MY SEMINARS AT THE *COLLÈGE*

From 1984 to 1989, I gave regular seminars on *traductologie* at the *Collège international de philosophie* [...]. [These] seminars at the *Collège* [...] were very much led by my own research and writing. Like all the other seminars given at the institution, [they] were aimed at an audience of auditors (a mixed group of students; translators; researchers; psychoanalysts; semiologists etc.) and did not feed into a particular specialisation (whether part of a formal degree programme or not). Over the course of these five years, I covered the following topics:

- the idea of literalism in translation (Winter 1984)
- translation, mother tongue, foreign language (Spring 1984)
- philosophy and translation (a commentary on 'The Task of the Translator' by Walter Benjamin) (Winter 1984–85)
- the *défaillance* [failings] of translation (Spring 1986)
- the history of translation in France (Spring 1987)
- translational Babel: specialised translation and literary translation (Spring 1988)
- a commentary on the translations of John Donne and Friedrich Hölderlin (Spring 1989)

Before explaining the logic behind this series of seminars, I should explain that they formed part of the *Collège*'s 'translation' programme, of which I was the director, and that for the *Collège international de philosophie*, this programme, in accordance with the wishes of its founders François Chatelet, Jacques Derrida and Jean-Pierre Faye, occupied a central, or at least a privileged position in a certain respect, as an official document published by the *Collège* in 1988 makes clear:

> The international politics of the *Collège* are constructed around three kinds of problematic: tradition, translation, communication. How are we to interpret

the endless reiteration of differentiation, the local character of our apparatus for investigating problems? Is there such a thing as a polymorphism of the truth? Translation and translatability are a privileged axis, as theoretical as they are practical.

This summary appears to echo a report that I wrote for the *Collège*'s 'authorities' in 1987, a report that takes up the ideas sketched in *L'Épreuve de l'étranger* in 1984:

Of all the programmes at the *Collège international de philosophie*, the 'translation' programme has a particular status. This particular status resides first of all in the fact that all of the other programmes (and the seminars that belong to them), irrespective of theme, are concerned with translation: wherever and whenever we look, our intellectual work encounters the 'problem' of the translation of certain texts.

But the importance of translation for the *Collège* is more genuinely located in the fact that these various epistemologies or enquiries all encounter the question of translation (whether these are epistemologies that take an institutional form like philosophy, psychoanalysis, the sciences, law, literature and literary criticism, or the intersciences that exist only within the *Collège*). Let us start with those epistemologies and enquiries that already have a name and a status in our society.

For philosophy, in the first instance, translation has become a central question where what is at stake is philosophy itself and its own development [*devenir*]. This can be seen, first of all, in certain major philosophical works, whether by Benjamin, Heidegger, Wittgenstein, Quine, Derrida or Michel Serres. Where modern philosophy posits itself as reflection (a very multiple reflection) on *le langage* and *les langues*, it faces an imperious encounter with translation as a question. Where it posits itself as reflection on tradition and the history of tradition, it faces a no less necessary encounter. Where it discovers, little by little, that it is constituted by the 'transmission' of its fundamental categories, by the transfer of *Grundwörter* – the fundamental words of Greek thought from Greek to Latin, and then from Latin into the modern languages – it also faces an encounter with translation as (problematic) tradition. Where it finds itself, even within the West, divided into very different linguistic and cultural traditions (German philosophy, French philosophy, English philosophy etc.) it also faces a (this time horizontal) encounter with translation as a question. Where it poses the question of dialogue with forms of non-European and non-philosophical thought (India, Japan etc.), it also faces an encounter with translation. And where, finally, it is confronted with the global dissemination of its categories and its texts (there is 'philosophy' in North America, in Latin America, in China, in Africa etc.), it also faces this encounter. This extremely loose enumeration suggests the six obvious areas within which philosophy has to contend with the fact that translation constitutes its most urgent fate.

From the beginning, translation has been no less essential for the *Collège's* reflection on science and technology. [...]

Where psychoanalysis is concerned, to begin with we know that ever since *The Interpretation of Dreams*, the concept of translation has occupied a central position in its corpus. One only has to look at the number of articles, special journal issues, colloquia and roundtables devoted to translation by psychoanalysts to establish that translating is a more than burning question for them.

For literature (and correspondingly for literary criticism), the question of translation is no less essential, all the more so because literature has been explicitly posited as an act of translation from the era of German Romanticism through to Proust, Valéry, Pasternak, Roa Bastos etc.

Finally, any reflection on the law, whether it addresses the history of the law (and therefore its transmission) or the plurality of existing systems of legal thought, encounters the question of translation just as forcefully."

The seminars I gave at the *Collège international de philosophie* between 1984 and 1989 attempted to engage, albeit partially, with this problematic. At the same time they followed their own path.

The *first seminar* attempted to elucidate what had been the unquestioned assumption of my own activity as a translator: that translating was first and foremost and in its essence 'work on the letter'. In this seminar, the concept of literality was approached via analysis of great historical translations like Hölderlin's Sophocles, Chateaubriand's Milton and Klossowski's *Énéide*.

The *second seminar* interrogated the notions of 'mother tongue' and 'foreign language' and their relationship to translation. It studied representations of the mother tongue and translation in Dante, Nebrija, Du Bellay, Grimm and Schleiermacher; furthermore it looked at puzzling historical phenomena such as polylingualism in the Renaissance, self-translation at the beginning of the Age of Reason, and the practice of the 'variation' in the sixteenth and seventeenth centuries.

The *third seminar* was essentially devoted to a commentary on a major text about translation, Benjamin's 'The Task of the Translator'. The commentary pertained both to the German original and to the existing French translation (by Maurice de Gandillac). This seminar was highly instructive because commentary as a traditional mode of textual explication is also 'work on the letter' that is very close to translation. It allows for a micrological analysis of a translated text which has a considerable pedagogical impact. But what this seminar revealed was an unexpected phenomenon that surprised those who attended: the translation of Benjamin's text, although carried out by a distinguished Germanist philosopher (the author, among other things, of translations of Meister Eckhart and Novalis) displayed inexplicable 'faults': the omission of key sentences, misinterpretations verging on misrepresentation, shortcomings and terminological ruptures, the domestication of foreign words, rewritten citations and other puzzling errors. Where did these mistakes that so disturbed us as we encountered them over the course of the commentary come from? Not from the translator's incompetence but, it seemed, from his *psyche*. What was it about the act of translation that prevented its realisation?

These were the questions that led to a *fourth seminar* on the *défaillance* [failings] of translation, which attempted to develop an analytic of the translating subject. Attempted ... because it was as though an impenetrable fog weighed on any reflection relating to the subjectivity of the translator.

The *fifth seminar* took as its theme the origins and birth of translation in France, studying the works of the two great 'founding fathers', Nicole Oresme in the fourteenth and Jacques Amyst in the sixteenth century.

The *sixth seminar*, initially called translational Babel, brought together (and contrasted) specialised translation and literary translation. Within this framework the translation of children's literature was the subject of in-depth analysis (Grimm's fairytales in the versions by Armel Guerne and Marthe Robert).

The *seventh and final seminar* was a commentary on two love poems, one by John Donne, 'Going to bed', and the other by Hölderlin, 'Wenn aus der Ferne', and contrasted the originals with the French versions and one Spanish version (for Donne).

With this final commentary, my cycle of seminars at the *Collège* reached its conclusion.

Unedited text by Antoine Berman
Drôme, April 1991

Overture

CAHIER 1

Cahier 1 is Antoine Berman's 'overture' to his commentary on 'The Task of the Translator' and offers a general introduction to Walter Benjamin's thought. Berman argues for the suitability of the commentary form on two grounds, one of which has to do with the complexity of Benjamin's text which is 'not quotable, nor can it be summarised' (2008:31); and the other with the traditional link between translation and commentary, a link that Berman is keen to reinstate. The commentary contains re-translations by Berman (into French) of excerpts from Benjamin's text, which are sometimes directly contrasted with Gandillac's self-revised 1971 translation but more frequently stand independently. Berman argues, in an early articulation of the controversial 're-translation hypothesis' that would be proposed by Berman and Paul Bensimon in the journal *Palimpsestes* in 1990, that re-translation is the 'most critical, most accomplished vein that translation has to offer' (2008:20). The dual notion that re-translations necessarily represent an improvement on previous translations and that subsequent translations become more foreignising may be highly problematic, but some aspects of the re-translation hypothesis do merit further consideration. Re-translating a text when one has access – if indeed one chooses to access – previous translations is undoubtedly a task of a different order than translating a text that has never been translated before. Expectations of the translation are also of a different order. The translator does not come to the text unaffected by earlier readings and may well be influenced – deliberately or unconsciously – by the language of earlier translations. But acknowledging the influence of previous translations does not imply acceptance of teleological improvement. A more important point, and one that is illustrated more fully later on in the commentary, is that Berman's thinking on re-translation is ultimately a reflection on the relationship of tension that a literary text has with the natural language in which it is written at the time of its appearance, and on the translator's ability to represent that tension in the translating language. The re-translation hypothesis is ultimately founded on an enquiry into literariness that cannot be as easily dismissed as the hypothesis that grows out of it.

This introductory cahier also meditates on the gap between translation discourse – Berman further differentiates between translation 'reflection' and translation 'theory' – and the practice of translation. This gap is metonymically suggested by the absence of any reference to Benjamin's translations of Baudelaire in the 'prefatory' text that is 'The Task of the Translator'. It is indicative of a wider problem which, Berman argues, cannot in fact be overcome, since whenever discourse on translation is not methodological, that is, not concerned with how the transfer of meaning is to be effected, it is no longer 'homogenous with its object' (ibid.:38) and an unavoidable fissure between discourse and practice opens up.

In this cahier, we can also trace a trajectory from Antoine Berman to Lawrence Venuti, from Berman's discussion of the 'effacement' or 'self-obliteration' of the translator and of the translated text (2008:37) to Venuti's discussion (1998, 2008) of the 'invisibility' of the same. It is interesting that Berman discusses this issue at length but continues to assert the primacy of the source text for the pursuit of commentary, which 'by its very nature […] is commentary-on-the-letter' (2008:19). The letter of the translation remains 'untrustworthy' in Berman's eyes because it is not fixed like the letter of the original. Both Venuti's foreignising translation (2008) and Clive Scott's translation-as-experimental-writing (2012a, 2012b) suggest ways in which the translator takes responsibility for the letter of the translation, instituting new signifying networks that merit analysis. Arguably, also, Berman's insistence on the primacy of the letter over meaning in the translated text is a naïve relapse into the binary division of content and form.

In the section on concept and image in Benjamin's work, Berman ponders why 'the essence of translation is more satisfactorily illuminated through images than concepts' (2008:28) and why translation is so often defined by metaphor. In a lecture given at the University of Warwick on 25 October 2017, Lawrence Venuti argued that translation proverbs – themselves metaphorical entities – are a means of framing translation in a particular way, of locking it down to prevent us from rethinking what it is and what it might do. But the images that we will encounter in Benjamin's text – the mountain forest, the royal robe, the fragmented vessel – are of a different order than the clichéd and gendered *traduttore traditore* and *les belles infidèles*, not to mention the ubiquitous 'lost in translation'. The mountain forest in particular requires some work on the part of the reader, work that Berman exemplifies by engaging with it in detail in Cahier 8. In the language of cognitive metaphor theory, the reader has to consider which entailments are being mapped from the source domain onto the target. Translator Maureen Freely has argued that we resort to translation metaphors because 'it's very hard to define or even to describe the place in which [translation] puts you, the place from which you have to act, from which you have to think, from which you have to translate, from which you have to read' and that 'whatever metaphor you have for what [translation] is and what it involves, that metaphor only ever works for a while and then you go beyond it' (Freely and Wright 2017:98). This may well be one answer to Berman's question.

In this seminar series, we will be working towards a commentary on Walter Benjamin's 'The Task of the Translator' ['Die Aufgabe des Übersetzers'] (1991a).[1] I consider this text to be *the* twentieth-century text on translation. It may well be that each century produces but a single text of this calibre: an unsurpassable text; a text that becomes the point of departure for all further meditation on translation, even for those who disagree.[2] Benjamin's text sees the convergence of a range of encounters with translation: Bible translation; the translational experiences of German Romanticism (A.W. Schlegel and Tieck), and those of Goethe, Hölderlin and Stefan George. In fact, the entire *German* experience of translation is gathered together in this text. There are other texts on translation from roughly the same period – texts by Rosenzweig and Schadewaldt – and they too endeavour to gather together this experience. But even though Benjamin's text went almost unnoticed at the time of its publication, his is more radical than theirs.

In an article published in *Littoral*, Michel Cresta (1984) makes two pertinent observations. The first is that 'The Task of the Translator' can only be approached via *commentary*.[3] That Benjamin's text should reveal itself only through commentary is a crucial point. It is not in the least immaterial that a text concerned with translation can only be illuminated in this fashion.

Why?

There is an essential link between translation and commentary that extends back to (without being the exclusive purview of) the philosophical and theological (or religious) tradition. Any commentary on a foreign work entails translation – *is* translation, one might even say. Conversely, all translation entails an element of commentary, as medieval 'translations' exemplify. A fine example of an interlacing translation and commentary can be found in Proust's version of Ruskin (1906) where, page after page, the translated text is accompanied by all manner of observations. Proust's work (which is, moreover, extremely subjective) reminds us of something we have almost forgotten.

When critical discourse established itself as an autonomous entity, the traditional link between translation and commentary was broken. The time is ripe for it to be reinstated. There are Freud translations in France which point in this direction: I am thinking here of W. Granoff and J.-M. Rey's work in *L'Occulte, objet de la pensée freudienne* (1983), which admirably thematises commentary's return to translation. There is no reason why this radical interlacing of commentary and translation should not be extended to poetic and literary works – since these are the kind of works that legitimise this approach.[4]

Let us return to Benjamin. The fact that his essay reveals itself only through commentary is an implicit indicator of the close link between commentary and translation. Benjamin wrote about this immemorial link in *One-Way Street* [*Einbahnstrasse*] (1991b), and did so by linking it to the immemorial:

> Kommentar und Übersetzung verhalten sich zum Text wie Stil und Mimesis zur Natur: dasselbe Phänomen unter verschiedenen Betrachtungsweisen. Am Baum des heiligen Textes sind beide nur die ewig rauschenden Blätter, am Baum des profanen die rechtzeitig fallenden Früchte.
>
> *(Benjamin 1991b:92)*

> Commentary and translation are to the text what style and mimesis are to nature: the same phenomenon observed from different viewpoints. On the tree of the sacred text they are merely the eternal rustling of the leaves, on the tree of the profane, the timely falling of the fruit.[5]

If there is any truth to these remarks about commentary, then it follows – and this brings me back to Cresta's second observation – that commentary on a foreign text has to take the original, the work-embedded-in-its-language, as its point of departure.

There can in fact be no such thing as a legitimate commentary on a translated text. Not only because such a text would be 'untrustworthy', but because commentary operates within the realm of translation: it illuminates the original and its translation step by step as it unfolds. Every explanation of a word, sentence or expression is simultaneously their translation. Commentary on a translated text (which is commonplace) can only be a movement through meaning, whereas by its very nature, commentary is *commentary-on-the-letter*. In a translated text, the relationship between meaning and the letter is such that it allows only for analysis of the former, not for commentary on the latter. Since the text of a translation is not the 'letter', there can be no commentary *stricto sensu* on a translation. The dogmatic tone of these assertions will soften as we penetrate 'The Task of the Translator'.

What *is* possible, however, is a commentary on the source text accompanied by an analysis of its translation or translations. This is actually the most fruitful mode of commentary for a foreign text. It is more open; it opens up the original for those with no knowledge of the language of the source text. It is more radical, and on several levels. Working on the source text and on its translation gives access both to the *language* of the source text – to the manner in which poetry and thought operate within it – and to one's own translational *work*. This is where the commentary acquires a dual focus: it becomes a commentary on the source text (on the letter thereof) and an analysis of its translation (of the manner in which the letter of the source text has been transmitted). The commentary is then inevitably driven to re-translate, or rather to *translate in the vein of re-translation*, which is to say in the most critical, most accomplished vein that translation has to offer. Furthermore, engaging with the source text both in its own language and in another language allows for *illumination* of the text on multiple levels, and brings commentary closer to its translational essence.

To date there has been a single French translation of 'The Task of the Translator', a translation by Maurice de Gandillac, the person who introduced Benjamin into France. There is a general consensus that this translation is 'bad'. As we will conclude over and over again, it displays *the structural weaknesses of a first translation*. Cresta quite rightly says: 'His [Benjamin's] most important texts are badly translated, or at least they are deserving of re-translation (which is not quite the same thing)' (Cresta 1984:54).[6] It is *not* the same thing, and this is crucial for any translational thought. It is no less crucial that we recognise our debt to Maurice de Gandillac and the gift he gave us in the 'sixties.[7]

I will be working with the German text and with Gandillac's version thereof. Thus my comments on a text devoted to translation will be accompanied by the work of re-translating that text. Nonetheless, my work will not stray into territory that is more properly the purview of re-translation proper.

I have not defined what a *commentary* is. A definition will arise of its own accord as this commentary unfolds, its nature emerging little by little, since any commentary is a commentary on commentary.

There has also been no mention of methodology, precisely because questions of method are foreign to commentary. It should gradually become clear that this category of relationship to a text has its own laws, which are as rigorous and as restrictive as those of any method, if not more so.

There are certainly models for this sort of commentary, or at the very least sources of inspiration: the commentaries by Alain, Michel Alexandre, Heidegger, Romano Guardini, Levinas, Derrida, admittedly all very different from one another, are the ones that most readily come to mind as I embark on this endeavour.

But these readings, which have been so influential over the years, are not as important as the passage from *One-Way Street* that I cited earlier, and which I will cite again here because each of its sentences will dominate my commentary on 'The Task of the Translator':

> Commentary and translation are to the text what style and mimesis are to nature: the same phenomenon observed from different viewpoints. On the tree of the sacred text they are merely the eternal rustling of the leaves, on the tree of the profane, the timely falling of the fruit.
>
> *(Benjamin 1991b:92)*

Why has this passage had such a profound effect on me? The answer is of no consequence. I can only hope that my engagement with 'The Task of the Translator' will be *rechtzeitig*.[8]

I will broach 'The Task of the Translator' through a series of preliminary reflections. The first concern certain characteristics of Benjamin's thought, his *mode-de-penser*; the second, the position occupied by translation in his life and work.

The metaphysics of language

In addition to 'The Task of the Translator', my commentary assumes that you will be familiar with two further texts by Benjamin: 'On Language as such and on the Language of Man' ['Über Sprache überhaupt und über die Sprache des Menschen'] (1991c)[9] and 'On the Mimetic Faculty' ['Über das mimetische Vermögen'] (1991d).[10] I would also recommend that you read Benjamin's *Correspondence*.[11] Even though, strictly speaking, one should have read all of Benjamin's writings before attempting any interpretation of 'The Task of the Translator', reading these particular texts will place you on a solid footing. They contain the essentials of what Benjamin has to say about language and translation.

In Benjamin's eyes 'The Task of the Translator' was part of a greater whole, a metaphysics of language in which translation would occupy a pivotal position – more so than in conventional philosophies of language. To a certain extent 'translation' would come to replace 'communication', a notion that Benjamin spurned. This metaphysics of language underpins all of his writing, from beginning to end, but Benjamin never developed it systematically. Nonetheless, it presides over 'The Task of the Translator', and this explains the extreme importance that the author attached to this text. In a letter to his friend Scholem, Benjamin wrote:

> This subject is so pivotal for me that I do not yet know if I can develop it with sufficient freedom at this current stage of my thought – that is even assuming that I can succeed in illuminating it.
>
> *(Benjamin 1978:259)*[12]

Benjamin's metaphysics of language is founded on a credo that he once expressed in the following fashion to Hofmannsthal: 'every truth has its house, its ancestral palace, in language' (ibid.:329).[13]

This credo in turn points us to a more fundamental postulate, one that Benjamin never thematised as such: that language is above all a 'house', an 'ancestral palace'. Benjamin's critique of a theory of language that reduces language to a means of communication or a mere system of signs proceeds from this postulate. If language is a 'house', it is neither a tangible means … nor an instrument. Benjamin expressed this elsewhere, differently, by saying that language is a 'medium', a *milieu*. Language is the milieu of all communication, but it is not communication itself. It is not a homogenous medium: it contains zones of varying densities. Translation is the movement from a less populous zone to a more populous one.

The primordial metaphor of language that runs through the entire German tradition, from Luther to Grimm and Heidegger, is easily recognisable within the image of the 'house'. For Benjamin, and within this tradition, language has to be a 'house'. Or rather: *the* house.[14]

Benjamin is in fact tackling the problematic of language just as Hamann did with Kant in the eighteenth century: the 'pure reason' with which this philosopher occupied himself is rooted in language and its forms. Hamann said:

Language, the mother of reason and *revelation*, their A und Ω.
(Hamann as cited by Benjamin 1991c:147)[15]

If I were as elequent as Demosthenes, I would still only have to repeat a single word thrice: reason is language, λóγος. I chew on this marrowbone and I will chew myself to death on it.
(Hamann as cited by Heidegger 1959:13)[16]

The reference to Hamann is explicit in 'On Language as such and on the Language of Man', and the development of a metaphysics of language as an extension of Kant's metaphysics of reason features in another text from the same period: 'On the Programme of the Coming Philosophy' ['Über das Programm der kommenden Philosophie'] (1991f):

In his awareness that philosophical knowledge is absolute, certain and *a priori*, in his awareness that these aspects of philosophy are equal to mathematics, Kant has lost sight of the fact that all philosophical knowledge finds its only expression in language and not in formulae and figures.
(Benjamin 1991f:168)[17]

Within this context, translation is one of the royal roads leading to a metaphysics of language.

This metaphysics is a metaphysics of pure language, *reine Sprache*. This choice of expression – which first appears in 'On Language as such' and which plays a central role in 'The Task of the Translator' – not only evokes the Adamic language which, in the Bible, pre-exists the fragmentation of languages at the Tower of Babel: it correlates precisely with the Kantian term 'pure reason', *reine Vernunft*. Pure reason is founded on pure language, the language that pre-exists all empirical languages and makes languages of them. Pure language is the ultimate object of philosophical reflection, the language of truth. Empirical languages both contain it and conceal it, they gesture toward it and debase it. The task of philosophy is to discover it – and that is also the task of translation, as we will see. This, for Benjamin, is how philosophy and translation relate to one another.

The metaphysics of pure language is also complemented by a theoretical, practical and ethical *critique* of the ways in which language is being degenerated, a critique of all those things in the fields of literature, philosophy, politics etc., that threaten to reduce language to pure chatter, to a pure system of signs with no essence. Benjamin quite rightly observed that the 'house' of language was under threat, and more radically so in our epoch than at any other time; he quite rightly saw translation as one way of preserving language's 'house'. Defending language as a fundamental medium of experience and human existence was a categorical imperative for him. This critique threads through his work, from the beginning to the end of his life.

But, as I have already said, Benjamin's metaphysics of language was never fully developed. It is present in all of his texts in either a programmatic, fragmentary or a latent form.

Five characteristics of Benjamin's thought

Torso and fragment

If there is an image that characterises Benjamin's work, then it is that of the 'torso' or 'fragment'. Everything Benjamin wrote is governed by this sign; occasionally, he was moved to theorise it. A torso is a mutilated statue of which only the central section, the chest, heart and genitals remain. One of Rilke's poems, one of the few that Benjamin liked, 'Archaischer Torso Apollos' (1908),[18] celebrates the glorious power of this form, a broken piece of art reaching for fulfilment in its brokenness.[19] Benjamin's texts are not, however, fragmentary in the sense of being incomplete. Rather it is precisely because each of these texts *is* complete, rounded and finished that they are also irremediably fragmentary: torsos. The reader is confronted with *definitive sketches* – but sketches nonetheless. Whenever Benjamin wishes to develop a different axis of his thought, he has to reformulate it completely, using other means. There is no continuity between one text and another in the sense of progression. A text develops, forms a self-contained unit and comes to an end. The next text develops in a similar fashion and writes itself, in non-sequential fashion, into some kind of constellation with Benjamin's other texts. Benjamin's correspondence, and even his translations – given that he judged his translations of Baudelaire to be inadequate – display these traits too.[20]

This applies – *mutatis mutandis* – to *all* of Benjamin's texts. The French translator of the *Correspondence* very succinctly wrote: 'It is like a thread that is constantly broken by perfect chapters, the pages of an unwritten book' (Petitdemange 1979:346).[21]

This paradoxical state of incompleteness – paradoxical because it does not exclude a certain state of completeness – is also found at the level of *concepts*, which are rarely expounded or developed. 'Understanding' Benjamin therefore means finding the places where a particular thought appears under a different terminological guise, and attempting to (re)establish the constellation to which the concept belongs. This, by the way, is what Benjamin did with respect to Novalis's labyrinthine *Fragments* and with Schlegel.

It is a matter of seeking out the underlying systematicity of this broken writing, which draws its strength from its brokenness.

Diversity and sameness

Benjamin's oeuvre is extremely diverse, both from a thematic point of view and from the point of view of genre. It is hard to recognise the author of 'The Task of the Translator' in the author of an article on toys, or the author of *One-Way Street* or *Berlin Childhood around 1900* [*Berliner Kindheit um 1900*] (1991h) in Benjamin's speculative essays on language. This diversity cannot simply be explained in terms of the evolution of Benjamin's thought. There is a gulf between the abstraction of the big theoretical texts and the minutious sense of the concrete on display in *Berlin Childhood around 1900*. But there is more to it than this: irrespective of its content and its form, all of Benjamin's writing moves within the same element, to the extent that his thought is at the same time heterogenous and one. This is hinted at in a particularly fine passage in *Berlin Childhood around 1900* in which Benjamin recalls his childhood stockings, which were rolled up and tucked into themselves in such a manner that they looked like a 'small purse'. The little boy digs in this purse to find the 'sock on the inside', the 'contents'.[22] He discovers that once,

> the 'contents' had been wrested from their purse, the purse itself was no longer there. I could not put this puzzling truth to the test often enough: that form and content, outside and inside, 'the contents' and the purse were one. One – but in fact a third entity: the stocking that they had turned into.
>
> *(Benjamin 1991h:284)*[23]

Youth and maturity

The passage that I have just cited shows how a statement of the most abstract thought is rooted in a concrete – and child-like – perception. This is an (indirect) reminder of something that we should never forget: the majority of Benjamin's texts were written during his youth, at an age when Nietzsche, for example, was still confusedly formulating his intuitions. Benjamin could not be more different: almost from the beginning, his texts display a staggering maturity. His Hölderlin essay,[24] whose ideas far outstrip the most modern criticism, dates from 1914, when Benjamin was 22 years old. The essay on language dates from 1916 and 'The Task of the Translator' from 1921; Benjamin was 29 at the time. His key works were all written between the ages of 20 and 40. Extreme youth – extreme maturity; the latter sometimes makes us forget the former, another vital component of Benjamin's work, which explains the interest he displayed in youth (he wrote a 'Metaphysics of Youth' ['Metaphysik der Jugend'])[25] and childhood. This in turn explains the fragmentary, unfinished nature of his writings. When reading 'The Task of the Translator', one should bear in mind that its author was still quite young, young in translation as well, having translated only a handful of Baudelaire's poems.

Concept and image

Benjamin's thought operates within a sphere of extreme *conceptuality*. We will return to the opacity that is peculiar to this conceptuality in a moment. But above all else Benjamin's thought is distinguished by the occurrence of key *images*, which are themselves opaque. Benjamin also thinks via images, and these serve to buttress his thought. He spoke, in *Berlin Childhood around 1900*, of 'the images and allegories that preside over my thought like the caryatids on the balconies above the courtyards of West Berlin' (Benjamin 1991h:294).[26]

'The Task of the Translator' is rich in images foregrounded within a thought process that is highly abstract. This is why it is necessary not only to eluci-date the conceptual labyrinth of Benjamin's thought, but also the images that are scattered throughout it. The same is true for the passage from *One-Way Street* cited above, where the relationship of commentary, and of translation, to the source text is fixed both conceptually (but without being made explicit) and metaphorically. As it happens, this text is one of the finest examples of Benjamin's writing.

The question is: why is the essence of translation more satisfactorily illuminated through images than concepts? Why is translation so often defined – not only by Benjamin – through metaphor?

Moreover, the definition of translation through metaphors and images occurs in an opaque and obscure fashion.

Obscurity and illumination

Benjamin's reader cannot help but be struck by the obscurity of his texts. It may well be that his texts cannot be completely 'understood'. But they are illuminating nonetheless. What form does this illumination, tempered to a significant degree by obscurity, take? This will remain a puzzle. Benjamin has an esoteric bent. But he is not in control of it, even though he made something of a 'theory' of it. Several factors feed in to this esotericism.

The first is that there is no didactic aim to Benjamin's writing. Despite the existence of interlocutors such as Scholem, Hofmannsthal or Adorno, his thought unfolds in solitude. It is enclosed within itself.

There are two essential categories in Benjamin's life and work: *secrecy* and *mystery*. These categories are also present in his writing. Very early on he writes to Buber: 'Everything that is wholesome about writing, every effect of writing that isn't profoundly devastating, is rooted in its (the word's, language's) mystery' (Benjamin 1978:126).[27]

Elsewhere – in his thesis on German tragic drama – he says: 'Truth is not an exposé that destroys mystery but a revelation that does it justice' (Benjamin 1991k:211).[28]

There is no conflict between this quasi-sanctification of mystery – of language *as* mystery – and a desire for dialogue. But there is a rejection of communication in the modern sense, in the sense that is predicated on the assumption of a referen-tial sphere. There is no referential sphere in Benjamin, and no effort to open up his thought to the reader. In the same letter to Buber, he writes:

> I can understand writing poetically, prophetically, materially, with reference to its effect – but in any case only *magically*, in other words, im-*mediate*-ly. [...] No matter in which forms language proves itself effective, it will not do this

by mediating content but through the purest exploration of its dignity and
its essence.

(Benjamin 1978:126–7)[29]

In other words (and with an emphasis on the word 'pure', which often crops up in
Benjamin when language is being discussed), language only exists as *reine Sprache*,
rein, pure, indicating a refusal to communicate anything, to express anything, to
signify anything, a refusal to enter into the referential sphere. But language as pure
language exists as mystery and – in as much as language has agency – as *magic*. The
unexpected correlate of the notion of 'mystery' is – and this is key in Benjamin –
magic. The word may well come as a surprise.

That which is magical achieves its effects without any mediation. All Benjamin's
texts are written at a level where the language is magical, which is to say unmediated
by reason or illumination. They deal with concepts first by rendering them opaque,
by withdrawing them from the communal sphere of use. In a second step, they render
them more discursive, or more illuminating. Benjamin borrows almost all of his categories from tradition, but works them over in such a manner that they become almost
undecodable or hermetic. Within this hermeticism, his texts are replete. Benjamin was
perfectly aware of this tendency in his thought. He explains himself to Hofmannsthal:

> Years ago I tried to liberate the old words 'fate' [*Schicksal*] and 'character'
> [*Charakter*] from the terminological fray and to do justice to the life they
> originally enjoyed within the German spirit of language. But today this very
> attempt makes it extremely clear to me which difficulties one encounters in
> this manoeuvre, difficulties that have remained unsolved. At those junctures
> where insight proves inadequate to the task of loosening the petrified con-
> ceptual vice, it finds itself tempted, so as not to fall back into the barbarism of
> formulaic language, not only to dredge the linguistic and conceptual depths
> but to drill them. This forcing of insight clearly undermines the essay in
> question[30] and I ask you to consider me sincere if I attribute the cause of cer-
> tain obscurities therein to myself.
>
> (Benjamin 1978:329–330)[31]

In other words, it is a matter of giving words an *aura* in which clarity and obscurity come together. Benjamin talks about Friedrich Schleiermacher in terms of
'mystical terminology'. The same applies to Benjamin, especially if we can listen for
the word 'mystery' in 'mystical'. His terminology is organised along the lines of an
unfinished labyrinth.

Torso and fragment
Sameness and diversity
Youth and maturity
Image and concept
Obscurity and illumination

These five dimensions of Benjamin's thought should be at the forefront of our minds, both because we will come across almost all of them in 'The Task of the Translator' but also because certain critics have attacked what they call the 'cryptic' character of this text, seeing in it only cleverly disguised banalities. 'The Task of the Translator' is cryptic in a very particular sense – the one that Nicolas Abraham and Maria Torok (1978) have bestowed on the notion of '*crypte*'. 'The Task of the Translator' is a crypt in the sense that it both reveals and *hides* the essence of translation. Turning a text about translation into a crypt that conceals the very essence of translation was Benjamin's way of speaking to what he called, in his doctoral thesis on German Romanticism, 'the infinitely enigmatic nature of translation'.

It is the cryptic character of his text that necessitates a *commentary*. This is the only way of doing justice to the obscurity of 'The Task of the Translator'. Today the text is often quoted as if it were truth. But it cannot be 'quoted' because none of its statements can be separated from the rest without them immediately becoming gratuitous and baseless. 'The Task of the Translator' is not quotable, nor can it be summarised. But it can be commented upon. Its non-quotability, its irreducibility and, conversely, its commentability, are its essential characteristics, and this must be borne in mind as we analyse its contents.

Benjamin as translator

There are three elements to Benjamin's relationship with translation. We have seen that translation interests him as part of the framework of his speculative reflection on language and art. But he is also interested in it as a *reader-of-translations*.[32] His correspondence shows that he read Hölderlin's translations from Greek (which Germany was rediscovering at the time) very closely, as well as the translations of the German Romantics, with whose spiritual world he was intimately acquainted. He also read Stefan George's translations (Baudelaire, Shakespeare, Dante), and these, alongside Hölderlin's translations, could be said to have informed his own translations and his thinking about translation. Finally, he read, year after year, his friend Scholem's translations from the Hebrew (fragments from the Bible, texts by Agnon) and it was in the framework of a discussion of Scholem's translations, in 1917, that he formulated his vision of translation for the first time:

> Principally it should not be impossible for two languages to enter into the same sphere: on the contrary, that is the hallmark of all great translation and forms the basis of the few great works of translation that we have. In the spirit of Pindar, Hölderlin located for himself the same sphere in both German and Greek: love of two languages became *one*. But you are not as close to the German language as you are to the Hebrew and that is why you are not the person *called* to translate the Song of Songs; yet thanks to your reverent and critical attitude, you have not turned into one of those who translate without a calling.
>
> *(Benjamin 1978:142)*[33]

I should add that he also read Buber and Rosenzweig's attempts at translating the Bible – and didn't think much of them.

The third strand of his relationship to translation is *the act of translation itself.* From 1914–15 to 1921, Benjamin translated Baudelaire. This resulted in the 1923 publication of his translation of *Tableaux Parisiens* and its prologue 'The Task of the Translator'. This publication, to which we will return, marked the beginning of his 'translation years', which featured Proust (a co-translation)[34], Perse's *Anabase*, Balzac's *Ursule Mirouët*, Tzara, Bloy, Jouhandeau etc. Benjamin became a translator 'of the French'. Nonetheless, the enthusiasm he was able to muster for translation lay far beneath that which he felt for his critical work, which began to develop at the same time. Why?

The Baudelaire translation proved to be a failure, both in his own eyes and in the eyes of his closest confidantes. In the letter to Hofmannsthal cited above, Benjamin attempts to identify the reasons for his failure:

> Nine years have gone by from my first attempts at translating the *Fleurs du Mal* to the printing of the book, a period in which I was able to improve many aspects but which in its last phase also allowed me to see what was inadequate yet not open to 'improvement'. I have the simple but important fact in mind that the translation is metrically naïve. By that I do not mean simply the metrical stance of the translations as the fact that they did not trouble me in the manner announced in the prologue vis-à-vis literalism. [...] I am convinced that ultimately only metrical thoughtfulness in the translation of the *Fleurs du Mal* would make Baudelaire's style, a style that I would call the Baroque of banality, more intensely present than is the case in my translations.
>
> *(Benjamin 1978:330)*[35]

One only has to read his translations of several of Baudelaire's finest poems to realise the extent to which Benjamin's work remains formulaic and quasi-scholastic, especially when compared with George's efforts.

In the *Correspondence*, discussion of his Proust translation is characterised by a lack of enthusiasm for the most part. For Benjamin it was by turns an onerous task ('At bottom,' he wrote to Scholem, 'Proust makes me ill'), an 'unproductive encounter'[36] and a pointless undertaking, since he came to the conclusion that the essence of the author could not be conveyed in German. He wrote to Hofmannsthal:

> Without reflecting on the difficulty of translation in general – the limits of potential achievement [...] seem in this case particularly fiercely circumscribed by the fact that the sustained Proustian phrasing that lends the original text a good portion of its character through its relationship of tension with the linguistic spirit of French cannot have the same effect of tension and surprise in German. To the extent that what might be the most important thing about Proust for the German reader can scarcely be conveyed in German.
>
> *(Benjamin 1978:412)*[37]

For a while, Benjamin thought of writing a text entitled 'En traduisant Marcel Proust'[38] in which he would reflect on his own translation, but this project metamorphosed into a reflection on Proust's oeuvre instead of Benjamin's translation thereof.

It was as though the *speculative* passion that Benjamin felt for translation in general, and the burning enthusiasm that he felt for Hölderlin's translations, disappeared as soon as he found himself confronted with the *concrete* work of translation, which struck him as an onerous obligation, sterile and secondary. This can be heard in these lines addressed to Rilke, striking for their platitudes:

> I am very happy, thanks to your goodness, to be able to make a small contribution to the relationship between German and French letters. The path of translation, particularly of such a difficult text is, with this goal in mind, certainly one of the most difficult, but precisely because of this all the more worthwhile than that of, say, journalism.
>
> *(Benjamin 1978:391)*[39]

And in these lines, surprising coming from the author of 'The Task of the Translator', addressed once again to Hofmannsthal:

> I think I am convinced that any translation work that is not undertaken for the highest and most urgent practical purposes (like Bible translation – as a type) or for pure philological study – necessarily has something absurd about it.
>
> *(Benjamin 1978:445)*[40]

One thing is certain: whenever Benjamin's writings on translation proceed from his metaphysical horizon, then the result is a profundity of thought. But as soon as his writing draws on his own experience as a translator, his interest appears to wane. The man who chastised a German university for labelling translation a 'derivative act', calling this 'shameful', is saying exactly the same thing when he talks about his Proust translation as an 'unproductive encounter'.

In this respect Benjamin cannot be said to be a *translator*: where a translator displays an *urge-to-translate*, Benjamin shows no sign of it, nor any ambition to develop it. What *is* apparent, however, is his ambition to become 'the premier critic of German literature' (Benjamin 1978:505),[41] as he wrote – in a letter composed, somewhat bizarrely, in French – to Scholem.

We will come back to the conflicting but related positions of criticism and translation in Benjamin's work. The fact remains that what we have here is a great translation *thinker* who is not a great translator. The opposite is more frequently the case. And, what is more, his thinking on translation is not in the least grounded in his experience as a translator. There is a gulf between Benjamin's translating self and Benjamin the philosopher of translation. This gulf requires further investigation.

Some scholars claim that one can refute Benjamin's theoretical writings on translation on the grounds that they are not borne out by his translations. This will not be my position here. Nonetheless, we must enquire into how the vision outlined in 'The Task of the Translator' relates to the one that reigns in the *Correspondence*. How is it possible to describe translation simultaneously as productive *and* unproductive? To assign it 'messianic' intentions and also declare that it necessarily has 'something absurd about it'? This contradiction must be located within 'The Task of the Translator' and points towards a contradiction that is not of Benjamin's making, but which lies at the heart of translation itself.

'The Task of the Translator': a prologue

'The Task of the Translator' is the *prologue* to the author's translation of Baudelaire or, to be more precise, to a partial re-translation of the *Fleurs du Mal*. Strangely enough, however, this is not stated anywhere in the prologue. The prologue talks exclusively about translation in general, even though it is clear that its focus is on poetic or literary translation.

Normally, when a translation prologue aims to have a more general or theoretical reach, it focuses on the translation that it is introducing. This is almost a law of the genre: consider Humboldt with Aeschylus' *Agamemnon*, George with *Die Blumen des Bösen*, Bonnefoy with Shakespeare's *Hamlet*, Meschonnic with *Le Chant des Chants* ... Always, without exception, when translators preface their work, they discuss the translations they have created. We find nothing of the sort in Benjamin, and because this is too out of the ordinary not to have been deliberate, it indicates a desire to produce a *different* kind of discourse on translation.

We might be tempted to call 'The Task of the Translator' an essay or – as Todorov has suggested – a 'manifesto'. But no. It is not even a theory in the manner of Schleiermacher's lecture, which is a systematic essay on translation that surveys the entire field. It is not an essay, because Benjamin is interested in expounding truths that bear no relation to the hypothetical and provisional nature of the thoughts in an essay. It is not a manifesto expounding new translational principles. It is not a theory that systematically investigates the structure of the act of translating in all of its facets.

Moreover, this text, which is neither essay, nor manifesto, nor work of theory, does not partake in the independence of these forms: it occupies a *position-as-prologue* and this would remain its essential nature even if it were published in an anthology of Benjamin's texts. This means that its pronouncements are vitally linked to the translations that follow. But in what manner? The prologue might be the lesson drawn from the translations or, conversely, the translations might be examples of the type of translation outlined in the prologue. In the first instance, the emphasis would be on the translations; in the second, on the prologue. But the prologue and the translations turn a reciprocal blind eye to one another, while being and remaining bound to one another within this reciprocal ignorance. If the prologue had proceeded from the translations, if the translations reflected the prologue, this would be apparent. But this is not the case. *There is a gap between Benjamin's discourse-on-translation and the translation itself.* This gap creates a tension that cannot be reduced to the fact – historically established – that Benjamin's translations are not equal to his vision of the act of translation. This gap, in so far as it is *intentional*, indicates, necessarily perhaps, that discourse on translation that reflects the essence of translation cannot simply consist of describing the 'how', in other words, it cannot be methodological in the broad sense. This indicates that there is a gulf – which cannot be ignored – between the experience of translation and translation thought. But perhaps it also signals an important *limit* in Benjamin's thinking about translation that connects to his philosophy of language.

Thus we find ourselves confronted with the *paradox* of a prologue that does not discuss the work that it prologues, and which positions itself as a 'pure' discourse on translation, removed from all empiricism, from all reference to examples.

This was undoubtedly the type of text Benjamin had in mind when he was working on Proust; we know that he abandoned it, as if by this route – that of an empirical treatise on translation drawing on examples – one could learn nothing about translation, nor about the work in question. Benjamin was perfectly capable of writing in the empirical manner that characterises the majority of texts on translation: he did it in his works of criticism, which are often very concrete, as is the case in his commentary on Goethe's *Elective Affinities* [Goethes Wahlverwandschaften] (1991g). Why didn't he do the same here?

The paradox deepens when one considers the title of the prologue: 'The Task of the Translator'.

As it happens, this is a text that is more preoccupied with translation than with the translator. We could perfectly well replace each occurrence of the word 'translator' with the word 'translation'. Armand Robin's, Valéry's and Bonnefoy's texts on translation are attempts at reflection on the *translator*. With Benjamin, the prologue bears no relationship to the work that it prologues, and the title bears no relationship to the entity bearing that title.

This paradoxical lack of correspondence between title and prologue, between prologue and translations brings us back to the *tension* that exists between the problematic of translation and that of the translator, to the problematic of the experience of translation and that of translation thought.

Translator and translation

Let us approach this from a Platonic perspective. This perspective is implicit to 'The Task of the Translator' and explicit in many other of Benjamin's texts. 'The Task of the Translator' thinks within the Platonic tradition, which is not to say that it is dependent on it in a sterile manner.

In what sense is there a state of tension here?

The answer is obvious if one considers the current understanding of translation, which sees it as a *transparent* rendering of meaning. In order to achieve this transparency, translation has to be *subjectless*, because the presence of a subject would *deform* the translation process. If we are able to identify, for example, the translator's mark in the translation, then this is considered a flaw which has implications for the translation's fidelity and veracity. This promotes a psychology in which the translator is wedded to *effacement*. Like an imperative thrown down to the translator, effacement literally signals that the translator must not 'be' so that the translation can effectuate itself, so that the translation can 'be', or rather, that the translator's only 'being' is that of pure *function*: that of bringing about the decorative passage of meaning. The translator's visibility is always seen negatively, the translator stands in the way of the translation's fulfilment. *Traduttore traditore*: of all the betrayals committed by the translator, the greatest and most flagrant is the betrayal of the translation itself.

Here we find ourselves in a space of striking obliteration: to the fact that translation must not appear to have been carried out by anybody, we can add the fact that it must not appear to be a translation. *The self-obliteration of the translation corresponds to the self-obliteration of the translator*. And because this double self-obliteration is obviously an impossible situation, a state of tension arises. A translation is, after all, a translation and not an original, and it is the work, the action of a subject. From the Platonic perspective – that of the transfer of meaning – it is considered neither a translation, nor the action of a subject.

So then: a choice has to be made. The translation or the translator. There is no escape from this paradoxical choice.

Conventionally in translation the translator is the source of mistakes, infidelities and deformities. We cannot counter this with an insistence that a translating subjectivity is an indispensable agent who makes choices, interprets, modulates etc. since it is precisely this interventionist role that comes in for criticism. And yet … what would a translation be without this agency?

This puts us in an awkward situation: all analyses of translated texts reveal a subjectivity at work, but this subjectivity primarily manifests itself negatively. At the same time, it is obvious that this agency is not exclusively negative.

By calling his text
'The Task of the *Translator*'
rather than
'The Task of *Translation*',
Benjamin is pointing out that translational subjectivity is an essential constituent of translation. But, as we will see, he eschews any *ethical* definition of the *task* of this translator. He leaves this unarticulated, thus following a long tradition.

Experience of translation and thought on translation

Let us briefly return to the traditional structure that continues to dominate theoretical and non-theoretical discourse on translation.

This discourse, from its basic premises and *a priori* definitions, tends to be confined to technical precepts on the one hand and empirical descriptions on the other. If translation is about the transfer of meaning then it is simply a question of knowing how to effect this transfer. We can formalise this somewhat: the 'how' is a *method. Conventional discourse on translation is fundamentally methodological.* Furthermore, translation method only exists within a Platonic definition of translation, and from the perspective of this definition, all discourse-on-translation is necessarily method. Where method reigns, the translator as an independent subjectivity never appears, because method requires only an abstract agent.

This methodological discourse distinguishes itself in its *attachment* to its object. Translation as transfer-of-meaning produces a discourse that is homogenous with its object and that can be expressed in principles, rules, norms, examples etc. But this homogeneity of discourse and object only exists within the traditional Platonic definition. Its limits are *the same.* As soon as we postulate that translation is something other than the transfer of meaning, discourse on translation ceases to be a method because the question of its purpose arises (why translation?) and its object (what should I translate? Or: should I translate?). As soon as it ceases to be a method, attached to a pre-defined object, a gap opens up between translation (the experience thereof) and discourse on translation. This discourse cannot master translation, nor can it illuminate it. And that creates both tension and a paradox.

The tension that exists is between the experience of translation and discourse on translation, since the latter cannot determine the former (although it can guide it), nor can it analyse it in its entirety. This leads us to the paradox that the *essence* of translation is more appropriately represented in statements that are neither concrete nor pragmatic, such as those one finds in Goethe and indeed in an entire tradition. Nonetheless, 'example' will necessarily continue to play a role in discourse-on-translation.

We can formulate 'regulatory principles' for the translation of the letter but these principles are *not* methodical. Between the space devoted to principles and the act of translating there is an obscure elective space where subjectivity and the unconscious intervene. Discourse cannot touch this space, nor can it explore this area where the essential nature of translation has *manifested itself. Discourse on translation is therefore not homogenous with the experience of translation.*

'The Task of the Translator' is a keen manifestation of this tension and this gap, and in one sense it is naïve to say: But the prologue and the text don't match! There will always be a gap of this kind. Its renunciation of methodologising discourse of whatever kind indicates that, fundamentally, 'The Task of the Translator' will question the Platonic theory of translation. And it will do this in the name of hyper-Platonism.

The title

We have already touched upon the content of the title, but not on its language. For this we have to return to the German:

'Die Aufgabe des Übersetzers'
which translates, very literally, as

The Task of the Translator.
Aufgabe: task, *Übersetzer*: translator.

The title implies that the translator has a *task*, and that this task is very specific. And the entire text is a response to this question: what is the specific task of the translator? There is of course a polemical and a critical note: the (true) task of the translator must be distinguished from erroneous or secondary tasks.

At least two things are implied by the fact that the translator has a specific task, as we will see: delimiting the sphere of translation in relation to that of 'poetry'; delimiting it in relation to the sphere of criticism. This is because an entire tradition, from Novalis to Proust, amalgamates the two, to the extent that it is impossible to speak of a specific task accorded the translator. *The title of the text therefore pronounces a critical delineation.* This delineation concerns the 'task' of the translator.

But haven't we known for a long time what the task of the translator is? Why revisit it? If Benjamin feels it necessary to do this, it is because he wants to redefine it. *The title of the text therefore announces a critical redefinition of translation.* What kind of redefinition is this? Tradition has long defined the task of the translator as effecting the faithful transfer of works from one language to another. Bowing to the law of fidelity, the translator is charged with a *responsibility*. The word 'task' implies 'responsibility': 'duty'.

But Benjamin understands something different by the word 'task'.

The German word for 'task' is *Aufgabe*. This term, which I will translate using the French word '*tâche*' [task], acquired an important meaning in the Romantic era, with Novalis, a meaning with which Benjamin was perfectly well acquainted. This meaning has nothing to do with the realm of duties and responsibilities – or at least with the realm of morals and ethics. In the Romantic terminological cosmos, the task, the *Aufgabe*, is connected to another term, *Auflösung*, which translates as both 'resolution' and 'dissolution'. The 'task' is always confronted with a state of affairs that needs 'resolving'. Under 'resolution' or 'dissolution', we can include:

solution in the logical sense (of a problem)
(dis)solution in the chemical sense (of a substance)
(re)solution in the sense of musical harmony.

The 'task' is therefore confronted either with a problem (to solve), with a hostile materiality (to dissolve), or with dissonance (to resolve musically). Each of these elements can be traced back to a theme in Novalis. But in which domain do we find *Aufgabe* and *Auflösung* specifically? In a famous fragment, Novalis writes: 'Poetry dissolves the foreign within itself' (Novalis 1954:22).[42]

The task of poetry is the dissolution of the foreign in its true essence, language.

Where Romanticism is concerned, we can identify four domains where the dialectic of task and solution plays out: philosophy, poetry, criticism and translation. It is there, and only there, that we find 'tasks', in a metaphysical sense. These four 'spiritual' activities have a common element: language. The task is a search for a solution within the domain of language. And the 'task of the translator' should not be reduced to a vague function or role but to action that concerns the 'dissolution' of a primordial 'dissonance' in the sphere of language. As this sphere is related to that of truth, the task of the translator, in turn, has a relationship with truth. What kind of a relationship? That remains to be seen.

In his Hölderlin essay, Benjamin also uses the concept of task and that of 'resolution'. On the subject of the poem, he writes that the 'idea of task' corresponds

> to the idea of resolution, which is the poem. (For task and resolution are only separable in the abstract.) This idea of the task, for the creator, is always life. The other extreme functional unity lies within it. The poetic composition therefore proves itself to be the transition from the functional unity of life to the functional unity of the poem. Within the poetic composition life determines itself through the poem, the task through the resolution.
>
> *(Benjamin 1991i:107)*[43]

This is not yet the place to illuminate this extremely obscure passage. But 'task' and 'solution' certainly appear to be fundamental constituents of poetry. They will reappear in 'The Task of the Translator' and if we apply Benjamin's correlation to that text, we come to the conclusion that translation (in the sense of the translated text) is a resolution. And that the translator's agency, far from being determined by a purpose or goal of some kind (transmission, communication etc.), is rather determined by the 'resolution' immanent in translation. Translation, as a result, constitutes a (re) solution in the linguistic order.

That is what we can conclude if we read the concept of 'task' not in terms of its current meaning but from its Romantic origins. There is a re-definition of the 'task' of the translator here; right from the start we find ourselves in a sphere that no longer has anything to do with the usual understanding of translation as an act of transmission. The beginning of the text itself will confirm this interpretation, and its relationships to language and truth will gradually emerge, relationships which until now have only been outlined or hinted at.

It remains to be seen why Benjamin talks of 'The Task of the Translator' rather than of *translation*. If we connect it back to the task–poetry correlation, it would seem more appropriate to talk of the task of translation.

Notes

1 [Steven Rendall's (1997/revised 2012) English translation of Benjamin's essay opts for the title 'The Translator's Task' but I will be referring to the essay throughout using the title adopted by its other translators Harry Zohn (1968), James Hynd and E.M. Valk (1968) and J.A. Underwood (2009), which is also the title by which it has become most commonly known in English. For the German titles of works by Walter Benjamin that are referred to and cited from in Berman's commentary, and for bibliographical details of the most commonly available English translations of these works, see the prefatory note 'Texts by Walter Benjamin discussed in *The Age of Translation*'. German titles are also given in the body of the commentary when a text is first mentioned. Generally, as I have

done with 'The Task of the Translator', I adopt the English titles most commonly in use to refer to Benjamin's texts.]

2 The nineteenth century had Schleiermacher's lecture, 'Über die verschiedenen Methoden des Übersetzens' (1813). [This lecture has been translated into English by Susan Bernofsky as 'On the different methods of translating' (2004). Berman himself translated this lecture into French as 'Des différentes méthodes du traduire' (1985); this translation was re-published in 1999 in an edition revised by Christian Berner.]

3 Jacques Derrida delivered a similar type of commentary in a seminar at the *École normale supérieure*. See Derrida 1987.

4 A caveat is necessary here. Lacoue-Labarthe notes of Celan: 'I believe these poems to be strictly untranslatable, even within their own language; for the same reason, one cannot comment on them. They necessarily resist interpretation; they forbid it. They are written to forbid it' ['Je crois ses poèmes strictement intraduisibles, y compris à l'intérieur de leur propre langue, et pour cette raison d'ailleurs incommentables. Ils se dérobent nécessairement à l'interprétation, ils l'interdisent. Ils sont écrits, à la limite, pour l'interdire.'] (Lacoue-Labarthe 1986:23).

5 [All translations from French and German texts cited in Berman's commentary are my own unless otherwise indicated.]

6 ['Ses textes capitaux sont mal traduits, ou du moins mériteraient d'être retraduits (ce qui n'est pas tout à fait la même chose.']

7 [The first French translation of 'Die Aufgabe des Übersetzers', by Maurice de Gandillac, was published in *Œuvres choisies* (1959). Antoine Berman's discussion references a revised version of this translation – the revisions were carried out by Gandillac himself – that was published in *Œuvres I, Mythe et violence* (1971). A more recent version of Gandillac's translation, revised by Rainer Rochlitz, was published in *Oeuvres I* (2000). The text has subsequently been re-translated by Martine Broda (1990) in *Po&sie* 55.]

8 [Berman has borrowed this word from the passage in *One-Way Street* that he cites twice in the opening section of Cahier 1 ('die *rechtzeitig* fallenden Früchte', literally, 'the timely falling fruits'). In Benjamin's sense, *rechtzeitig* means both 'mature/ripe' and 'timely'.]

9 [Jennings, Eiland and Smith date this essay as having been written in 1916 and first published posthumously.]

10 [Jennings, Eiland and Smith date this essay as having been written in 1933 and first published posthumously.] Benjamin returns to the theme of resemblance (a few months later, or earlier, since there is some uncertainty surrounding the date …) in another essay, 'Doctrine of the Similar' ['Lehre vom Ähnlichen'] (1991e). [Jennings, Eiland and Smith date this latter essay as having been written January–February 1933 and first published posthumously.]

11 [The standard English translation is *The Correspondence of Walter Benjamin 1910–1940* (2010). All translations from Benjamin's correspondence in this commentary are my own; references are to the two-volume German *Briefe* (1978). The English *Correspondence* follows the system adopted by the *Briefe*, in which each letter has a numerical identifier.]

12 ['Nur handelt es sich um einen Gegenstand, der so zentral für mich ist, daß ich noch nicht weiß, ob ich ihn, im jetzigen Stadium meines Denkens, mit der ausreichenden Freiheit entwickeln kann, vorausgesetzt, daß mir seine Auklärung überhaupt gelingt.']

13 ['jede Wahrheit [hat] ihr Haus, ihren angestammten Palast, in der Sprache.']

14 See 'On Language as such and on the Language of Man'. 'The Task of the Translator' contains a further image, that of the 'forest of language'. This is another fundamental way of conceptualising language – but it is not specifically German (see Formentelli 1985). How does the experience of language conveyed by these two images differ: how can language be both a 'house' and a 'forest'?

15 ['*Sprache, die Mutter* der Vernunft und *Offenbarung*, ihr A und Ω.' The emphasis is Benjamin's own.]

16 ['Wenn ich so beredt wäre wei Demonsthenes, so würde ich doch nicht mehr als ein einziges Wort dreymal wiederholen müssen: Vernunft ist Sprache, λόγος. An diesem Markknochen nage ich und werde mich zu Tode darüber nagen.' Heidegger cites this as an excerpt from a letter that Hamann wrote to Herder, dated 10 August 1784.]

17 ['Über dem Bewußtsein daß die philosophische Erkenntnis eine absolute gewisse und apriorische sei, über dem Bewußtsein dieser der Mathematik ebenbürtigen Seiten der Philosophie ist für Kant die Tatsache daß alle philosophische Erkenntnis ihren einzigen Ausdruck in der Sprache und nicht in Formeln und Zahlen habe völlig zurückgetreten.' Jennings, Eiland and Smith date this essay as having been written in 1918 and first published posthumously.]

18 [This poem has been variously translated into English under the titles 'Archaic Torso of Apollo', 'Apollo's Archaic Torso' and 'Torso of an Archaic Apollo'.]

19 Benjamin writes: 'That which smashes the work to pieces, breaks it into fragments of the real world, into the torso of a symbol, is what effects its completion' [Dieses erst vollendet das Werk, welches es zum Stückwerk zerschlägt, zum Fragmente der wahren Welt, zum Torso eines Symbols] (1991g:181). 'Fragments of a symbol': this is how Benjamin defines natural languages in 'The Task of the Translator'. [Gandillac translates 'Torso' as 'débris' [fragments, rubble] (Gandillac 1971:234), in other words 'fragments of a symbol' could also be rendered 'torso of a symbol'.]

20 See note 32, infra.

21 ['On dirait une trame sans cesse rompue de chapitres parfaits, les feuillets d'un livre resté non écrit.']

22 The German word that I have translated as 'contents' is *das Mitgebrachte*, literally, the thing brought along, from the verb 'mitbringen', to bring along.

23 ['"Das Mitgebrachte" seiner Tasche ganz entwunden, jedoch sie selbst nicht mehr vorhanden war. Nicht oft genug konnte ich so die Probe auf jene rätselhafte Wahrheit machen: daß Form und Inhalt, Hülle und Verhülltes, "Das Mitgebrachte" und die Tasche eines waren. Eines – und zwar ein Drittes: jener Strumpf, in den sie beide sich verwandelt hatten.' Jennings, Eiland and Smith date this essay as having been written in 1932–4 and revised in 1938. It was first published posthumously.]

24 ['Two Poems by Friedrich Hölderlin' ['Zwei Gedichte von Friedrich Hölderlin'] (Benjamin 1991i:105–126).]

25 The original of this text is lost but a copy (which may well be incomplete), made by Gerschom Scholem, exists. 'Metaphysik der Jugend' is included in Benjamin's *Gesammelte Schriften* II.I. (1991j:91–104). [Jennings, Eiland and Smith date this essay as having been written in 1913–14.]

26 ['die Bilder und Allegorien […], die über meinem Denken herrschen wie die Karyatiden auf der Loggienhöhe über die Höfe des Berliner Westens.']

27 ['Jedes heilsame, ja jedes nicht im innersten verheerende Wirken der Schrift beruht in ihrem (des Wortes, der Sprache) Geheimnis.']

28 ['Wahrheit [ist] nicht Enthüllung, die das Geheimnis vernichtet, sondern Offenbarung, die ihm gerecht wird.']

29 ['Schrifttum überhaupt kann ich mit dichterisch, prophetisch, sachlich, was die Wirkung angeht, aber jedenfalls nur *magisch* das heißt un-*mittel*-bar verstehen. […] In wievielerlei Gestalten auch die Sprache sich wirksam erweisen mag, sie wird es nicht durch die Vermittlung von Inhalten, sondern durch das reinste Erschließen ihrer Würde und ihres Wesens tun.']

30 The essay in question is 'Schicksal und Charakter' (Benjamin 1991l:171–179).

31 ['So versuchte ich vor Jahren, die alten Worte Schicksal und Charakter aus der terminologischen Fron zu befreien und ihres ursprünglichen Lebens im deutschen Sprachgeiste aktual habhaft zu werden. Aber gerade dieser Versuch verrät mir heute auf das klarste, welchen, unbewältigt in ihm verbliebnen, Schwierigkeiten jeder derartige Vorstoß begegnet. Dort nämlich wo die Einsicht sich unzureichend erweist, den erstarrten Begriffspanzer wirklich zu lösen, wird sie, um in die Barbarei der Formelsprache nicht zurückzufallen, sich versucht finden, die sprachliche und gedankliche Tiefe, [...], nicht sowohl auszuschachten als zu erbohren. Diese Forcierung von Einsichten [...] beeinträchtigt unbedingt den fraglichen Aufsatz ['Schicksal und Charakter'] und ich bitte Sie, es für aufrichtig zu halten, wenn ich in diesem Sinne die Ursache gewisser Dunkelheiten darin bei mir finde.']

32 Reading-in-translation is a fundamental mode of relating-to-translation. We cannot even think of experiencing translation if we do not read in translation. The latter should be a prerequisite for any translation pedagogy. Reading translations is not simply a matter of comparing them to their source texts. It is an act *sui generis*.

33 ['Es wäre nun prinzipiell nicht unmöglich daß zwei Sprachen in eine Sphäre eingehen: im Gegenteil das konstituiert alle große Übersetzung und bildet die Grundlage der ganz wenigen großen Übersetzungswerke die wir haben. Im Geiste Pindars erschloß sich Hölderlin die gleiche Sphäre der deutschen und der griechischen Sprache: eine Liebe zu beiden wurde *eine*. [...] Ihnen jedoch ist die deutsche Sprache nicht gleich nahe wie die hebräische und darum sind Sie nicht der *berufene* Übersetzer des Hohen Liedes, während Sie es eben dem Geiste der Ehrfurcht und der Kritik verdanken, daß Sie kein Unberufener geworden sind.']

34 [With Franz Hessel.]

35 ['Von meinen ersten Versuchen einer Übersetzung aus den Fleurs du mal bis zur Drucklegung des Buches sind neun Jahre verflossen, eine Zeit, die mir die Möglichkeit gab, Vieles zu bessern, in ihren letzten Ablauf aber auch die Einsicht in dasjenige, was, unzureichend, dennoch keiner »Besserung« zugänglich war. Ich habe dabei das ebenso einfache wie gewichtige Faktum im Sinne, daß die Übersetzung metrisch naiv ist. Damit meine ich nicht sowohl die metrische Haltung der Übertragungen als die Tatsache, daß sie mir nicht im selben Sinne zum Problem geworden war, wie die Vorrede dies von der Wörtlichkeit ausspricht. [...] Ich bin der Überzeugung, daß zuletzt nur die metrische Besonnenheit einer Übersetzung der Fleurs du mal intensiver als die meinigen des Baudelaireschen Stils teilhaft macht, eines Stils [...] den ich den Barock der Banalität nennen möchte.'] Hofmannsthal was disappointed by Benjamin's translations of Baudelaire but liked the prologue very much.

36 [Berman does not reference this citation but it appears to come from Letter 157 to Scholem: 'sie [macht] mich im gewissem Sinn krank. Die unproduktive Beschäftigung' (Benjamin 1978:431).]

37 ['Ohne auf die Schwierigkeit des Übersetzens im Allgemeinen zu reflektieren – die Grenzen der möglichen Leistung [...] scheinen mir in diesem Falle besonders streng dadurch umschrieben, daß die lang ausgehaltnen Proustschen Perioden, die dem Originalwerk ein gut Teil seines Charakters durch die Spannung mitteilen, in der sie zum französischen Sprachgeist überhaupt stehen, im Deutschen ähnlich beziehungsvoll und überraschend nicht wirken können. Derart daß, was gerade dem deutschen Leser an Proust das Wichtigste sein könnte, in dessen Sprache kaum zu übertragen ist.']

38 This was to be an article written in French, hence the French title.

39 ['Ich bin sehr glücklich, an einem kleinen Teile, dank Ihrer Güte, an der Verbindung deutschen und französischen Schrifttums wirken zu dürfen. Der Weg der Übersetzung,

zumal der eines so spröden Werkes, ist zu diesem Ziele gewiß einer der schwersten, eben darum aber auch wohl weit rechtmäßiger, als etwa jener der Reportage. ']

40 ['Ich glaube mir darüber klar zu sein, daß jede Übersetzungsarbeit, die nicht aus höchsten und dringendsten praktischen Zwecken (wie Bibelübersetzung – als Typus) oder aus rein philologischer Studienabsicht unternommen wird, etwas Absurdes behalten muß.']

41 ['le premier critique de la littérature allemande.']

42 ['Die Poesie löst fremdes Dasein im eigenen auf.']

43 ['entsprechend der Idee der Lösung, als welche das Gedicht ist. (Denn Aufgabe und Lösung sind nur in abstracto trennbar.) Diese Idee der Aufgabe ist für den Schöpfer immer das Leben. In ihm liegt die andere extreme Funktionseinheit. Das Gedichtete erweist sich also als Übergang von der Funktionseinheit des Lebens zu der des Gedichts. In ihm bestimmt sich das Leben durch das Gedicht, die Aufgabe durch die Lösung.']

Bibliography

Abraham, N. and Torok, M., 1978. *L'Écorce et le noyau*. Paris: Flammarion.

Benjamin, W., 1978. *Briefe I und II. Herausgegeben und mit Anmerkungen versehen von Gershom Scholem und Theodor Wolfgang Adorno*. Frankfurt am Main: Suhrkamp.

Benjamin, W., 1991a [1923]. Die Aufgabe des Übersetzers. In: R. Tiedemann and H. Schweppenhäuser, eds. 1991. *Gesammelte Schriften*. IV.I. Frankfurt am Main: Suhrkamp. pp.9–21.

Benjamin, W., 1991b [1928]. *Einbahnstrasse*. In: R. Tiedemann and H. Schweppenhäuser, eds. 1991. *Gesammelte Schriften*. IV.I. Frankfurt am Main: Suhrkamp. pp.83–148.

Benjamin, W., 1991c. Über Sprache überhaupt und über die Sprache des Menschen. In: R. Tiedemann and H. Schweppenhäuser, eds. 1991. *Gesammelte Schriften*. II.I. Frankfurt am Main: Suhrkamp. pp.140–157.

Benjamin, W., 1991d. Über das mimetische Vermögen. In: R. Tiedemann and H. Schweppenhäuser, eds. 1991. *Gesammelte Schriften*. II.I. Frankfurt am Main: Suhrkamp. pp.210–213.

Benjamin, W., 1991e. Lehre vom Ähnlichen. In: R. Tiedemann and H. Schweppenhäuser, eds. 1991. *Gesammelte Schriften*. II.I. Frankfurt am Main: Suhrkamp. pp.204–210.

Benjamin, W., 1991f. Über das Programm der kommenden Philosophie. In: R. Tiedemann and H. Schweppenhäuser, eds. 1991. *Gesammelte Schriften*. II.I. Frankfurt am Main: Suhrkamp. pp.157–171.

Benjamin, W., 1991g [1924–5]. Goethes Wahlverwandschaften. In: R. Tiedemann and H. Schweppenhäuser, eds. 1991. *Gesammelte Schriften* I.I. Frankfurt am Main: Suhrkamp. pp.123–201.

Benjamin, W., 1991h. Berliner Kindheit um Neunzehnhundert. In: R. Tiedemann and H. Schweppenhäuser, eds. 1991. *Gesammelte Schriften*. IV.I. Frankfurt am Main: Suhrkamp. pp.235–304.

Benjamin, W., 1991i. Zwei Gedichte von Friedrich Hölderlin. In: R. Tiedemann and H. Schweppenhäuser, eds. 1991. *Gesammelte Schriften* II.I. Frankfurt am Main: Suhrkamp. pp.105–126.

Benjamin, W., 1991j. Metaphysik der Jugend. In: R. Tiedemann and H. Schweppenhäuser, eds. 1991. *Gesammelte Schriften*. II.I. Frankfurt am Main: Suhrkamp. pp.91–104.

Benjamin, W., 1991k [1928]. Ursprung des deutschen Trauerspiels. In: R. Tiedemann and H. Schweppenhäuser, eds. 1991. *Gesammelte Schriften*. I.I. Frankfurt am Main: Suhrkamp. pp.203–430.

Benjamin, W., 1991l [1921]. Schicksal und Charakter. In: R. Tiedemann and H. Schweppenhäuser, eds. 1991. *Gesammelte Schriften*. II.I. Frankfurt am Main: Suhrkamp. pp.171–179.

Benjamin, W., 2012 [1994]. *The Correspondence of Walter Benjamin 1910–1940. Edited and annotated by Gershom Scholem and Theodor W. Adorno*. Translated from German by M.R. Jacobson and Evelyn M. Jacobson. Chicago: University of Chicago Press.

Berman, A., 2008. *L'Âge de la traduction*. Paris: Presses Universitaires de Vincennes.

Broda, M., trans. 1990. La tâche du traducteur. *Po&sie*, 55, pp.150–158.

Cresta, M., 1984. Au-dessus des fragments d'un langage plus grand. *Littoral*, 13, pp.53–62.

Derrida, J., 1987. *Psyché. Inventions de l'autre*. Paris: Galilée.

Freely, M. and Wright. C., 2017. Translators are the Jazz Musicians of the Literary World: Translating Pamuk, Literary Translation Networks and the Changing Face of the Profession. *The Translator*, 23(1), pp. 95–105.

Gandillac, M. de, trans. 1959. La tâche du traducteur. In: *Œuvres choisies*. Paris: Juillard. pp. 57–74.

Gandillac, M. de, trans. 1971. La tâche du traducteur. In: *Œuvres I, Mythe et violence*. Paris: Denoël/Les Lettres Nouvelles. pp.261–275.

Gandillac, M. de and Rochlitz, R., trans. 2000. La tâche du traducteur. In: *Œuvres I*. Paris: Gallimard. pp.244–262.

Formentelli, E., 1985. Bilinguisme et poésie. In: J. Bennani, A. Boukous, A. Bounfour, F. Cheng, E. Formentelli, J. Hassoun, A. Khatibi, A. Kilito, A. Meddeb and T. Todorov. *Du bilinguisme*. Paris: Denoël. pp.99–115.

Granoff, W. and Rey, J.-M., 1983. *L'Occulte, objet de la pensée freudienne*. Paris: P.U.F.

Heidegger, M., 1959. *Unterwegs zur Sprache*. Pfullingen: Verlag Günther Neske.

Hynd, J. and Valk, E.M., trans. 1968. The Task of the Translator, *Delos*, 2, pp.76–96.

Lacoue-Labarthe, P., 1986. *La Poésie comme expérience*. Paris: Christian Bourgois.

Novalis, 1954. *Werke. Fragmente II*. Heidelberg: Verlag Lambert Schneider.

Petitdemange, G., 1979. Treize facettes de Walter Benjamin au fil de ses lettres. In: W. Benjamin. 1979. *Correspondance 1929–1940*. Translated from German by G. Petitdemange. Paris: Aubier. pp.345–358.

Rendall, S., trans. 1997. The Translator's Task. *TTR*, 102, pp.151–165.

Rendall, S., trans. 2012. The Translator's Task. In: L. Venuti, ed. 2012. *The Translation Studies Reader*. 3rd ed. Abingdon: Routledge. pp.75–83.

Rilke, R.M., 1908. Archaischer Torso Apollos. In: R.M. Rilke. 1913. *Neue Gedichte. Der neuen Gedichte anderer Teil*. Leipzig: Insel Verlag. p.1.

Ruskin, J., 1987 [1906]. *Sésame et les lys*. Translated from French and with notes by M. Proust. Paris: Complexe.

Schleiermacher, F., 1813. Über die verschiedenen Methoden des Übersetzens. In: M. Rössler with L. Emersleben, eds. 2002. *Kritische Gesamtausgabe*. XI. *Akademievorträge*. Berlin and New York: Walter de Gruyter. pp.67–93.

Schleiermacher, F., 1985 [1813]. Des différentes méthodes du traduire. Translated from German by A. Berman. In: A. Berman, G. Granel, A. Jaulin, G. Mailhos and H. Meschonnic. 1985. *Les Tours de Babel: Essais sur la traduction*. Mauvezin: Trans-Europ-Repress. pp.277–347.

Schleiermacher, F., 1999 [1985]. Des différentes méthodes du traduire. Translated from German by A. Berman and revised by C. Berner. In: C. Berner, ed. 1999. *Des différentes méthodes du traduire et autre texte*. Paris: Seuil. pp.30–93.

Schleiermacher, F., 2004 [1813]. On the Different Methods of Translating. Translated from German by S. Bernofsky. In: L. Venuti, ed. 2004. *The Translation Studies Reader*. 2nd ed. Abingdon: Routledge. pp.43–63.

Scott, C., 2012a. *Translation and the Rediscovery of Reading*. Cambridge: Cambridge University Press.

Scott, C., 2012b. *Translating the Perception of Text*. London: Legenda.

Underwood, J.A., trans. 2009. The Task of the Translator. In: W. Benjamin. *One-Way Street and Other Writings*. London: Penguin. pp.29–45.

Venuti, L., 1998. *The Scandals of Translation*. London and New York: Routledge.

Venuti, L., 2008 [1995]. *The Translator's Invisibility*. London and New York: Routledge.

Zohn, H., trans. 1968. The Task of the Translator. In: H. Arendt, ed. *Illuminations*. New York: Harcourt Inc. pp.69–82.

The commentary

CAHIER 2

In Cahier 2, where Berman's commentary on the letter of Benjamin's text begins in earnest, the lacunae between the German verbs *gelten* and *verlangen* and their French and English translations demonstrate how thinking Benjamin's text trilingually may help draw attention to key conceptual nodes within it. The verb *gelten*, which first occurs – in the third person singular form – at the end of Benjamin's first paragraph, 'Denn kein Gedicht *gilt* dem Leser, kein Bild dem Beschauer, keine Symphonie der Hörerschaft' (Benjamin 1991a:9, emphasis added) [No poem pertains to the reader, no painting to the viewer, no symphony to the audience], and then again immediately at the opening of the second, '*Gilt* eine Übersetzung den Lesern, die das Original nicht verstehen?' (ibid., emphasis added) [Does a translation pertain to readers who do not understand the original?], has no natural English equivalent. *Gelten* can be a transitive or intransitive verb and has a variety of meanings. Possible English renderings, depending on the context, are 'to be valid', 'to count', 'to be worth', 'to apply'; or 'to be considered as', for example *die Fahrkarte gilt in allen Bussen* (the ticket is valid on all buses); *ihre Stimme gilt* (her vote counts); *das Geld gilt nicht viel* (the money isn't worth much or doesn't carry much weight); *hier gilt die StVO* (the Highway Code applies or is applicable here); *er gilt als Fachmann* (he's considered an expert). The relevant meaning in 'The Task of the Translator' is that of *gelten* as an intransitive verb meaning 'to be addressed to or destined for' with an overtone of one of its other meanings 'applies to'. The verb is often used with the impersonal subject 'es' in a similar fashion to the French verb *valoir* ['to be worth', 'to have value'], that is, *il vaut* or *ça vaut*, and *valoir* is the translation Berman suggests here. Berman points out that Gandillac's decision to render *gelten* with the verb *faire* ('to do' or 'to make'), while essentially leaving the meaning of Benjamin's text unchanged, fails to respect its weft. The need to be attentive to the patterns and rhetoricity of prose (and the frequent failure of translation to do so) is a familiar concept in Berman's work. We find it expressed in the negative analytic formulated in his essay 'La traduction comme épreuve de l'étranger' (1985), translated by Lawrence Venuti as 'Translation and the Trials of the Foreign' (2000). The verb *gelten* has a grammatical subject in Benjamin's text (*Gedicht, Bild, Beschauer,* and then *Übersetzung*) but it has no subject in the sense of an agent – and that is precisely the point. Benjamin is unpicking our desire to conceive of the work of art as a message (*eine Mitteilung* or *Aussage*), and as Berman underlines, a message consists of three parts: 'transmission by somebody, transmission of something, transmission to somebody' (2008:47). Through his choice of verb, Benjamin begins his dismantling of the notion of message by removing the transmitter, the agent, at the same time as he dismisses the importance of the receiver. Benjamin rejects the notion that works of art are or should be preoccupied with their audience, thus questioning the notion of the work of art as a communicative act and positioning himself against contemporaneous views of language as a communicative tool. In my translation of *gelten*, I have opted for the verb 'pertain', in the sense of 'belonging to' (as a legal right or a privilege), but also 'relating to'. Like *gelten*, pertain's sense of agency is vague and it avoids the subject implicit in verbs such as 'mean', 'intend' or 'aim'.

Benjamin defines *Übersetzbarkeit*, translatability, on two levels: the first level has to do with whether a literary text is able to find its appropriate translator; the second – the more important of the two translatabilities – has to do with whether the text permits translation and accordingly also demands it ('*demnach* [...] *auch verlange*', 1991a:10). The most common contemporary meaning of the verb *verlangen* is 'to demand', but it can also mean 'desire', particularly in its nominalised form *Verlangen*. Berman translates *verlangen* as 'désirer' throughout, a verb which favours the element of desire over the element of demand. There is no verb in English in which these two meanings coincide. Desiring translation and demanding translation are two very different things; the imperative to translate is stronger in the latter and since Benjamin's text argues that translation is necessary – not for the original text, but for the attainment of pure language – I have opted for 'demand'. But Berman's choice calls attention to the element of desire in the German verb that English cannot reproduce, an element that I might otherwise have overlooked or repressed. Again the trilingual approach makes visible latent meanings.

Finally, I have rendered the highly enigmatic statement '*Übersetzung ist eine Form*' as 'Translation is a form'. Harry Zohn's translation, which for copyright reasons was dominant in the English-speaking world for several decades, rendered this as 'Translation is a mode' (2000:16), which leads the reader along a very different trajectory. The other three English translations all opt for 'form' and Berman too opts for *forme*. The opacity of the statement, which Berman discusses at some length, seems best served by the semantic bounty of the word 'form', which is how I have translated *Form* throughout. The most

> prominent meaning of this *Form* appears to be that of 'incarnation' or 'mor-
> phological variant', in the sense that each translation is a fresh version of a text,
> and translation as such productive of such variants.

We have situated Benjamin's thinking on translation within the framework of his
metaphysics of language, listed defining characteristics of his thought and considered his general relationship to translation. We have also approached 'The Task
of the Translator' from the perspective of the paradoxes manifest in its status as a
prologue and in its title. What has emerged is that this text, which is the preface to
a translation of Baudelaire, makes no reference whatsoever to this translation and
conversely, that the translation fails to embody the statements found in the prologue. Consequently, there is a *gap* between Benjamin's experience-of-translation
and his discourse-on-translation.

This gap extends far beyond Benjamin. It begs the question: what kind of discourse on translation can simultaneously do justice both to the essence of translation and to its empirical forms?

A second gap has emerged with respect to the text's title and its relationship to the
body of the text. The title of the prologue announces that the text will be a reflection on the translator, but there is no trace of the translator in the preface. The focus
is purely on translation. This brings us back to the fact that, conventionally, translation theory makes an abstraction of the translator. Or rather, the translator features in
translation theory as the negative (deforming) element in the translation process, even
though it is apparent that translation cannot exist without the translator.

Then we tackled the concept of the task that features in the title by going back
to the German term *Aufgabe*.

We noted that this term, which translates conveniently into French as 'tâche',
acquired a specific meaning during the German Romantic era (in Novalis), and
that Benjamin's title has to be read against this background. Here, 'task' implies the
resolution or dissolution, *Auflösung*, of certain dissonances. Through the choice of
the term *Aufgabe*, the task of translation is implicitly established as the resolution of
certain dissonances in the order of *langue* or *langage*,[1] and not as the transmission –
viewed either ethically or aesthetically – of a text from one language to another.
Given that the dissonances in question have to do with the essence of language, the
task of the translator is of a metaphysical order. The very title of the prologue shows
that Benjamin's thinking about translation takes place within the framework of his
speculative reflection on language.

Today the commentary will focus on the first three paragraphs of 'The Task of
the Translator'. At the very beginning we encounter a series of statements which set
out, in categorical fashion, the sphere within which the text will operate:

> translation is the translation-of-literary-works;
> the essence of translation derives from the essence of the literary work;
> the essence of the literary work is not communication.

The first point draws an implicit line. The field of translation does of course extend beyond that of literary works: there are other, equally indispensable fields of translation such as legal translation and even, sometimes, scientific translation. But Benjamin's concern lies with literary translation. At the end of the text there is discussion of 'sacred' texts. We can therefore assume that his thinking relates – as the fragment from *One-Way Street* will go on to indicate – to the translation of profane (literary) texts and to the translation of sacred texts.

The distinction between the two is not absolute, however, because, for Benjamin, certain *poetic* works of art approach the sphere of the sacred (Hölderlin, Stefan George). The great translators invoked in the text – Luther, Voss, Hölderlin, A.W. Schlegel, Stefan George, Borchardt – straddle these two spheres. This, for Benjamin, is the domain of translation.

Nor is 'The Task of the Translator' a reflection on translation 'in general'. This type of thinking – which would resemble a translation theory in its structure – is alien to Benjamin.

If translation is exclusively the translation-of-literary-works, then it can only be grasped in terms of their essential nature. Since the literary work is a work-of-language, reflection on translation is necessarily reflection on language – on language as it is revealed and embodied in the text. Here Benjamin stands in radical opposition to all conventional theories of language, of the literary work and of translation.

As we have noted already, these theories understand language, the literary text and translation in communicative terms. Language is an instrument of communication, the text is a communicative act, a message, and translation is the interlingual transmission of that communication. This is why a number of theorists see translation as the 'communication of a communication'.

'The Task of the Translator' immediately dismisses this thinking. It immediately asserts that the literary work is not structured like a message. In a phrase that is so paradoxical (at first sight) that the French translator either forgot it or cut it, Benjamin says:

> Denn kein Gedicht gilt dem Leser, kein Bild dem Beschauer, keine Symphonie der Hörerschaft.
>
> *(p. 9. para 1)*[2]

> No poem pertains to the reader, no painting to the viewer, no symphony to the audience.[3]

> aucun poème ne vaut pour le lecteur, aucun tableau pour le spectateur, aucune symphonie pour l'auditoire.
>
> *(Berman)*[4]

[Literal translation of Berman's French translation:

> no poem is valid for the reader, no painting for the viewer, no symphony for the audience.]

If a poem, symphony or painting do not pertain to the public, this means that their *pour-quoi*, their essence, cannot be determined on the basis of their *reception*. They cannot be treated like messages. Any message, of course, contains three elements: transmission by somebody, transmission of something, transmission to somebody. The 'something' is itself structured in terms of form and content.

But the three elements of the message are not equal. Their totality is determined by the *final* element, that of the text's reception. Any transmission presupposes a receiver and structures the message according to its vision thereof. But where literary texts are concerned, the opposite is true, as the epigraph of Nietzsche's *Zarathustra* warns us – 'A book for all and none'.[5]

A work of art does not presuppose a receiver. The implied reader is characteristic only of secondary or generic works. Moreover, in its state of fulfilment, a literary text never concerns itself with a receiver. It does not 'turn' towards us. And that is precisely what makes us turn towards it.

If the work of art cannot be thought on the basis of its reception, then this situates Benjamin's thinking on art and translation *outside the realm of aesthetics*, if we recall that aesthetics is an approach that apprehends art via the senses, *aesthesis*. Today we can re-read the beginning of 'The Task of the Translator' in light of Heidegger's words:

> The work of art is conceived of as an 'object' intended for a 'subject'. The relationship between subject and object – a relationship of feeling – is decisive for contemplation of the work. The work becomes an entity via the surface that it presents to those who experience it.
>
> *(Heidegger 1961:93)*[6]

The point here is not to bring these two thinkers together arbitrarily, but to demonstrate more clearly the scope of a mode of thinking about works of art that refuses to take reception as its point of departure. The point here is to think about the work itself rather than its effects.

This dismissal of a theory based on reception is absolutely essential for translation thought. In no other field have theories (or ideologies) of reception caused so much damage. For centuries, deforming tendencies that do even more damage to the meaning of translations than to original works have been practised in the name of the receiver. Ethnocentric translation and hypertextual translation are in fact rooted in the ideology of reception.[7] Ethnocentric translation that pivots on the reader transforms the literary work into a message. A critique of translation theories that focus on the reception of texts is key for any contemporary reflection on translation.

In his second paragraph, Benjamin writes:

> Was »sagt«[8] denn eine Dichtung? Was teilt sie mit? Sehr wenig dem, der sie versteht. Ihr Wesentliches ist nicht Mitteilung, nicht Aussage.
>
> *(p. 9. para 2)*

> What does a literary work 'say'? What does it communicate? Very little to the person who understands it. Its essence is not communication, nor pronouncement.

> Mais que «dit» une œuvre littéraire? Que communique-t-elle? Très peu à qui la comprend. Ce qu'elle a d'essentiel n'est pas communication, n'est pas énonciation.

> *(Gandillac 1971:261)*

[Literal translation of Gandillac's French translation:

> But what does a literary work 'say'? What does it communicate? Very little to the person who understands it. Its essential feature is not communication, not pronouncement.]

The attack on translation as communication that will follow is rooted in the above assertion, but the assertion is not developed further. It has to be re-read in light of the final sentence of the first paragraph, according to which the work of art is never 'addressed'. This phrase does not imply that the work of art will not be read, listened to or contemplated. Rather it formulates something that takes place within the work itself, and shapes how it is received. In a letter addressed to the musician Benvenuta, Rilke writes:

> When music speaks, it does not speak to us. The complete work of art only relates to us in so far as it outlasts us. Poetry steps into language from within, from a side that is always turned away from us, it replenishes language in wonderful fashion, it ascends to the very edge of language – but it no longer tries to reach us. The colours are stamped onto the painting but they settle into it like rain into the landscape; and the sculptor can only show his stone the most splendid way of closing in upon itself.

> *(Rilke 2000:83)*[9]

The parallels with Benjamin's thought are quite striking in their intensity.

In a poem, language is in a self-contained state of fulfilment, and this comes about on one condition: that it no longer transmits anything, no longer communicates anything, no longer even 'means' anything. It is so fully realised that it is content to rest within itself. *This* is the language – language that turns away from us and from utilitarian purposes – that is encountered by the translator.

The question arises as to whether this is true of every literary text or if it is characteristic of a particular historical constellation that extends, let's say, from German Romanticism to Mallarmé, Rilke, George and Benjamin himself. A constellation that establishes the work as a self-referential, hermetic, monologic totality, whose '*mot total*', to cite Mallarmé, is a 'stranger to language' (1945:368),[10] that is to say, to natural language. This is an important question for a theory of literature and poetry; it is just as important for a theory of translation, because if the language of a text has become monologic and un-communicative, even un-signifying, what might or can the translator hope to achieve? If the translator's agency no longer consists of transmitting meaning ad absurdum, meaning that is now seen as inessential, what else might it consist of?

Let us leave aside this question for the moment: we will return to it later when we discuss one of George's translations of Baudelaire and one of Celan's translations of Supervielle. The analysis of these two translations will demonstrate what a translation can do when it is confronted by a poem's monologic essence. It might also demonstrate that translation uncovers the dialogism immanent in the poem – and which runs deeper than its (modern) monologism.

At the beginning of paragraph two – as the opening gambit in his critique of communication – Benjamin asks a question that is both essential and odd. It is a question that goes unanswered. To be more precise, he uses the interrogative form to lay out the assumption that underlies all conventional theories of translation: a translation is made for readers who do not understand the original text.

Benjamin interrogates this statement (literally and figuratively).

> Gilt eine Übersetzung den Lesern, die das Original nicht verstehen?
>
> *(p. 9. para 2)*

Does a translation pertain to readers who do not understand the original? Gandillac translates:

> Une traduction est-elle faite pour les lecteurs qui ne comprennent pas l'original?
>
> *(1971:261)*

[Literal translation of Gandillac's French translation:

> Is a translation made for readers who do not understand the original?]

But Benjamin doesn't say 'made' ['est-elle faite']; he uses the verb *gelten* [*valoir*], as he does in the final sentence of the first paragraph when he talks about the poem, the picture and the symphony. And this verb will appear again later on. What we have here is one of those foundational terms that make up the lexical fabric of the text *beneath* its conceptual fabric. The translation has to pay attention to these foundational terms and consistently translate *gelten*, in so far as this is possible, with an equivalent verb.

Re-translated this would read:

> Une traduction *vaut-elle* pour les lecteurs qui ne comprennent pas l'original?

[Literal translation of Berman's French translation:

> Does a translation *apply to* readers who do not understand the original?]

My critique of Gandillac's translation has nothing to do with meaning (translating *gelten*, here, with *faire* [to do] is not wrong or misleading) but with its failure to respect the linguistic weft of the text. Translating prose is *above all* about replicating the weft through which the text derives its consistency, its systematicity, its logicalness and, of course, its singularity. Saying 'vaut-elle' in this commentary instead of 'est-elle faite' barely changes the meaning; but in highlighting the frequency of the verb *gelten* in 'The Task of the Translator', we are paying attention to its language. The verb *verstehen* [*comprendre*: understand], which occurs in the same sentence is another one of these foundational terms. Benjamin uses it in the context of foreign languages and, a few lines further down, of poetry. Do we 'understand' a foreign language in the same way we 'understand' a poem? Benjamin certainly uses the same verb in both contexts, in quite a lax fashion. The same thing will happen with the term *Ausdruck* [*expression*: expression]. There is a tension between this *basic fabric* of the text, which is underdefined, and the more rigorous conceptual network which is, so to speak, embedded within it. The translation should respect the way in which this network is inserted into the fabric of the text.[11] This will shortly become apparent with respect to the concept of *Übersetzbarkeit* [*traduisibilité*: translatability].

But let us return to Benjamin's question and to the fact that he uses the interrogative form to present something which all translation theory takes as a given – or as a point of departure. This question is laden with significance, because the nature of the response determines both the purpose and the essence of the act of translation (as well as its forms and its 'how').

Traditionally the answer to this question has been self-evident: a translation is addressed to those who do not understand the language of the original. Why on earth would we bother translating otherwise? Translation is, above all, a communicative act.

Let us entertain, for a moment, an absurd premise, namely that we all understand each and every language. If this were the case, then we would be able to read literary texts in the original. And how can we deny that literary texts speak more fully in their language of composition?

In affirming this, however, we are forgetting several things. Firstly, that the big languages (the *koinai*) are always languages-of-translation: they are translated and they translate; they have been caught up in translation from their very beginnings. How then can we postulate that the text has a 'pure' relationship to its language (posited as an unadulterated reality) if this language has been shaped, to a significant extent, by translation?

Furthermore (and this is even more important), each literary text, in its own way, contains the 'presumption' of its own translation. By this I mean that each literary text can speak *beyond* its own language. But some texts are resistant to this.

However, even if we accept the conventional thesis that a literary work can only speak in its own language, the question of *our* relationship to the foreign language remains. Even if I could 'understand' German, English or Japanese perfectly … these languages would always be fundamentally *foreign* to me. I will never read Shakespeare like an English speaker. But my access to the original will be constrained irrespective of whether I read the text in the original or in translation: I will come up against a boundary in both cases (albeit of two different kinds). The belief that translation – reading a text in translation – is inferior to 'direct' reading, is misguided.

If it is highly unlikely that a text can speak only in its own language, and if it is unlikely that it speaks to me more fully in its own language than in translation, then this undermines the thesis that the sole purpose of translation is to give me access – of whatever quality – to the foreign work. This is certainly *one* of translation's purposes, but is it its essential purpose? The polylingual cultures of the sixteenth and seventeenth centuries translated texts that they were able to read perfectly well in the original language. For them, translation was a way of 'modulating' a work. For them, a text was only fully realised in its *variations* – and, in turn, these variations could *only* be linguistic.

Conventional theory dictates that translation is not essential for the literary text. 'The Task of the Translator' will show that translation is not an arbitrary event that comes about because human beings have decided to disseminate a text written in one language in another language. This dissemination is only possible because the work demands it – and allows it. And the paradoxical explanation for this can be found in the following observation: communication is not the essence of translation because the literary text is *untranslatable*.

All our empirical experience of the act of translation attests to this: the linguistic flesh of the text (the flesh that constitutes the true meaning of the literary work) cannot be transmitted because there is no real equivalence between languages. *Aufgabe* does not equate to *tâche* because these two words have a different history and it is this history that determines their true meaning. Those who seek to relativise this state of affairs are wrong. But those who conclude that translation is futile are even more wrong. Translation takes place within the sphere of untranslatability – without negating itself.

This means two things.

First of all, translation is not a search for equivalents, but a movement towards the kinship of languages. It *produces* this kinship without presupposing it. In this respect, translation is the most significant upheaval that a language can experience within the textual realm.

Secondly, the literary work is connected to its language in a double, contradictory manner: it is rooted in its language and it transcends it, sets itself against it. Proust said that great texts always appear to have been written in a foreign language. The text roots itself by burrowing into the density of the mother tongue; it sets itself against it by tearing itself away to produce a different language, a language which is foreign to the communal language. In its rootedness, the literary work is untranslatable. This is even more the case when it subverts its own language. And this gives rise to a peculiar dialectic. Translation, first and foremost, only intensifies this subversive tendency. Its purpose is to carry the text even further away from its language. But the more a work is translated, the greater the potential for it to become rooted in its own language and appear untranslatable. This rarely happens at the moment of its birth when its travels have not yet begun. The text only takes on the appearance of a work-in-its-mother-tongue when it is (re)translated. We can therefore argue that translation *effectuates the literary text's relationship to its own language*.

Have we strayed too far from Benjamin? We have, but in an attempt to respond – digressively – to the provocation posed by his question. *All commentary should digress.* The Moroccan writer Khatibi says: 'Commentary moves with the text, each on its own account' (1985:187).[12]

Through our digression we have sought to establish the purpose of translation, or rather what its purpose *would be* if we happened to be able to read works of literature in their original language. And what have we concluded? That even then translation would remain indispensable for the literary text and for the way we relate to it. Its true purpose would become even clearer. This is because translation is primarily carried out for those who are able to read the original text: it is in the back-and-forth between the original and its translation(s) that our relationship to the foreign work is fully realised.

The third paragraph begins with the following phrase:

Übersetzung ist eine Form.

(p. 9. para 3)

Translation is a form.

Une traduction est une forme.

(Gandillac 1971:262)

[Literal translation of Gandillac's French translation:

A translation is a form.]

What does Benjamin understand by 'form'? Is he implying that translation is a literary form? It would be inappropriate, incorrect even, to think of it as such. Translation is not a genre. To grasp the meaning of the term, we have to look to Goethe, for whom 'form' leads to 'organisation', 'organism', 'ensemble' – both in the artistic sphere and, above all, in the sphere of living matter. Translation is a type of organism. As such, it is governed by an organisatory principle, by a *law*.

Sie als solche zu erfassen, gilt es zurückzugehen auf das Original. Denn in ihm liegt deren Gesetz als in dessen Übersetzbarkeit beschlossen.

(p. 9. para 3)

To grasp this, it is pertinent to go back to the original, because the original contains this law of translation in its translatability.

Pour la saisir comme telle, il est bon [*gilt*, again] de revenir à l'original. Car c'est lui qui contient sa loi, en tant que celle de sa traduisibilité.

(Berman)

[Literal translation of Berman's translation:

To seize it as such, it is good [*gilt*, again] to come back to the original. Because it is [*the original*] that contains its law, in the sense of [*the law*] of its translatability.]

Gandillac translates this more elegantly as:

Pour la saisir comme telle, il y a lieu de revenir à l'original. Car c'est lui qui contient la loi de cette forme, en tant qu'elle est enclose dans la possibilité même qu'il soit traduit.

(Gandillac 1971:262)

[Literal translation of Gandillac's translation:

To seize it as such, we need to come back to the original. Because it is [*the original*] that contains the law of this form, in the sense that it is enclosed in the very possibility of [*the original*] being translated.]

On the one hand Gandillac's translation obscures (in trying to explain) the fact that the 'law' governing translation is, straightforwardly, the 'translatability' of the original. On the other hand, it translates *Übersetzbarkeit* as 'possibilité même qu'il soit traduit' [the very possibility of [*the original*] being translated], thus transforming via periphrasis one of the fundamental concepts of the text. I will translate (further on Gandillac himself suggests 'traductibilité') *Übersetzbarkeit* by 'traduisibilité', derived from 'traduisible' [translatable].

A form, therefore, has a law. This law could be immanent within it, as is the case in living matter or the text, or transcendent, as is the case with translation, which finds its 'principle' elsewhere: in the original text. Benjamin calls this law the *translatability* of the original. As the structuring principle of the text, translatability allows the form that is translation to emerge through a process of engendering. The original text is the originary form that can engender other forms: translation, but also criticism. For example, the 'critiquability' of the literary text (a concept that Benjamin explores in *The Concept of Criticism in German Romanticism* [*Der Begriff der Kunstkritik in der deutschen Romantik*]) (1991b) is what makes critical discourse – that other form that derives from the literary text – possible.

Translation therefore emerges organically from the original. For Benjamin, translation, as a form, belongs to the sphere of life. Where there is form, there is life, and vice versa. By 'life', of course, Benjamin understands something very specific. And by 'form' he does not understand a formal – complete, dead and frozen – structure. Living matter is form and, I would like to add, echoing Goethe once again – *metamorphosis*.

The domain of forms is the domain of metamorphoses. Metamorphosis is the self-transformation of form. Form, in fact, only exists through metamorphosis: this is Goethe's 'die and become'.[13]

To say that translation is a form is to affirm that it is a sort of metamorphosis of the original text and not a transformation that is external to the literary work. And the principle by which the text goes beyond (*meta*) itself to assume another form is what Benjamin calls 'translatability', *Übersetzbarkeit*.

Übersetzbarkeit is not simply the (linguistic) possibility of being translated. This possibility, in so far as it exists, can only be relative. Benjamin is thinking of a radical and absolute translatability which cannot be determined (except superficially) on the basis of linguistic criteria. In a moment I will illustrate, using two examples, that linguistic translatability is merely the consequence of another translatability that is singular to the literary text as literary text.

Benjamin continues:

> Die Frage nach der Übersetzbarkeit eines Werkes ist doppelsinnig. Sie kann bedeuten: ob es unter der Gesamtheit seiner Leser je seinen zulänglichen Übersetzer finden werde? Oder, und eigentlicher: ob es seinem Wesen nach Übersetzung zulasse und demnach – der Bedeutung dieser Form gemäß – auch verlange.
>
> *(pp. 9–10. para 3)*

> The question of the translatability of a text is double-layered. It can mean: will the text ever find its appropriate translator among the ranks of its readership? Or, and more importantly: does its nature permit translation and therefore – as accords with the significance of this form – demand it?

> La question de la traduisibilité d'une œuvre est double. Elle peut signifier: parmi la totalité de ses lecteurs, trouvera-t-elle le traducteur adéquat ? Ou bien, plus proprement: de par son essence, admet-elle (*zulasse*) la traduction et – conformément à la signification de cette forme – la désire-t-elle (*verlange*)?
>
> *(Berman)*[14]

[Literal translation of Berman's French translation:

> The question of the translatability of a text is a double one. It can mean: will it find a suitable translator among the totality of its readers? Or rather, more correctly, by its essence, does it allow translation and – in accordance with the significance of this form – does it desire it?]

The first of the questions above may come as a surprise because this appears to be a purely empirical matter. Whether or not a text finds its translator depends upon a series of factors, none of which is insignificant but none of which affect its essential translatability. In fact, whether or not a work finds its translator depends on the nature of its internal translatability, as well as on *kairos*, the 'right moment'.

This category of the 'right moment' – the moment in which a translation is both permitted and desired – is crucial. The 'right moment' is not the sum of favourable and verifiable empirical circumstances. It is an indication that a translation's moment has come. Of course Benjamin does not speak of *kairos* (to use the old Greek term) as such, but he implicitly invokes it in the fragment from *One-Way Street* that I cited earlier when he says that commentary and translation fall from the 'tree' of the profane text at the right moment, *rechtzeitig*. If we run with this metaphor, we could say that both commentary and translation, like fruit, fall from the tree of the text when they are *ripe*. The good translation emerges in the autumn of the text. I will return to this in my discussion of translation's lateness, its *Spätheit*. *Kairos* is connected to this ripening. There are moments in the history of a language and a literature when the translation of a work is impossible and premature, and there are other moments when it is possible after all. This 'possible' is linked – on the part of the translating language – to a *desire*. When this desire manifests itself, all the supposed objective impossibilities, linguistic and other, disappear. *Kairos* determines translatability. When the right moment arrives, the translator will always be there.

What I mean when I say that *kairos* is not the product of verifiable empirical circumstance is that it is not the object of objective knowledge. *Kairos* is apprehended via premonition. This premonition relates to the very movement of time (of the text and its language). Suddenly, translation becomes possible, desirable and desired. The translation that is out of time will not find the right translator, editor – or reader.

Studying the circumstances that permit translation is fruitful up until the point where we get to *kairos*. The concept of *kairos* touches all of human existence. It is as old as Greek thought and is the object of its own distinct branch of study.

The study of the *kairos* of translation leads us to the historicity of translation of course (we see how Benjamin thinks this historicity primarily in terms of literary texts). Re-translation inevitably forms a part of any such study. *It is a law that any great translation is a re-translation.* Put more globally, translation is realised through re-translation. The necessity of re-translation cannot simply be explained on the basis of changing tastes and demands. It correlates with the fairly enigmatic state of affairs that 'first' translations always fail to do justice to their texts, and that their radical imperfection is the ground that makes re-translation possible. From the perspective of *kairos*, this means that any 'first' translation is premature. Benjamin admittedly does not talk about re-translation, but we will see that he indirectly touches upon this issue when he says that a text never finds its 'chosen' translator 'at the time of its emergence'.

As I stated earlier: *kairos* makes something 'possible' and this correlates with the emergence of a desire. This is a double desire: the desire to translate and the desire to be translated. The text becomes translatable in the space opened up by these two desires. This raises several questions: what are the implications for translatability if this desire fails to appear? Can one speak of a 'desire' to be translated on the part of the text? Let us begin with the first of these questions.

The fact that a text fails to find a translator does not mean it is untranslatable. Can we say that men who never find a partner are ill-suited to married life? Perhaps they met the right person but at the wrong time. My marital comparison is not as arbitrary as you might think: in *Die Schrift und Luther* (1926), Franz Rosenzweig spoke of *hieros gamos* in relation to translation, a sacred marriage between two languages.

The fundamental translatability of a text is not undermined by the fact of its non-translation. This is how we should read paragraph three, where Benjamin develops an idea of which he was very fond – the idea of the *unforgettable*. A life or a moment remain 'unforgettable' even if the entire world has forgotten them. They remain unforgettable because they are unforgettable in their essence. The unforgettable is an objective category: it is not that which cannot be subjectively forgotten, because everything can be forgotten, but that which asks to be remembered, to be recalled. The fact that we cannot always rise to the challenge of this unforgettability changes nothing. We have all experienced unforgettable moments that we have forgotten, or not forgotten. Perhaps the unforgettable is the most easily forgotten: like intense moments of besottedness that we desperately want to remember but whose intensity, by rendering them unforgettable, destines them to be forgotten. There is a covert link here between Benjamin's digression and translation, if we recall the manner in which the sixteenth-century French translator, Des Essarts, signed his translations:

> *Acuerdo*
> *Olvido.*[15]

This is a memorable signature that places translation under the double sign of memory and forgetting and which goes beyond the translational experience of the sixteenth century. All translation is remembrance. Think, in our own century, of Klossowski's *Énéide* (1964) or Jean Beaufret's *Parménide* (1955). Translation is commemoration even when the translations concerned are not of great historical texts, for at the point when a translation comes about, the original text is always distant.

If, as Benjamin asserts, no text finds its chosen translator within its lifetime, then the commemorative dimension comes to the fore. We could go further and say that translation is connected to the unforgettability of the text. This unforgettability is what Benjamin calls the text's 'fame' (*Ruhm*). Everything that is unforgettable is famous – and vice versa.

Translation is therefore the *memory of the unforgettable*.

What about the text's *desire* for translation? Benjamin introduces the concept of *desire* with the verb *verlangen*. This desire is strictly that of the text – whether or not an author wishes to be translated is another matter. If this desire becomes inscribed in the writing of the text then it belongs entirely to the text. But how can we talk about what a text desires? A text is not, after all, a subjectivity but the product of a subjectivity! And yet all translators experience a text's desire to be translated. The call of this desire, the *translate-me*, is mute but perceptible. The use of the verb *verlangen* is not metaphorical. Just as the unforgettable constantly asks to be remembered, the text constantly asks for its translation.

One might object that certain texts are (or appear to be) indifferent to translation and that others, greater in number, resist it, wishing to remain in their mother tongue. Benjamin modifies his assertion by saying:

> Wenn Übersetzung eine Form ist, so muß Übersetzbarkeit gewissen Werken wesentlich sein.
>
> *(p.10. para 3)*

> If translation is a form, then translatability has to be an essential feature of *particular* texts.

> Si la traduction est une forme, la traduisibilité doit être essentielle à *certaines* œuvres.
>
> *(Berman, emphasis Berman's own)*

[Literal translation of Berman's translation:

> If translation is a form, translatability must be essential to *certain* works.]

Particular texts? Not all texts? This qualification is even more noteworthy than another qualification which follows immediately on from it:

> Übersetzbarkeit eignet gewissen Werken wesentlich – das heißt nicht, ihre Übersetzung ist wesentlich für sie selbst, sondern will besagen, daß eine bestimmte Bedeutung, die den Originalen innewohnt, sich in ihrer Übersetzbarkeit äußere. Daß eine Übersetzung niemals, so gut sie auch sei, etwas für das Original zu bedeuten vermag, leuchtet ein.
>
> *(p.10. para 4)*

> Translatability is an essential feature of certain texts – this does not mean that their translation is essential for them, but rather signifies that a particular meaning that inhabits the originals expresses itself via translation. It is evident that a translation, no matter how good it is, can never have any significance for the original.

> Que la traduisibilité soit essentiellement propre à certaines œuvres – cela ne veut pas dire que leur traduction soit essentielle pour elles-mêmes, mais qu'une signification déterminée, immanente aux originaux, s'exprime dans leur traduisibilité. Qu'une traduction, si bonne soit-elle, ne puisse jamais rien signifier pour l'original, cela est évident. [I have re-translated once again here.]

[Literal translation of Berman's French translation:

> That translation is essential to certain works – this does not say that their translation is essential for them, but that an importance that has been determined and is immanent in the originals, is expressed in their translatability. That a translation, as good as it might be, can never mean anything for the original, that is obvious.]

Let us leave aside the second qualification for one moment and come back to the first. It is important for translation thought, because one of the essential postulates of translation thought – irrespective of the diversity of texts and text-type – is that translatability is a structure that is common to all texts and is part of what defines them as such. Saying that translatability is specific to certain texts (and therefore not to others) is to enter into a typological schema that has the potential to ruin any possibility of systematic reflection on translation. It is true that each text poses specific 'problems' of translatability – which is why there can be no method in this field. It is even possible to maintain that the appropriate mode of translation for a text is dictated by the mode of translatability inherent in each work. But this does not take anything away from the validity of a principle that sees translatability as a principle that structures every text. A text without translatability would be a contradiction in terms. It goes without saying that this translatability has infinite articulations and co-exists in a variety of ways with the structure of untranslatability.

In terms of desire, one can say that the text desires *and* does not desire its translation. But its non-desire is not symmetrical with its desire. It is *resistance*. This resistance exists in every text. It so happens that the desire to translate only acquires force and significance when it comes into contact with works that put up the fiercest resistance to translation, texts that are considered untranslatable. Yes indeed, the more a work resists translation, the more it attracts it: Shakespeare's *Sonnets* is a revelatory case in point. This leads us to conclude that this resistance contains a mute call to translation. The intensity of the resistance is an indirect indication that the text enters into translation with every fibre of its being.

This dialectic can be illuminated and illustrated by contrasting pieces of *écritures* in which translatability and untranslatability, consent and resistance to translation are clearly apparent. My examples are taken from the work of two Argentine authors, Jorge Luis Borges and Roberto Arlt. Comparing passages from their texts and the translations thereof shows how desire for translation and resistance to translation are always manifest as contrasting entities, without us being able to label either text 'translatable' or 'untranslatable'. This comparison also allows us to differentiate between linguistic translatability and 'literary' translatability and to show how, for a text, linguistic translatability is merely a consequence of its internal translatability.

Here is an extract from a novel by Roberto Arlt, *El juguete rabioso* (1926), (which I have recently translated with Isabelle Garma-Berman as *Le jouet enragé* (1994)):

Despacio consideraba sus encantos avergonzados de ser tan adorables, su boca hecha tan solo para los grandes besos; veía su cuerpo sumiso pegarse a la carne llamadora de su desengaño e insistiendo en la delicia de su abandono, en la magnífica pequeñez de sus partes destrozables, la vista ocupada por el semblante, por el cuerpo joven para el tormento y para una maternidad, alargaba un brazo hacia mi pobre carne; hostigándola, la dejaba acercarse al deleite.

(Arlt 1981:46)

An initial, literal translation would read as follows:

Lentement je considérais ses charmes honteux d'être si adorables, sa bouche faite seulement pour les grands baisers; je voyais son corps soumis se coller à la chair appelant sa désillusion et insistant sur le délice de son abandon, sur la magnifique petitesse de ses parties destructibles, la vue occupée par la face, par le corps jeune pour le tourment et pour une maternité, j'allongeais un bras vers ma pauvre chair.[16]

Whereas the beginning of this sentence can be translated, the middle of the sentence is resistant and sinks into confusion in French. This resistance to translation is not irremediable: it demands a degree of work in the translating language so that it becomes capable of matching the very unlinear structure (and for that matter the borderline 'incorrectness') of the original sentence. The original is written in a non-classical Spanish, a vernacular (Argentine) Spanish which has a *double aim*: to preserve, in writing, the free modes of the vernacular but, at the same time, to construct *literature* with this vernacular. Or rather to work with the heterogenous myth of Argentine Spanish to construct a *form* that both does it justice and goes beyond it so that it is not a written imitation of its vernacular orality. To the extent that this form is – linguistically – composed of the vernacular, it is resistant to translation and its translatability is problematic. But to the extent that it is a form, it is *a priori* translatable. It is apparent that the problem of the text's translation lies in its design: Arlt's text is, literally, *a literary universal embedded in the specificity of a vernacular*. This embeddedness is both a mode of fulfilment and a mode of imprisonment. The translation is the trial that the text fears but through which it can also affirm its literariness and reaffirm its rootedness in its linguistic universe. It is the text that determines *a priori* the pertinent (and complex) translational problematic. The text does not reject translation; it does not consider it inessential. On the contrary. But it calls for it via the mode of resistance.

Let us now move on to the Borges text, taken from a book called *El hacedor* (1960), literally: the doer [*le faiseur*] (Caillois translated it as *L'auteur* [The author] (1965)).

Días y noches pasaron sobre esa desesperación de su carne, pero una mañana se despertó, miró (ya sin asombro) las borrosas cosas que lo rodeaban e inexplicablemente sintió, como quien renonce una música o una voz, que ya le había occurido todo eso y que lo había encarado con temor, pero tambien con júbilo, esperanza y curiosidad. Entonces descendió a su memoria, que le pareció interminable, y logró sacar de aquel vértigo el recuerdo perdido que relució como una moneda bajo la lluvia, acaso porque nunca lo había mirado, salvo, quizá, en un sueño.

(Borges 1972:14)

Des jours et des nuits passèrent sur ce désespoir de sa chair, mais un matin il s'éveilla, regarda (déjà sans surprise) les choses floues qui l'entouraient, et il sentit inexplicablement, comme qui reconnaît une musique ou une voix, que tout cela lui était déjà arrivé et qu'il l'avait affronté avec crainte, mais aussi avec joie, espérance et curiosité. Alors il descendit dans sa mémoire, qui lui parut interminable, et il parvint à tirer de ce vertige le souvenir perdu qui brilla comme une monnaie sous la pluie, sans doute parce qu'il ne l'avait jamais regardé, sauf, peut-être, en un rêve.[17]

Here one could say that there is – seemingly – almost no resistance to translation. We could translate word for word and end up with a translation that works. This is a text that *consents* instead of resisting. There is even a sort of *a priori* agreement between the French and the Spanish, as if the former were present in the latter, without Borges's language being at all frenchified. It would be more precise to say that the text contains its French translation *a priori* and interlineally. From the beginning Borges's writing asserts its translatability into French. There is nothing surprising about this given the intensity of the author's relationship to the French language and its literature. This relationship has produced a text which, in its textuality, is wholly translatable, because its goal is realisation within a language *where no particularising element is retained* (where Spanish is concerned, and only Spanish).

The text is not entirely successful in its goal of course. But it fulfils it partially and consequently its resistance to translation, which always stems from a rootedness in the particular, in what is unique to a given language, is minimal. It consents to translation and calls to be translated. In reality, one might say that the text is *already translated.*[18] The text is nothing other than the way in which the translation is realised; whereas Arlt's linguistic untranslatability leads to a more intense untranslatability, the untranslatability of a work that is rooted in the strata of the vernacular.

But in the same way that Arlt's untranslatability is relative, and his resistance to translation a particular mode of calling for translation, Borges's translatability is misleading and is partnered by an untranslatability that is just as radical, since no French translation is able to preserve the secret *immanence* of French within the Spanish that constitutes the essence of Borges's texts. In translation, this pre-translatability into French, the interlinear presence of Spanish in the French version, disappears irremediably. This is undoubtedly the fulfilment of the destiny manifest in the call of the original text to *make me even more French or even more of a translation!* Borges's translatability is therefore a trap, a trap that benefits the original text (because it wanted to be translated, and was written – unconsciously – with this in mind) and undermines the translation.

This is a truth that is doubtless applicable to all translation. It might be necessary to distinguish between *the original text's goal in being translated* (what the text, desirous of translation, expects from it) and *the goal of translation* (as an act). The former is the ultimate truth of translation, because the text's mode of translatability (ideally) always imposes itself, whereas the *usual* aim of translation – reproducing the text 'as it is' – is its greatest illusion.

The task of the translator will be to disengage him- or herself from this illusion and to work from the translatability (and the untranslatability) posited by the original text. And this, it goes without saying, is a very risky move.

Notes

1 On the difference between the French terms 'langue' and 'langage', both of which translate into English as 'language', see the entry on Language in the *Dictionary of Untranslatables* (Cassin 2014:541–549).

2 [Each citation from 'Die Aufgabe des Übersetzers' in Berman's commentary will be accompanied by a paragraph number and a page number referencing the *Gesammelte Schriften* IV.I. (1991a).]

3 [All English translations from 'Die Aufgabe des Übersetzers' and other German texts cited in Berman's commentary are my own unless otherwise specified.]

4 All citations from 'La tâche du traducteur' will be accompanied by the original German text for reasons that are essential to commentary. And because, as we will see, the authority of a citation can never rely on a translation.

5 ['Ein Buch für Alle und Keinen' (Nietzsche 1883).]

6 ['Das Kunstwerk ist als "Objekt" für ein "Subjekt" angesetzt. Maßgebend für seine Betrachtung ist die Subjekt-Objekt Beziehung, und zwar die fühlende. Das Werk wird Gegenstand in seiner dem Erleben zugekehrten Fläche.']

7 Nida and Taber's theories provide the model that functions as the caricature of this ideology – but it is an influential model nonetheless. According to them: 'When a high percentage of people misunderstand a rendering, it cannot be regarded as a legitimate translation' (Nida and Taber 1974:2). For them the question 'is this a good translation?' is dependent on the answer to another question: 'Good for whom?' This theory leads to a form of adaptation which, in turn, is a form of manipulation guided by the infamous 'receiver'. This does not mean, of course, that any and all engagement with the reception of a translation is devoid of value. It is only when this element takes over that it becomes fatal.

8 I will come back to this *sagen*, placed in quotation marks, and to the fact that it has been placed in quotation marks. The verb *sagen* is a key word in Rilke's poetry.

9 ['Wenn aber die Musik spricht, so spricht sie doch nicht zu uns. Das vollendete Kunst-Gebild hat nur *darin* mit uns zu thun, dass es uns übersteht. Das Gedicht tritt von innen, an einer uns immer abgekehrten Seite, in die Sprache hinein, es füllt sie wunderbar an, es steigt in ihr bis an den Rand, – aber es strebt doch nie mehr zu uns über. Die Farben schlagen sich nieder ins Bild, aber sie sind ihm eingewirkt wie der Regen der Landschaft; und der Bildhauer zeigt seinem Steine nur, wie er sich am herrlichsten verschließt.']

10 ['étranger à la langue']

11 This is a matter of distinguishing those terms that make up the text's lexical fabric from the ideas that make up its conceptual fabric – and taking a rigorous approach to the translation of both.

12 ['Le commentaire tourne avec le texte, chacun sur son compte.']

13 ['Stirb und werde!' From the poem 'Selige Sehnsucht' in the collection *West-östlicher Divan* (1998:21).]

14 *Zulassen: admettre, permettre* [allow, permit]. *Verlangen: désirer, exiger* [desire, demand]. *Nach etwas verlangen: désirer vivement quelque chose* [to greatly desire something]. Here again, Gandillac's translation, which opts for 'exiger', suppresses something: desire.

15 Spanish for 'I remember/I forget'.

16 The definitive French text was as follows: 'Très lentement, j'examinais ses charmes confus d'être si adorables, sa bouche faite uniquement pour de longs baisers; je voyais son corps soumis se coller à ma chair qui appelait sa propre désillusion, et insistant sur les délices de son abandon, sur la merveilleuse petitesse de ses parties destructibles, le regard hanté par son visage et son jeune corps prêt aux tourments et à la maternité, j'étirais mon bras vers ma pauvre chair et, la harcelant, la laissais s'approcher du plaisir' (Berman and Berman 1994:78). [The English translation of this passage, by James Womack, reads: 'I would consider her charms slowly, charms that were ashamed of being so adorable: her mouth made for nothing other than lengthy kisses; I imagined her willing body holding tight to the flesh of another person, flesh that called for her to abandon herself, and imagined her insisting that she would enjoy her abandonment; I saw the magnificent smallness of her vulnerable parts, my vision filled with her face, with her body that was so young for torment and for motherhood; I would stretch out an arm to my own poor flesh: in punishing it, I allowed it to attain pleasure' (Womack 2013: 56–57).]

17 [The footnote that appears at this juncture in Berman's commentary gives a page reference to Caillois's translation (pp.18–19), but also states 'translation by Isabelle and Antoine Berman'. This passage does indeed feature on pp.18–19 of Caillois's translation, but the French translation cited in the commentary is that of the Bermans. The English translation of this passage, by Mildred Boyer, reads: 'Over this desperation of his flesh passed days and nights. But one morning he awoke; he looked, no longer alarmed, at the dim things that surrounded him; and inexplicably he sensed, as one recognizes a tune or a voice, that now it was over and that he had faced it, with fear but also with joy, hope, and curiosity. Then he descended into his memory, which seemed to him endless, and up from that vertigo he succeeded in bringing forth a forgotten recollection that shone like a coin under the rain, perhaps because he had never looked at it, unless in a dream' (Boyer 1964:22).]

18 Or rather: it is the immanent desire for translation that forms the basis of linguistic translatability in Borges. This desire, in turn, interpellates the translator, provoking the desire to translate. In Arlt's case, we have the inverse structure: resistance to translation provokes resistance on the part of the translator, a resistance that *kairos* will undo when the 'time is right', Arlt's 'untranslatability' is transformed into a *call* for translation (on the part of the work) and a *desire* for translation (on the part of the translator). The empirical proof of this state of affairs is that Arlt was translated very late, and Borges very early. The linguistic translatability of the latter points to a more significant translatability.

Bibliography

Arlt, R., 1981 [1926]. *El juguete rabioso*. Buenos Aires: Centro Editor de América Latina.

Beaufret, J., 1955. *Le Poème de Parménide*. Paris: Presses Universitaires de France.

Benjamin, W., 1991a [1923]. Die Aufgabe des Übersetzers. In: R. Tiedemann and H. Schweppenhäuser, eds. 1991. *Gesammelte Schriften*. IV.I. Frankfurt am Main: Suhrkamp. pp.9–21.

Benjamin, W., 1991b [1920]. Der Begriff der Kunstkritik in der deutschen Romantik. In: R. Tiedemann and H. Schweppenhäuser, eds. 1991. *Gesammelte Schriften*. I.I. Frankfurt am Main: Suhrkamp. pp.7–122.

Berman, A., 1985. La traduction comme épreuve de l'étranger. *Texte*, 4, pp.67–81.

Berman, A., 2000 [1985]. Translation and the Trials of the Foreign. Translated from French by L. Venuti. In: L. Venuti, ed. 2000. *The Translation Studies Reader*. 1st ed. New York: Routledge. pp.284–297.

Berman, A., 2008. *L'Âge de la traduction*. Paris: Presses Universitaires de Vincennes.

Berman, A. and Garma-Berman, I., trans. 1994. *Le jouet enragé*. Grenoble: Cent Pages.

Borges, J. L., 1972 [1960]. *El hacedor*. Madrid: Alianza Editorial.

Boyer, M. and Morland, H., trans. 1964. *Dreamtigers*. Austin: University of Texas Press.

Caillois, R., trans. 1982 [1965]. *L'Auteur et autres textes*. Paris: Gallimard.

Cassin, B., 2014. *Dictionary of Untranslatables*. Princeton: Princeton University Press.

Gandillac, M. de, trans. 1971. La tâche du traducteur. In: *Œuvres I, Mythe et violence*. Paris: Denoël/Les Lettres Nouvelles. pp.261–275.

Goethe, J. W. von, 1998 [1819/1827] *West-östlicher Divan*. In: K. Richter, ed. 1998. *Sämtliche Werke*. Band II.I.2. München: Carl Hanser Verlag. pp.7–127.

Heidegger, M., 1961. *Nietzsche. Erster Band*. Pfullingen: Verlag Günter Neske.

Khatibi, A., 1985. Incipits. In: J. Bennani, A. Boukous, A. Bounfour, F. Cheng, E. Formentelli, J. Hassoun, A. Khatibi, A. Kilito, A. Meddeb and T. Todorov. *Du bilinguisme*. Paris: Denoël. pp.171–195.

Klossowski, P., 1964. *Virgile. L'Énéide*. Paris: Gallimard.

Mallarmé, S., 1945. Variations sur un sujet. In: S. Mallarmé. *Œuvres complètes*. Paris: Gallimard. pp.353–420.

Nida, E. and Taber, C. R., 1974. *The Theory and Practice of Translation*. Leiden: E.J. Brill.

Nietzsche, F., 1883. *Also Sprach Zarathustra*. Chemnitz: Verlag von Ernst Schmeitzner.

Rilke, R.M., 2000. *Briefwechsel mit Magda von Hattingberg*. Frankfurt am Main/Leipzig: Insel.

Rosenzweig, F., 1936 [1926]. Die Schrift und Luther. In: M. Buber and F. Rosenzweig. 1936. *Die Schrift und ihre Verdeutschung*. Berlin: Schocken. pp.88–129.

Womack, J., trans. 2013. *The Mad Toy*. London: Hesperus Press.

Zohn, H., trans. 2000 [1968]. The Task of the Translator. In: L. Venuti, ed. 2000. *The Translation Studies Reader*. 1st ed. New York: Routledge. pp.15–25.

CAHIER 3

In the fourth paragraph of Benjamin's 'prelude', which is the focus of Berman's third cahier, the noun *Zusammenhang* appears three times in short succession and is implied but elided on a fourth occasion. The related verb *zusammenhängen* also makes an appearance.

> Dennoch steht sie mit diesem kraft seiner Übersetzbarkeit im nächsten *Zusammenhang*. Ja, dieser *Zusammenhang* ist um so inniger, als er für das Original selbst nichts mehr bedeutet. Er darf *ein natürlicher* [*Zusammenhang*] genannt werden und zwar genauer ein *Zusammenhang* des Lebens. So wie die Äußerungen des Lebens innigst mit dem Lebendigen *zusammenhängen*, ohne ihm etwas zu bedeuten, geht die Übersetzung aus dem Original hervor.
>
> *(Benjamin 1991a:10, emphasis added)*

Nonetheless, the translation has the closest possible *interrelation* with the original thanks to the original's translatability. Indeed, this *interrelation* is all the more intimate since it no longer has any meaning for the original. It can be called a natural *interrelation* and more precisely an *interrelation* of life. Just as the expressions of life are intimately *interrelated* with that-which-is-alive, without having any significance for it, so the translation proceeds from the original.

Translation has no meaning for the original text, Benjamin writes, but it has 'the closest possible *interrelation*' [*Zusammenhang*] with the original thanks to the original's translatability. The rarefied term 'interrelation' is my rendering of the more prosaic *Zusammenhang*. In modern German usage, *Zusammenhang* normally translates as 'context', 'relation' or 'connection'. The Duden gives the following examples: *man nannte ihn in Zusammenhang mit einem Verbrechen* [he was named in connection with a crime]; and *nur noch eins möchte ich in diesem Zusammenhang erwähnen* [I only want to mention one more thing in this context]. The verbal form *zusammenhängen* literally means 'to hang together'. *Zusammenhang* and *zusammenhängen* are such everyday words that one rarely stops to consider them, and Benjamin's usage of *Zusammenhang* is, in a sense, unremarkable; it is in English that a certain artificiality creeps in. This is a common problem when translating from German (a problem that has famously affected Freud translations, for example) and has to do with the fact that German can use everyday words in more abstract – and particularly in philosophical and scientific – contexts, whereas English tends to reserve a distinct lexis for these different levels of discourse. Benjamin's sentences here are constructed around the nominal form rather than the verb. Berman, too, adopts a nominal form, *co-relation* (2008:70), which references Gandillac's *corrélation* (co(r)relation) and is also not an everyday term in French, and for this reason an English noun suggested itself as the best way to follow the nominalisation in Berman's commentary. The 'inter' in 'interrelation' represents the *zusammen* [together] in *Zusammenhang*, the sense that there is a tie between original and translation. 'Relation' seemed more appropriate than 'relationship' since it suggests non-elective kinship rather than desire. The original does desire [*verlangen*] translation but is ultimately indifferent to the forms that ensue from it, and since kinship is such an important concept in Benjamin's essay, 'relation' is a way of strengthening this network of signification within the text.

The use of the term 'afterlife' to describe a particular stage in the literary text's existence stems from Harry Zohn's 1968 translation of 'The Task of the Translator' (2000:16) and is Zohn's rendering of the nominalised verb *Überleben*, from *über* meaning 'over', 'above' or 'beyond', and *Leben/leben*, meaning 'life'/'to live'. The resulting widespread adoption of the term 'afterlife' in the English-speaking world in its reception of Benjamin's essay has been accompanied by the erroneous reading that translation creates an 'afterlife' for the literary text. What Benjamin actually argues is that translations emerge from the *Überleben* of the text. The English 'afterlife' is problematic on a number of levels. It has religious connotations that are not present in the conventional usage of the German term – although one might argue that 'afterlife' strengthens the broader Messianic framework of Benjamin's text. *Überleben* typically means 'survive', 'outlive', and in a more minor, idiomatic usage, 'to go out of fashion'. The word 'after' suggests a linear movement or development that is not contained in *über*. There are several things to note about Benjamin's usage of the term *Überleben*. The first is that the particle *über* is also present in the German words for 'translation' and 'to translate' [*Übersetzung* and *übersetzen*, literally 'placing over' and 'to place over'] and is a key term in German Romantic thought, as Berman discusses at some length in this cahier. The second is that Benjamin is contrasting *Leben, Überleben* and *Fortleben*, all of which represent different stages of the literary text's existence. A text's *Fortleben* is the fact of its continued existence over time, beyond the era in which it was created and, we are led to understand, after the death of its author. Berman argues that '*Fort* is less semantically charged than *über*. [...] The *Überleben* that precedes it in the text designates an act (that of surviving), whereas *Fortleben* appears to express merely a state of continuation' (2008:79). Gandillac translates both *Fortleben* and *Überleben* as *survie* [survival], placing *survie* in guillemets whenever *Überleben* is intended. Berman initially translates *Überleben* as *survie*, but then argues the need to differentiate between *Fortleben* and *Überleben*, coming to the conclusion that *survie*, the nominal form, should be more properly reserved for *Fortleben*, and *survivre*, the verbal form, used for *Überleben*, to indicate the act of surviving, as contrasted with mere continuation. French is able to mimic the structure and semantics of the German with its *sur-vie* [above-life]. However, *sur-vie* also has the religious connotations of 'afterlife' that the German does not. I have chosen to translate *Fortleben* as 'continuing life' and *Überleben* as 'sur-vival'. The latter is a more artificial term than either the German term or the French translation, but it gestures towards the *über* of *Überleben* while remaining a homonym of the everyday word 'survival'. Part of Benjamin's rhetorical strategy is to make familiar, everyday terms strange, to invest them with meanings that stray from their everyday usage or to group them with prepositions that defy convention. I am marking this tendency in the ordinary-strange 'sur-vival'. The same translational strategy was employed by Joseph F. Graham in his translation of Derrida's essay on Benjamin 'Des tours de Babel' (1985).

Last week we discussed the first three paragraphs of 'The Task of the Translator' (1991a) and attempted an initial *re-translation* of certain sentences. The aim of this commentary is to offer an interpretation of the text by reflecting on its *language*, thus simultaneously preparing the way for its re-translation.

This is the point we have reached today.

A *commentary* is not the same thing as a *critical analysis*. The latter focuses above all on ideas. Commentary, by contrast, focuses on the language – the *letter* – of the text. Critical analysis takes on the text in its entirety, citing from it on occasion. Commentary follows the text line by line, even though this line-by-line approach is not strictly linear and sometimes purposefully jumps a few lines. Commentary is, in fact, a search for *pivotal lines. It seeks out the letter embedded within those lines.*

Commentary's line-by-line approach and the attention that it pays to the letter of the text make it a very close relation of translation; translation, too, proceeds line by line, seeking out the letter of the text.

Where foreign texts are concerned, in fact, commentary and translation are inseparable, to the point that it is impossible to say that one 'precedes' the other. *In this case, all interpretation is translation and all translation is interpretation.*

But *my* commentary has an additional dimension: it is a commentary on an *already translated text*. The commentary therefore becomes a commentary both on the translation *and* on the original. The lacunae in the first translation invite reflection on the notion of first translations and re-translation. And on commentary itself more generally. All good commentary is also *a commentary on itself.*

This is also *a text about translation.* The commentary occupies a space in-between translation and original and is thus situated as close as possible to what is being *said* in the original text. Consequently, it does not share in the distance that characterises both theory and critical analysis. Or rather (and we will return to this) it gives the translation both distance from and *intimacy* with the text.

Somewhat paradoxically, this means that the commentary itself is situated in *the untranslatable.* Its micrological – so to speak – reflection on the language of the original text and, correlatively, on the language of the commentary as it goes about translating the language of the original word by word, sentence by sentence, means that the commentary, in turn, cannot be translated without it being profoundly altered. Commentary, a thinking confrontation between two languages, cannot be translated. We would do well to ponder this.

Commentary cannot be translated and indeed *it cannot be summarised.* The fundamental aspects of what it has to say can only be grasped line by line, either by listening to it or by reading it. Not only does each line in the commentary interpret and translate the original text, the commentary also follows its path via detours and digressions, often forgetting the text it is discussing. This *'gives [pause for] thought'* as Heidegger (1961:2) says.[1] And this gift of something to think about allows us to *move away* from the commentary to think for ourselves. Far from being a servile, paraphrasing explanation of the text, the commentary is the best way not only of thinking it, but of thinking from it. Perhaps even against it.

This thinking *against*, however, is secondary. *Commentary is about paying attention to the text and cherishing it*, it is about paying attention to what the text is thinking and cherishing its thoughts.[2] From the start the commentary is joined to the original in the subject of its thought; in this particular instance that subject is translation, approached in a manner distinct from mere opinion.

This mode of reading is a very old one, of course. There is a particular gratification to be found in re-rooting oneself in this *traditional* mode of thought (and reviving it). Commentary is a gratifying *experience* in which one moves forward without knowing what is coming next. Walter Benjamin was perfectly familiar with the gratifying nature of this experience; he once talked of his 'commentator's nature' in a letter.

At the beginning of paragraph four, Benjamin endeavours to define the concept of 'translatability'. Here are the first two sentences again:

> Translatability is an essential component of certain texts – this does not mean that their translation is essential for them, but rather signifies that a particular meaning that inhabits the originals expresses itself via translation. It is evident that a translation, no matter how good it is, can never have any significance for the original.

> Que la traduisibilité soit essentiellement propre à certaines œuvres – cela
> ne veut pas dire que leur traduction soit essentielle pour elles-mêmes, mais
> qu'une signification déterminée, inhérente à l'original, s'exprime dans leur
> traduisibilité. Qu'une traduction, aussi bonne soit-elle, ne puisse jamais rien
> signifier pour l'original, cela est évident.[3]
>
> *(Benjamin 1991a:10)*

Translatability does not mean, therefore, that translation (in itself, as an act and as
an end result) means (*bedeutet*) something for the text. Firstly let me draw your
attention to the terms *bedeuten, Bedeutung* [*signifier, signification*; to mean, meaning].
For even though, according to Benjamin, the best translation can never 'mean' anything for the original text, a certain meaning inherent in the original expresses itself
in its translatability.

This takes us back to the previous paragraph:

> The question of the translatability of a text is double-layered. It can mean: will
> the text ever find its appropriate translator among the ranks of its readership?
> Or, and more importantly: does its nature permit translation and therefore –
> as accords with the significance of this form – demand it?
>
> *(Benjamin 1991a:9–10)*

Here again the term *Bedeutung* is used.

But if, as its essence dictates, the text allows and desires its own translation, how
can Benjamin assert that translation 'means' nothing for the original? How can the
text desire something that is devoid of significance?

First of all we might say – on the basis of the very experience of translation – that once the text has been translated, it closes in on itself in an even more
'splendid' way (to borrow Rilke's expression).[4] Translation, *stricto sensu*, does not
touch the text. The text 'allows itself' to be translated, 'allows itself' to be the
object of criticism, 'allows itself' to be interpreted and 'allows itself' to be read, but
its hermetic singularity and existence makes it look upon all of this with infinite
indifference. This is the sense in which none of this means anything for the original
text. The original text is the original text, and the mass of textual 'derivatives' (this
is how the law defines them) proliferates from it and beyond it. The fundamental
characteristics of these derivatives are their perishability and their multiplicity. The
original text, the finished form, generates and calls forth all of these unfinished
forms, each of which, in its own way, attempts to grasp the original. But the original cannot be *grasped*. The relationship of the text to its translational and critical
derivatives is one of desire, but this desire is pervaded by *irony*. This irony resides
in the fact that the text, in its state of fullness and completion, relativises, through
the simple fact of its being, both translation and criticism, which will forever lack
these qualities.

We may well be the victims here of the ambiguity that surrounds the terms
'translation' and 'criticism', in so far as both conflate (and with good reason) process

and product. What the original text calls for with all of its strength, so that the meaning immanent in its translatability can come into being, is the *act* of translation. But the *product* of this act is regarded with ironic indifference, as if it had nothing to do with the original text.

Why? Could it be that the product fails to live up to the promise of the act? Could it be that translation, as an act, is more fundamental than its end result? The text's indifference is ultimately a verifiable fact. The original has been transferred from one language to another and at the same time *it has not moved*: it resurfaces behind the translation, intact, untouched, untamed, ready for other translations. This might well be one of the most painful experiences a translator can have: to see the text with which he or she has been in the most intimate contact − an intimacy that one might call infinite, an intimacy that one might call the most intimate of intimacies that one can possibly have with a text − withdraw from the translator disdainfully, as though it has not been translated. *What appears to have taken place has not taken place.*

This is how we might read the fact that, for Benjamin, translation has no meaning for the original text. We might add that via translation the text has reaffirmed and corroborated its *base untranslatability*, confirming that translation is a hopeless act. Just as translatability structures the text, just as the desire to be translated is inscribed within the original, like the original's desire to be torn away from itself and its language, untranslatability structures the text too; we might even say that it is *its most intimate source of pride*. We cannot say the same of translatability. Untranslatability is one of the ways in which the text asserts itself as an inaccessible and untouchable reality. Its untranslatability is somewhat analogous to its *non-critiquability*. No matter how good the translation, no matter how good the piece of criticism, they will never exhaust the text. From this point of view, the text is inexhaustible: it contains an infinite number of translations and works of criticism, of which only a miniscule number actually come into being. Goethe was of the opinion that criticism could never grasp or comprehend the essential nature, the *core*, of the text. There was no work of criticism that could uncover or analyse the textual core that addresses us brusquely, without mediation. Goethe looked at criticism ironically, from the point of view of the text. But the irony generated by the text's untranslatability weighs more heavily on the translation.

The text finds its deepest kernel in its untranslatability − it is the very thing that allows us to attribute a 'kernel' to the text. Just as translatability expresses a partic- ular meaning inherent in the text − both its claim to universality and an essential lack which the act of translation is supposed to fill − untranslatability also expresses a particular meaning, a meaning that one might define as the text's drive to partic- ularity (uniqueness) and an assertion of its fullness (or self-sufficiency). In the face of this drive to particularity and assertion of fullness, translation has, once again, no meaning for the text. It cannot even have a negative meaning, because transla- tion can never come close to, let alone exhaust, the closing-in-on-itself expressed, linguistically, by the text's untranslatability. The more translation, in its radicalness, tries to exhaust the untranslatability of a text, the more this untranslatability reveals new layers of untranslatability, *ad infinitum*. The text is composed of an infinite number of layers of untranslatability which are also layers of translatability: as soon as the translation reaches the end of one layer of untranslatability, transforming it, or rather *revealing* its translatability, it finds, behind it or below it, a further layer of untranslatability, and so on. It goes without saying that at the end of all this there is a final kernel of untranslatability, and that this kernel is concealed under impenetrable layers.

The text's propensity for the particular is also a propensity for the infinite; this is why the text is proud of its untranslatability. For the text, of course, this propensity (in a predictable reversal) demands its opposite, which is the universality embedded in its translatability, for if the text simply closes back in on itself, it will be engulfed by its sheer specificity, by the abyss of its language.

When the drive towards untranslatability prevails over the drive towards translatability, the text as such vanishes: this can be quite clearly observed in certain poems from the second period of German Romanticism which are sheer *musicality*. It was with good reason that these poems were eventually put to music by Romantic and post-Romantic musicians, thus ensuring their continued life and even their fame, but it also meant that music reclaimed them. This could hardly have been avoided, however, since these poems were so deeply rooted in their musicality that they could no longer enjoy an independent existence.

Generally speaking, musicality has to be seen as the most untranslatable element of a text; it is also the element that should never be allowed to dominate if the text wishes to remain text. By emphasising the latent musicality of its language, the text loses its relationship to its mother tongue. Musicality amplifies an element of this mother tongue that is destructive for the text, because it comes at the expense of the way in which *it speaks and makes its meanings*. 'De la musique en toutes choses'[5] [music in everything] is a fatal principle for a text composed of language. The kernel of how the text speaks and makes its meanings is what should be untranslatable (because at some stage the untranslatable *can* shift into the translatable), not its kernel of musicality, which in its vague infinity constitutes the *absolute* untranslatability of an opaque, mute and unsignifying sphere.

This is how – on the basis of the experience of translation – we might parse Benjamin's statement. When I speak of the experience of translation, I do not mean the lived experience of the translator but rather *that knowledge of the text's essence that is revealed in translation and that has to do with the text's degrees of translatability and untranslatability*. This has nothing to do with the translator's subjective feelings about the text or its translation.

To shed some light on the paradox contained in his statement, Benjamin sets out on a very different path, one that goes beyond the sphere of translation. Immediately after having stated that a translation has no meaning for the original text, he adds:

> Dennoch steht sie mit diesem kraft seiner Übersetzbarkeit im nächsten Zusammenhang.

(p. 10. para 4)

Nonetheless, it [*the translation*] has the closest possible *interrelation* with the original thanks to its [*the original's*] translatability.

Cependant, elle se tient avec celui-ci, grâce à sa traduisibilité, dans la plus proche (*nächsten*) co-relation (*Zusammenhang*).

(*Berman*)

[Literal translation of Berman's French translation:

Nonetheless, it stands with it [*the original*], thanks to its [*the original's*] translatability, in the closest co-relation.]

Gandillac translates *Zusammenhang* as 'corrélation' [correlation] (1971:263). This judicious translation does not fully render the original term, which is one of numerous terms that are difficult to translate from the German. *Zusammenhang*, in German, is an everyday term, whereas the French 'corrélation' is almost a technical term, and is in any case more abstract than the German word. *Zusammenhang* indicates a 'se-tenir-ensemble' (standing/holding together) (*zusammen: ensemble* [together]), the mutual belonging of parties to an 'ensemble'. This is the 'corrélation', if we understand by this *a dynamic interrelation [une co-relation vivante]*.

What might one say about this dynamic *interrelation* between the translation and its original?

This relationship, Benjamin says, is determined by translatability. Translatability is somehow where the two texts meet, it is the thing that connects them across the gulf of their difference. Translation is grounded in translatability, and this is immanent in the text. But that does not change anything about the fact that Benjamin sees translatability as meaningful for the text but not translation, the end result of translatability.

Let me set this out again. By virtue of its translatability the work *engenders* its translation, with the following result: a relationship constituted by the greatest possible degree of *intimacy* (manifest in the fact of the engendering) and the greatest possible *distance* (because the translated text, though engendered by the original, has no meaning for it).

I cannot help but think, here, of the relationship between progenitors and children. Without wanting to go into this at any length, this is a relationship characterised by the fact that the 'flesh of my flesh' is simultaneously 'a different flesh'. It is significant that later on Benjamin talks of a *kinship without resemblance* where languages are concerned. The paradox of the child is that the child unites kinship and resemblance; the resemblance that the child manifests is the inessential (and dangerous) element, whereas kinship is essential (and salvational). The relationship that holds between a child and its progenitors is one of *perpetuation*.[6] As a father I perpetuate myself in my son, but at the same time my son is a separate being, and radically so. I am nothing to him (in the matter of his own existence) and vice versa, he is nothing to me (in the matter of my own existence). He perpetuates me (this is in fact the one true form of perpetuation) through the fact of his existence, an existence that is not, however, fundamentally directed towards me. Jacques Derrida once said to me (in conversation, not in writing): 'l'enfant est celui qui s'en va' ['it is in the nature of the child to leave']. In this 'leaving', the intensity of the child's relationship to me reaches its zenith.

I will not say that translations are the 'daughters' of original texts. But reflecting on kinship as an essential element of human historicity opens up a plane that allows us to think about the enigmatic relationship between the original and its translation. All of this belongs, Benjamin will say, to the same *Zusammenhang*, to the same space of *interrelation*.

This is the space of *life*. Not life in the purely biological sense but life as *historicity*. Historicity is not a straightforwardly linear notion, it is a process of metamorphoses, of stages of maturation, of engenderings. To think about historicity, we have to start out from the primordial categories of life, but conversely (so as not to fall into a historicising biologism such as Spengler did in Benjamin's epoch), we have to think about life – the life of youth, maturity, old age, sexuality,[7] family, natality – historically: that is to say as an entity that cannot be reduced to a simple vital *cycle* that is predetermined and instinctual.

What characterises this historical life – the historical life of man, his deeds, words and the entire human sphere in the broad sense – is that it gathers its meaning via *experience*. Unlike the animal world, humans live their paternity, maternity – natality in general – via example, via the mode of experience.

This is the framework of life, history and experience within which Benjamin will think the relationship between the translation and the original, a relationship in which the thing that is engendered, he says, means nothing for the engenderer, but enjoys the most intimate relationship with it nonetheless.

> Ja, dieser Zusammenhang ist um so inniger, als er für das Original selbst nichts mehr bedeutet.
>
> *(p. 10. para 4)*

> Indeed, this *interrelation* is all the more intimate since it no longer has any meaning for the original.

> Oui, cette co-relation est d'autant plus intime (*innig*) qu'elle ne signifie plus rien pour l'original.
>
> *(Berman)*

[Literal translation of Berman's French translation:

> Yes, this co-relation is all the more intimate because it no longer means anything for the original.]

We should pause here on:

> intimate (*innig*) [*intime*]
> and
> no longer/nothing more (*nichts mehr*) [plus rien].

Innig is translated here as 'intime' [intimate]. But this German word is untranslatable. The French 'intime' is hopelessly subjective and *intimiste*. *Innig*, in German, takes us straight to the inter-belonging of beings implied, amongst other words, by *Zusammenhang*. It is an ontological category.

Innig is a significant word in Hölderlin's poetry (and thought) ('*alles ist innig*', he wrote, 'everything is *innig*' (1951:321)) and Rilke's late poetry is the poetry of the *Innigkeit* of things.

We cannot tarry any longer with *Innigkeit*. But it is obvious that this word does not coincidentally issue from Benjamin's pen in a context where *Zusammenhang* and, one line further on, 'natural *Zusammenhang*' is at stake, for Nature (in the Spinozean sense of *natura naturans*, not Nature as the object of science) is the space where Hölderlin and Rilke locate *Innigkeit*. For these poets, the space of *Innigkeit* is specifically one of distance. Intimacy between things comes about through distance – through what Rilke calls 'pure relation' (*reiner Bezug*).

The intimacy between the original and its translation is therefore all the greater because it creates an irremediable distance between them. This is because theirs is an *interrelation*, or a 'natural' co-belonging.

> Er darf ein natürlicher genannt warden und zwar genauer ein Zusammenhang des Lebens.
>
> > *(p. 10. para 4)*

> It can be called a natural *interrelation* and more precisely an *interrelation* of life.

> Elle doit être appelée une co-relation naturelle, et certes, plus exactement, une co-relation de la vie.
>
> > *(Berman)*

[Literal translation of Berman's French translation:

> It should be called a natural co-relation, and indeed, more exactly, a co-relation of life.]

Zusammenhang des Lebens: every essential *Zusammenhang* is a *Zusammenhang* of life.

I think that it is becoming more and more obvious that the re-translation that forms part of this commentary is only served by the commentary and conversely that the commentary is only served by being a translation. This is the *Innigkeit* of commentary and translation that we discussed at the beginning.[8]

Zusammenhang des Lebens is more precise than *natürlicher Zusammenhang* because the reference to Nature can be misleading, making us lose sight of the historicity of the sphere that has been evoked.

Is *Vie* [Life] preferable to *Nature* [Nature] here? Let us leave that aside for the moment. For Benjamin (and his epoch) there is no doubt that this was the case.[9]

But we should return to the *nichts mehr* that I forgot along the way, doubtless because it is subtle.

> Indeed, this *interrelation* is all the more intimate since it no longer has any meaning for the original.
>
> *(Benjamin 1991a:10)*

If this '*interrelation*' 'no longer' means anything for the original text, during which *period of time* does it hold sway? Was there a period of time when it did mean something for the text? Absolutely not. Or, structurally speaking, always. Either the relationship between the original and the translation always means something for the original text or it never means anything for it.

But then why the temporal designation *no longer*?

Firstly, it evokes death. Everything that meant something to me during my lifetime 'no longer' means anything once I am dead. But does a text die? Isn't it (at least partially) 'immortal'? Let's take this a step further. If I am given something that I have desired for a long time but which is no longer the object of my desire, then this thing (this gift) 'no longer means anything' to me. Death is present here, but it is the death of my desire, of my expectation. 'It is too late.' I have reached a stage where this gift no longer has any meaning. Does translation come *too late*? Later on we will see that translation is always 'late'. But no matter how we interpret it, the sentence is troubled by this temporal designation:

> a translation, no matter how good it is, can *never* have any significance for the original.
>
> *(Benjamin 1991a:10)*

Niemals, never. And then *nichts mehr*, nothing more/no longer. It is true that in writing this sentence, Benjamin has not yet entered into the paradox of the un-meaning intimacy that exists between the original and the translation; he has not yet thought through the temporality of the original text and the translation. So we have to try to think of the *niemals*, the never, as a mode of temporality rather than as an assertion of an atemporal structure, and state, bringing Benjamin's two sentences together, that translation can *never* (ever) mean anything for the original, because it comes about in a period when it can *no longer* mean anything for the original text.

But what does that mean?

Benjamin continues:

> So wie die Äußerungen des Lebens innigst mit dem Lebendigen zusammenhängen, ohne ihm etwas zu bedeuten, geht die Übersetzung aus dem Original hervor.
>
> *(p. 10. para 4)*

> Just as the expressions of life are intimately *interrelated* with that-which-is-alive, without having any significance for it, so the translation proceeds from the original.

> Tout comme les expressions de la vie co-appartiennent (*zusammenhängen*) au plus intime (*innigst*) avec le vivant (*das Lebendige*) sans signifier quelque chose pour lui, la traduction surgit (*hervorgeht*) de l'original.
>
> *(Berman)*

[Literal translation of Berman's French translation:

> Just as the expressions of life co-belong in the most intimate manner with living matter without meaning anything for it, translation emerges from the original.]

The first part of the sentence is too vague for us to discuss it now. Let us focus on these four words: *zusammenhängen* (again), *innigst* (again), *bedeuten* (again) and *das Lebendige*, that-which-is-alive. What kind of living matter might this be? A few years previously, Benjamin wrote a commentary on two of Hölderlin's poems that take *das Lebendige*, that-which-is-alive, as their central theme. *Le vivant par excellence, c'est l'homme. [Man is that which is most alive].*[10] What is an 'expression' of life? We will come to that presently.

Let us look at the second part of the sentence instead. We would normally – although this is not the case here – interpret this in light of the first part of the sentence because we are dealing with a comparison: *so wie*, just like … This is admittedly a subsuming comparison: the relationship between translation and the original text is analogous to the relationship between an expression and life, but this relationship also belongs, globally, to the domain of life. What we discover is:

expression ↔ life
translation ↔ original

What if these terms were mutually illuminating? What if we thought about life as the original and its expressions in terms of translation? We shouldn't forget the fragment from *One-Way Street*:

> Commentary and translation are to the text what style and mimesis are to nature.
>
> *(Benjamin 1991c:92)*

We could then write:

expression ↔ life
translation ↔ original
mimesis ↔ nature

Let us return to the text:

> die Übersetzung [geht] aus dem Original hervor.
>
> translation proceeds from the original.
>
> la traduction *surgit* de l'original.
>
> *(Berman)*

[Literal translation of Berman's French translation:

> translation *emerges* from the original.]

This statement is remarkable for its simplicity.

Here *surgir* is a tentative translation of the German verb *hervorgeht*, which evokes provenance from a source, an emergence from, a sudden bursting forth. Heidegger meditates upon this verb, specifically in the context of the name that the Greeks give to Nature, φύσις. What does this kind of emergence-from-a-source (the original, of course) have to do with expressions of life (*Äußerungen*)? Translation certainly issues from a source text in a manner that could be described as emergence, provenance, bursting forth. And it is a phenomenon of life, a *vital* manifestation. More precisely: *the life of the text*. But isn't discussion of the 'life' of a text metaphorical? No more so, as we will see, than talking about the text's 'desire'? The text is only desire because it is 'life'. But isn't the text ordinarily more properly considered to be one of life's 'expressions'? Benjamin will soon try to justify his statement – at length.

Prior to this, in order to delineate, from the outset, the sphere of the 'life' of the text, he writes this key sentence:

> Zwar nicht aus seinem Leben so sehr denn aus seinem «Überleben».
>
> *(p.10. para 4)*

Not so much from its life as from its *'sur-vival'*.

Certes pas tant de sa vie que plutôt de sa «survie».

(Berman)

[Literal translation:

Indeed not so much from its life but rather from its *«survie»* [survival/ afterlife].][11]

The term *Überleben* is so important to him that he deliberately places it in inverted commas. This is because there is obviously a connection, *Zusammenhang*, between *Überleben* and *Übersetzung*. Let me immediately stress that Benjamin does not mean that translation is the text's mode of survival.

An aside is necessary here: from Romanticism through to Heidegger, German thought has continuously reflected upon this *'über'* in the context of translation, criticism, thought and existence. Nietzsche's *Übermensch* requires no introduction. For Friedrich Schlegel (and Benjamin is the one who tells us this), criticism is governed by the sign of *'über'*. Schlegel's name for the piece of criticism that he considered to have come closest to the ideal of the genre – his study of Goethe's *Wilhelm Meister* (1798) – was the *Über-meister*. Matthias Claudius and Herder both reflected on the *über* of *Übersetzung*.[12] Finally, Heidegger links what he calls the *Überwindung* of metaphysics to this moment of *Übersetzung* when thought suddenly gains access to the Greek word. Listen to what he wrote in *What is Called Thinking?* [*Was heisst Denken?*] (1961), a text which is, to a large extent, the translation of a fragment of Parmenides:

> It is indeed superfluous to translate εόν εμμεναι into Latin or into German. But for us it is necessary to finally translate these words into Greek. This *Übersetzen* is only possible as *Über*setzen into what speaks from these words.
> *(Heidegger 1961:140)*[13]

Words with *Über-*, and verbs in particular, verbs like *überstehen* – endure – are fundamental in Rilke's poetry and correspondence.[14]

This is also the case for Benjamin. The *über* thread – of which we will gradually gather evidence – and reflection on the *über* of translation is fundamental both for translation and for much more besides.

> Ist doch die Übersetzung später als das Original und bezeichnet sie doch bei den bedeutenden Werken, die da ihre erwählten Übersetzer niemals im Zeitalter ihrer Entstehung finden, das Stadium ihres Fortlebens.
> *(pp.10–11. para 4)*

For the translation is later than the original and marks the stage of continuing life for those significant texts that will never find their chosen translator in the era of their creation.

> Car la traduction est plus tardive (*später*) que l'original et caractérise pour
> les œuvres importantes (*bedeutenden*), qui ne trouvent jamais (*niemals*) leur
> traducteur élu (*erwählten*) à l'époque de leur naissance (*Entstehung*), le stade de
> leur vie continuée (*Fortlebens*).
>
> (Berman)

[Literal translation of Berman's French translation:

> Because translation is later than the original and characterises for important
> works, which never find their chosen translator in the epoch of their birth,
> the stage of their continuing life.]

Gandillac translates *später* as 'après' [after], *erwählten* as 'prédestiné' [predestined],
entstehen as 'naissance' [birth] and *Fortleben* as 'survie' [survival] (1971:263). All these
choices can be critiqued to varying degrees and we will see why in a moment.
I would like to emphasise once again that the 'defaults' of Gandillac's translation
are those of any *first* translation and should not be blamed on this remarkable translator. Indeed, Gandillac's translation allows us to reflect on Benjamin's language.[15]

Später without a doubt implies 'after' ['après']. But *spät* is also 'late' ['tard'], late
in the sense of delayed ['tardif']. *Spät* contrasts with *früh*, early ['tôt']. The original
text (because it is the source) is in the *früh* category, the translation in the *spät* category, late ['tardif']. Translating *spät* as 'tardif' allows me to invoke translation as the
fruit which, in *One-Way Street*, falls *rechtzeitig*, at the right moment, from the tree
of the text, that is to say, in the autumn of the text. *L'automne est la saison tardive.*
[Autumn is the late season.] 'Late' art is autumnal art. 'Après' implies a succession,
the *nacheinander* of linear time. 'Tardif' points to the time of that 'life' of which
Benjamin speaks.

Erwählten is 'l'élu' [the chosen, elected one], not 'le prédestiné' [the predestined
one]. It is unnecessary – risky even – to introduce a notion that has so many theological and mythical connotations at this juncture.

Entstehung is more general than 'naissance' [birth]: it is an emergence [*surgissement*].
It would be better, therefore, to translate *hervorgehen* earlier on with 'provenir' [to
come from] or 'jaillir' [to burst, spurt, gush], and *entstehen*, which we encounter a
little further on, as 'surgir' [emerge].

We cannot translate *Fortleben* as 'survie' if we (perfectly correctly) translate
Überleben as 'survie' earlier on. *Fort* is less semantically charged than *über*.

Fort (in my opinion) contains the simple idea of continuation. The *Überleben* that
precedes it in the text designates an act (that of surviving), whereas *Fortleben* appears
to express merely a state of continuation. It would therefore be better to tentatively
translate *überleben* as 'survivre' [survive – verb] rather than 'survie' [survival – noun],
reserving the substantive form for *fortleben*.

Certes pas tant de son vivre que de son «survivre».

[Literal translation of Berman's French translation:

> Indeed not so much from its *vivre* [living > life: *vivre* is the verb meaning 'to live'] as its *survivre* [surviving > survival: *survivre* is the verb meaning 'to survive'.]

This sentence pronounces that the translation bursts forth – organically – from the '*survie*' [*Fortleben*], the active '*survivre*' [*Überleben*] of the text.

The sentence that follows it pronounces that translation 'characterises' (*bezeichnet*) the stage of the text's 'continuing life' because, for the original text, translation always comes 'later'. Benjamin is not simply saying that translation comes *after* the original text (which in any case would be an empty banality), but that this *after* falls into the late (in the sense of *tardif*) category.

This leads us to the following question: *why is translation always late?* Meaning, is lateness *part of its essence*? It is possible, after all, that this lateness is, chronologically speaking, not very late at all. The epoch in which the work comes to prominence can pass very quickly. But whether this epoch is brief or long in the conventional understanding of time, the translation of the original can only emerge when the epoch of the original is over.

The temporality of the translation, the period in which it emerges, is therefore dependent on the temporality of source texts. Benjamin defines this temporality briefly towards the end of the paragraph – after he has defined life as history. The temporality (or historicity) of the original text is not a location *in* time (in history). Rather it means that the work has its own temporal mode, *is in possession of its own historicity*. This historicity, at a particular moment of its 'maturity', provokes, allows and demands translation.

> Die Geschichte der großen Kunstwerke kennt ihre Deszendenz aus den Quellen, ihre Gestaltung im Zeitalter des Künstlers und die Periode ihres grundsätzlich ewigen Fortlebens bei den nachfolgenden Generationen. Dieses letzte heißt, wo es zutage tritt, Ruhm.
>
> *(p. 11. para 4)*

> The history of the great works of art recognises their provenance from sources, their creation in the epoch of the artist and the period of their life among subsequent generations that can principally continue in perpetuity. When the latter occurs, it is called fame.

> L'histoire des grandes œuvres d'art connaît leur descendance à partir des sources, leur formation à l'époque de l'artiste et la période de leur vie continuée et principiellement éternelle auprès des générations suivantes. Cette dernière s'appelle, lorsqu'elle vient au jour, la gloire.
>
> *(Berman)*

[Literal translation of Berman's French translation:

> The history of the great works of art knows their descent from sources, their creation in the epoch of the artist and the period of their continuing and in principle eternal life among the following generations. The latter is called, when it comes into being, glory.]

At the end of the paragraph, there is another implicit qualification: 'when it occurs'. The life of a text does not necessarily lead to a *Fortleben* therefore?

This is a parallel qualification to the one that announces in passing that translatability is only meaningful for certain texts. These are the same texts that enjoy a 'continuing life' and that call for and provoke their translation.

This continuing life of the text, Benjamin says, is called its 'fame'. We have seen that fame is linked to the *unforgettable*. If, by virtue of its essence, its plenitude, the text is unforgettable, something-worthy-of-not-being-forgotten, then the glory that is fame emerges, not necessarily at the time of the text's prominence, when the artist is alive, but among subsequent generations.

Aren't we at risk of returning to the plane of textual reception instead of staying with the immanent life of texts? What bestows 'fame' on a work if not its readers?

Perhaps there is a risk of this here. But Benjamin is clearly linking the *survie* of the text to the death of the artist here. We could counter this with examples of texts that have enjoyed fame while their authors were still alive. Joyce would be a twentieth-century example. However, if 'fame' indicates not so much the author's celebrity as *the sheer glory of the original text*, we would still have to posit that the work cannot truly enter into its glory until only the *name* of the author remains. While the author lives, the text will not attain the supreme autonomy that also designates its glory. The author casts a long shadow. To this we can add something that Benjamin knew better than anybody: that a text, linguistically speaking, is always ahead of its time, is always 'anticipatory' and that the era of its fame only begins when the time that it inhabits has aligned with ours. This is never the case in the author's lifetime. Any celebrity enjoyed by the author, as Valéry put it, is always built on misunderstandings.

The continuing life of the text is therefore the time when the text becomes glorious *on its own terms* and enters the sphere of its *autonomy*.

These two characteristics – the fact that the text has to wait for the death of the author for its glory; and that it possesses an anticipatory temporality – explain, quite aside from Benjamin, why a true translation of a text, one that does justice to its grandeur, is *not really possible* at the time of its birth.

The first of these two characteristics raises the problem of the *contemporaneity* of the author and the translator. This contemporaneity is always a serious problem for translation. Just as the author casts a shadow over his or her text and prevents, through his or her own existence, its autonomy, so too does the author cast a shadow over the text's translation. This issue is a long and difficult chapter in the history of translation thought.

Principally, the era of great translations of a text can only begin after the death of the author. This is not to say that translation cannot flourish during the author's lifetime, as was the case with Goethe, Joyce or Broch,[16] who not only took an interest in the translation of their works (and in translation in general) but made a significant contribution to these translations in a way that influenced the history of their texts and of the translations. Goethe clearly thought that living authors should translate each other's work, and this is something worthy of further consideration. But it does not alter the essential fact that great translations, and great translators, can only find their time and their space long after the author has disappeared. This is because translation can only operate in absolute *solitude* with the text – a solitude that matches the text's fame and its autonomy. The *intensity* of the translator's relationship to the text prevents anybody else from having a relationship with it. In fact, the disappearance of the author simultaneously allows the work to have a relationship with itself and the translator to have a relationship with it. *The disappearance of the author makes both the autonomy of the text and its translation possible.*

The anticipatory temporality of the text's language is also an obstacle to a (good) contemporaneous translation of the work. Faced with this language, the translator is just as helpless, initially, as the critic. What I have called the 'first translation' does not do justice to this language: first translations have a tendency to pull the text towards earlier languages; these might be the languages of texts in the translating language or in the translated language. This is because translation is restrictive on two fronts: *that of the contemporaneous state of the translating language, but also the state that the translated language is in immediately prior to the translation of the work.* To the extent that the text never simply constitutes a linguistic break, but is both a rupture and the continuation of a tradition, the first translation *accentuates* the conventional element of the work at the expense of its anticipatory element. In this respect any first translation (or contemporaneous translation of a text) is classicising in the academic sense.

We can summarise all this as follows: a true translation has to *wait*. It has to wait for the mode of temporality (and of being) signalled by the work's fame. This, as I have already said, is the work's true glory. This true glory, Benjamin suggests, classically, is 'eternal'.

But a strange kind of eternity it is. A poem by Pierre Emmanuel begins thus:

Oh fûts de tremblante éternité sur les collines[17]

[Oh trunks of trembling eternity on the hills]

The work's eternity is of this variety – *tremblante* [trembling] – and Emmanuel's poem, with its *fûts*, alludes to the semi-ruined colonnades of Greek temples.

With the enigmatic proposition that *translation comes to the work both as its fate and as a necessity during the period of its most radiant glory, which is also the period of its decline*, we return to the domain of the fragment from *One-Way Street* – but also the domain in which Goethe's thought operates. Glory is exhausting. Nobody knew this better than Goethe, who spoke of the aging process that accompanies the glory of the text.[18] The continuing life of the work is never an unchanging perennial splendour.

This 'trembling eternity' is a property of the *profane* text. We cannot attribute fame to *sacred* texts. Translation comes to them in another way, indicated by the image in *One-Way Street*: 'the eternal rustling of the leaves on the tree of the sacred text'. This is a way of suggesting that the tree knows neither fame nor decline and that commentary and translation are perpetually inscribed within it as part of its most intimate life. This is not the case with the profane text which thrives on its fame.

At this point it is worth emphasising what Goethe tells us: that translation, for the text that has petrified in its fame, is 'regeneration', 'rejuvenation', *Verjüngung*. It is not simply that the work petrifies in its own glory, but that it buries itself in its light and in its 'effects'. By 'effects', I mean what emanates or bursts forth from the text – *hervorgeht* – which is to say the mass of imitations, of works of criticism: everything that *descends* from it. It may well be a law governing the historicity of great texts that all the texts engendered by them in their own space (and that attest to, even celebrate their fame) end up concealing the works, suffocating them, or reducing them to mere names. Faced with something that conceals the work and prevents any relationship with it, translation represents a development which, by placing the text in an *other* linguisticity, liberates it from this suffocating vegetation, from the inviolable immobility of its own fame and which – literally – *transplants* it into fresh soil where it can regenerate. Yes, *translation is transplantation*. Goethe celebrates this in a poem, 'Ein Gleichnis' (Goethe 1988:862–864).

A regenerating and rejuvenating transplant of this kind is also a re-birth, which is to say that it returns the text to a more originary temporality, to the 'age of its own emergence'. This is empirical proof of the fact that, sometimes in order to escape the attrition in the relationship we have to our own language, we need to express ourselves in another language. Hofmannsthal put this magnificently in a text that utilises the same image as the one in Goethe's poem: that of the wilted and faded plant that revives when transplanted in foreign soil:

> When we have become deaf to the beauty of our own language, then any for-
> eign language has an indescribable magic; we only need pour our drooping
> thoughts into it and they come to life like flowers that have been thrown into
> fresh water.

> *(Hofmannsthal 1950:31)*[19]

Thus it happens – and this is the inverse of the same phenomenon – that when we hear our language spoken by a stranger it appears fresher, younger. This is the impression created by texts written in French by non-native-speakers, a phenom-enon that has a lot to do with translation. But translation is different in the sense that the shift is more specific and rigorous, a *re-deployment* of the text towards the 'era of its emergence'. Several translators have sensed this and formulated it in more or less psychological terms, even though the temporality of the shift is rigorously objective.

> The work of translation [...] does not lead us to compose a text on the basis of another, but rather to return the text to the virtual era of its creation.
>
> *(Valéry 1957:215)*[20]

> You would not believe the extent to which you can penetrate a text by struggling with it for a long period of time. You even come to believe that you can probe the secret of its genesis.
>
> *(Leyris 1974)*[21]

Translation, during the period of the text's glory and decline, is therefore a *rejuvenating commemoration*, a return to the origins of the text.

It does not appear that Benjamin, whose knowledge of Goethe's work was intensely specific rather than broad, was aware of his remarks on translation as *Verjüngung*; these remarks are admittedly few and dispersed. Benjamin was in any case closer to Romantic notions of translation which, without contradicting Goethe's ideas, go in another direction, that of translation as the work's 'elevation to power', its *Potenzierung*.

This is what the final lines of the paragraph discuss:

> Übersetzungen, die mehr als Vermittlungen sind, entstehen, wenn im Fortleben ein Werk das Zeitalter seines Ruhmes erreicht hat. Sie dienen daher nicht sowohl diesem, wie schlechte Übersetzer es für ihre Arbeit zu beanspruchen pflegen, als daß sie ihm ihr Dasein verdanken. In ihnen erreicht das Leben des Originals seine stets erneute späteste und umfassendste Entfaltung.
>
> *(p. 11. para 4)*

> Translations that are more than transmissions arise when, in the course of its continuing life, a work has reached the era of its fame. Translations thus do not serve this fame, as poor translators tend to claim of their work, so much as owe their existence to it. In them the life of the original reaches its constantly renewed, latest and most extensive development.

> Des traductions qui sont plus que des médiations (*Vermittlungen*: médiations, not 'communications' as Gandillac writes (1971:264), thus using the same French term to translate *Vermittlung* and *Mitteilung*), surgissent (*entstehen*) quand dans sa vie continuée une œuvre a atteint l'époque de sa gloire. Elles ne servent donc pas tant celle-ci, comme ont coutume de le revendiquer pour leur travail de mauvais traducteurs, qu'elles ne lui doivent leur existence (*Dasein*). En elles la vie de l'original atteint son développement constamment renouvelé le plus tardif et le plus étendu (*umfassendste*: literally: the most encircling, embracing).
>
> *(Berman)*

[Literal translation of Berman's French translation:

> Translations that are more than mediations emerge when in its continued life a work has reached the epoch of its glory. They therefore do not serve this [*its glory*], as bad translators are in the habit of claiming for their work, so much as much as they owe it their existence. In them the life of the original reaches its constantly renewed and latest, most extensive development.]

In a crescendo full of detours, Benjamin leads us into the next paragraph.

The first point here is that essential translation – translation that is not *Vermittlung*, *médiation* (a much broader concept and more philosophical than *Mitteilung*, communication, a word that does in fact express the essence of *Mitteilung*) – emerges during the period when the text has entered into the phase of its continuing life: its *Fortleben* makes *Übersetzung* possible.

The second point here is that translation does not facilitate the continuing life of the work and its fame *a fortiori*. 'Bad translators' make a claim to this.[22] Rather, it is the fame of the text that facilitates translation.

This brings us back to the fact that the text's translatability (*Übersetzbarkeit*) is determined by the temporal movement that leads the text into the fullness of its maturity and autonomy. As the work matures, it becomes translatable. *Übersetzbarkeit* is not an 'atemporal' structure. *It is born of the temporalisation of the text.*

This is where *kairos* and *translatability*, which we discussed separately, come together. The right moment for translation responds entirely to a particular moment of the text. This is what is expressed in the fragment from *One-Way Street*. A 'good' translator is one who responds to the call of the text when it is 'ripe' for translation. *The right moment and the right translator belong to each other.* A bad translator is one who has the audacity to translate *before* this moment. This audacity signals hubris, an immodesty on the part of the translator who is blind to the work's temporality – to the work as temporality. If the translator views the work as a petrified message bearing a content, then he or she fails to perceive that the text is a *living* being that has its own time, a time when it is ripe for translation, and a time when it is not yet ripe. A. W. Schlegel, Voss and Hölderlin were great translators because each, in his own way, perceived that Shakespeare, Calderón, Homer, Virgil, Sophocles, Pindar had reached the time of their translation in Germany.[23]

Benjamin's thinking on the place of translation here is completely in line with tradition.[24]

The final sentence of the paragraph introduces the dimension of *Überleben*, which is key throughout Benjamin's text.

Up until now we have distinguished, terminologically speaking, between *Überleben* and *Fortleben*. *Fortleben* simply indicates that the text has entered into the period of its ongoing reign. It continues on through time and this continuation is a phenomenon of maturity leading to fame. With translation, the text suddenly accedes to a more elevated life. Translation takes the text, or rather its sur-vival, to another level. The *über* of translation lifts the *über* of the life of the text – which was only a *fort*, a continuation – to an *elevated* state. Because *über* means above and beyond.

Über leben

Life   Continuing life in the sense of continuation   via

Über setzung

(*Überleben* = *Fortleben*)

There is a shift here from a perpetual temporality to an elevated temporality, that is to say to a different temporal 'sphere', a sphere where it is always the text that changes – it becomes, if not complete,[25] at least imbued with the *promise of completion*. This is the aspect that we will be reflecting upon in the remainder of the commentary. From this point on we can say that *the text itself is moving to another level*.[26]

One final remark: I have not discussed the middle of the paragraph, where Benjamin attempts to think through *life* – and (above all) the life of the text – as *history*. I will return to this later in the commentary.

Notes

1   ['gibt zu denken'.]

2   These two aspects – cherishing the text and its thought – mean that the commentary is *philo-logy* and *philo-sophy* in the original sense. No commentary is purely philological or philosophical.

3   Translation by Antoine Berman, slightly different from the version of this passage that he gives in Cahier 2. [The differences between the two translations are that 'immanente aux originaux' [immanent in the originals] has become 'inhérente à l'original' [inherent in the original], and 'si bonne soit-elle' has become the more or less equivalent 'aussi bonne soit-elle'.]

4   [This is a reference back to Rilke's letter to Benvenuta, cited in Cahier 2.]

5   [This citation from Verlaine should read 'De la musique avant toute chose' (Verlaine 1951:206).]

6   See the thoughts on 'natality' in *The Human Condition* (1958) by Hannah Arendt, Benjamin's friend.

7   Traditionally we spoke of gendered life rather than sexual life. On the replacement of gender by sex, see *Gender* by Ivan Illich (1983). Benjamin's thought on the subject of life operates in the realm of gender, not of sex.

8   Here I would like to come back to the remarks made by Granoff and Rey in their book *L'Occulte, object de la pensée freudienne* (1983:157). These remarks pertain to the argument that a translation, when faced with untranslatable terms in the original text, has to be accompanied by – or give way to – a commentary.

9   *Vie* is also a key term (*Grundwort*) in phenomenology, not to mention in Bergson and Simmel.

10 In the two poems that Benjamin discussed (Benjamin 1991b:105–126), *das Lebendige* actually designates man and not the 'biological realm'. The poem 'Dichtermut' begins with 'Sind denn dir nicht verwandt alle Lebendigen?' [Are all living things not related to you?] (Hölderlin 1977:141).

11 [Berman uses '*survie*' to translate '*Überleben*' here but later in the commentary states that '*survie*' should be reserved for *Fortleben* with *Überleben* more appropriately translated as 'survivre'.]

12 Think of the line by Matthias Claudius: *Übersetzen ist untersetzen*. Herder distinguishes between two types of translation, one where one emphasises the *über* and the other the *Setzung* in *Übersetzung*, the 'beyond' and 'the position': 'we have long since distinguished between two modes of translation. The first tries to bring us the original word by word and even, where possible, with the emphases of the words. This bears the name *Über*setzung, with the emphasis on the *über*. The other kind über*setzt*, that is to say that it presents the author as he would have written for us if our language had been his' (in Kloepfer 1967:49). ['Man hat längst eine zweifache Art der Übersetzung voneinander unterschieden. Die eine sucht das Urbild Wort für Wort, ja womöglich mit den Tönen der Worte herüberzutragen, man hat sie *Über*setzung genannt, indem man den Ton auf das Über legt. Die andere Gattung über*setzt*, d.i. sie drückt die Gestalt des Autors aus, wie er für uns, wäre ihm unsere Sprache zu Theil geworden, etwa sprechen würde.' Kloepfer gives the reference for this citation as *Sämtliche Werke*, ed. Suphan 1877 ff. (Kritische Wälder, 1. Wäldch. § 15).]

13 ['Es ist in der Tat überflüssig, ἐὸν ἔμμεναι in das Lateinische und in das Deutsche zu übersetzen. Aber nötig ist es für uns, diese Worte endlich ins Griechische zu übersetzen. Dieses Über*setzen* ist nur möglich als *Über*setzen zu dem, was aus diesen Worten spricht.' The Greek in the French translation cited by Berman is incorrectly rendered and has been corrected in this citation from the German source text.]

14 Cf. *Rilke* by Otto Friedrich Bollnow (1951) where an entire chapter is dedicated to terms containing *über*. For Rilke the poetic act is entirely governed by *über*.

15 Let me stress the term 'defaults' [*défaillances*]. We owe the remarkable expression 'Versagung der Übersetzung' (Freud 1986:219) to Freud (Freud's letter to Fliess no. 112 of 6 December 1896). [This letter is incorrectly referenced as letter no. 52 of 8 December 1896 in Berman's commentary.] Freud uses it in a context – that of the psychic apparatus – which does not directly concern us here. But it points to something essential in translation – which goes far beyond the 'mistakes' and 'faults' of the translator. *Translation's default consists of the fact that it does not deliver where it is supposed to (and could) deliver.* And this default is inherent in translation. *There is no translation without translation default.* The location of defaults can vary, but they always exist. Re-translation highlights them, but is not free of them. Further re-translation will also detect them. Why does this defaulting structure exist? And why does this structure, historically, culturally, become a *fault*, a fault attributed to the translation or the translator? We would have to jointly analyse the phenomena of the *defaults* and *deformations* in translation, which always occur together. Is censure at work? Once more we are circuitously led to psychoanalytic thought.

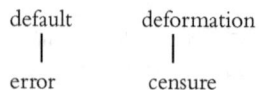

[The French term *défaillance*, which Berman uses to translate Freud's *Versagung*, can mean 'weakness' or 'incapacity', but is also a technical term referring to the non-execution of a clause in a legal contract. For this latter reason I have chosen 'default' as there is an element of refusal or non-compliance in the phenomenon that Berman is describing. Freud's *Versagung* is an unusual form of *Versagen* [failure].]

16 And Saint-John Perse, Guimarães Rosa.

17 [This line should read 'Fût de tremblante éternité sur les collines' (Emmanuel 2001:167). It appears in the poem 'Mourir', from the collection *Jour de Colère* (1942), but does not open the poem as Berman claims.]

18 'Every literature ends up exhausting itself if it is not regenerated by foreign participation.' Goethe, as cited in Strich 1946:32 and re-cited in French translation [with an incorrect page reference to Strich] by Berman 1984:106. ['Jede Literatur ennuyiert sich zuletzt in sich selbst, wenn sie nicht durch fremde Teilnahme wieder aufgefrischt wird.' Strich references this statement of Goethe's to a letter written to Carlyle dated 15 June 1828.]

19 ['Ja, wenn wir für die Schönheit der eigenen stumpf geworden sind, so hat die nächstbeste fremde einen unbeschreiblichen Zauber; wir brauchen nur unsere welken Gedanken in sie hineinzuschütten, und sie werden lebendig wie Blumen, wenn sie ins frische Wasser geworfen werden.']

20 ['Le travail de traduire [...] nous fait [...] non point façonner un texte à partir d'un autre; mais de celui-ci, remonter à l'époque virtuelle de sa formation.']

21 ['Vous ne pouvez pas savoir à quel point on pénètre un texte en luttant longuement avec lui. On croit même saisir le secret de sa genèse.' The citation comes from an interview by Françoise Wagner with Pierre Leyris, French translator of William Blake, to mark the publication of the first volume of the French translation of Blake's collected works.]

22 In 'The Task of the Translator' the shadow cast over translation by the figure of the 'bad translator' is key. Whenever Benjamin talks about the translator, he is generally talking about the 'bad translator'. A translator is bad by virtue of his *pretensions*. The 'good translator', in contrast, simply submits to the 'task' of translation. I will return to this point.

23 The greatness of Klossowski and his *Énéide* [*Aeneid*] is that he sensed the *kairos* of this text buried under the dust of the humanities and philology.

24 What I am trying to say here is that the theory that fame is an accomplishment of the work is traditional – like the theory of the aura – rather than modern. But it puts modernity and its disdain for fame and the aura in question.

25 For the German Romantics, translation is an accomplishment of the work. There is a reason why Novalis speaks of 'mythical translations'.

26 This is a level where one has to think of *Entfaltung*, this de-velopment, this de-ployment, this un-folding of the work effected by translation – and the neverending re-translations of the work. Translation shifts the text from *Fortleben* to *Überleben*. We are twisting Benjamin somewhat with this formulation. But the fact remains that he used these two terms, *Fortleben* and *Überleben*. For me, *Fortleben* is not *Überleben*.

Bibliography

Arendt, H., 1998 [1958]. *The Human Condition*. Chicago: University of Chicago Press.

Benjamin, W., 1991a [1923]. Die Aufgabe des Übersetzers. In: R. Tiedemann and H. Schweppenhäuser, eds. 1991. *Gesammelte Schriften*. IV.I. Frankfurt am Main: Suhrkamp. pp.9–21.

Benjamin, W., 1991b. Zwei Gedichte von Friedrich Hölderlin. In: R. Tiedemann and H. Schweppenhäuser, eds. 1991. *Gesammelte Schriften* II.I. Frankfurt am Main: Suhrkamp. pp.105–126.

Benjamin, W., 1991c [1928]. *Einbahnstrasse*. In: R. Tiedemann and H. Schweppenhäuser, eds. 1991. *Gesammelte Schriften*. IV.I. Frankfurt am Main: Suhrkamp. pp.83–148.

Berman, A., 1984. *L'Épreuve de l'étranger*. Paris: Gallimard.

Berman, A., 2008. *L'Âge de la traduction*. Paris: Presses Universitaires de Vincennes.

Bollnow, O.F., 1951. *Rilke*. Stuttgart: W. Kohlhammer Verlag.

Derrida, J., 1985. Des tours de Babel. Translated from French by J.F. Graham. In: J.F. Graham, ed. 1985. *Difference in Translation*. Ithaca, NY: Cornell University Press. pp.165–207.

Emmanuel, P., 2001. *Œuvres poétiques complètes*. Lausanne: L'Age d'Homme.

Freud, S., 1956. *La Naissance de la psychanalyse*. Translated from German by A. Berman. Paris: Presses Universitaires de France.

Freud, S., 1986. *Briefe an Wilhelm Fliess, 1887–1904*. Frankfurt am Main: Fischer.

Gandillac, M. de, trans. 1971. La tâche du traducteur. In: *Œuvres I, Mythe et violence*. Paris: Denoël/Les Lettres Nouvelles. pp.261–275.

Goethe, J.W. von, 1988 [1774]. Ein Gleichnis. In: *Sämtliche Werke. Gedichte (1800–1832)*. Frankfurt am Main: Deutscher Klassiker Verlag. pp.862–864.

Granoff, W. and Rey, J.-M., 1983. *L'Occulte, objet de la pensée freudienne*. Paris: P.U.F.

Heidegger, M., 1961. *Was heisst Denken?* Tübingen: Max Niemeyer Verlag.

Hoffmannsthal, H. von, 1950 [1897]. Französische Redensarten. In: H. von Hoffmansthal. *Reden und Aufsätze*. Wiesbaden: Insel Verlag.

Hölderlin, F., 1951. Alles ist innig. In: *Sämtliche Werke*. Stuttgart: Verlag W. Kohlhammer. p.321.

Hölderlin, F., 1977 [1801–1803]. Dichtermut. In: F. Hölderlin. *Gedichte*. Leipzig: Verlag Philipp Reclam jun.

Illich, I. 1983. *Gender*. London: Marion Boyars.

Kloepfer, R., 1967. *Die Theorie der literarischen Übersetzung*. Munich: Wilhelm Fink Verlag.

Leyris, P., 1974. Traduire, c'est s'en tenir parfois à une imperfection allusive. *Le Monde* [online], 12 July. Available at: www.lemonde.fr/acces-restreint/archives/article/1974/07/12/1755cadef7788208352176af04c1684b_2517903_1819218.html [Accessed 1 May 2017].

Schlegel, F. 1926 [1798]. Über Goethes Wilhelm Meister. [e-book] Bielefeld and Leipzig: Verlag von Belhagen und Klasing. Available at: Deutsche Nationalbibliothek http://d-nb.info/1088439675 [Accessed 12 September 2017].

Strich, F., 1946. *Goethe und die Weltliteratur*. Bern: A. Francke Verlag.

Valéry, P., 1957. Variations sur les bucoliques. In: *Œuvres I*. Paris: Gallimard. p.215.

Verlaine, P., 1951. Art poétique. In: *Œuvres poétiques complètes*. Paris: Gallimard. p.206.

Zohn, H., trans. 2000 [1968]. The Task of the Translator. In: L. Venuti, ed. 2000. *The Translation Studies Reader*. 1st ed. New York: Routledge. pp.15–25.

CAHIER 4

Two *interrelated* terms dominate the discussion in Cahier 4: *Darstellung* and *Bedeutung*. Both are ordinary, everyday words, but in their ordinariness, fiendishly complex. They are found together in the following sentence, which occurs in the fifth paragraph of Benjamin's text:

> Alle zweckmäßigen Lebenserscheinungen wie ihre Zweckmäßigkeit überhaupt sind letzten Endes zweckmäßig nicht für das Leben, sondern für den Ausdruck seines Wesens, für die *Darstellung* seiner *Bedeutung*.
> (Benjamin 1991a:11–12, emphasis added)

> All purposeful manifestations of life, just like their purposefulness as such, are ultimately not purposeful for life, but for the expression of its essence, for the performance of its meaning.

The German inseparable prefix *dar-* attaches to verbs and also features in their nominalised forms. It is related to the demonstrative pronoun 'da' and indicates presence or now-ness, a 'here' or a 'there'. The verb *stellen* means 'to place'. A *Darstellung* can be a portrayal (in words or via a visual medium such as painting or photography); a performance given by an actor; an account or a narrative; but it also has a chemical meaning: 'synthesis'. Benjamin uses it to describe something that translation does, contrasting it with *Herstellung* [production]. *Herstellung* is something that translation does *not* do. Translation is the *Darstellung* of the essence of a text, or of its *Bedeutung*. Gandillac's and Berman's approaches to this word are invaluable in crystallising the issues around its translation into English. Gandillac translates *Darstellung* as *réprésentation*, which broadly correlates with the meanings of the English 'representation' but can also translate as 'performance' in the sense of the performance of a theatrical production (rather than an individual performance by an actor). Berman dismisses this translation because it suggests the German *Vorstellung* (2008:89), which can also be the performance of a theatrical production, but which possesses a sense of artifice or remove that is not present in *Darstellung*. *Vorstellung* can also mean 'introduction', 'imagination' and 'understanding/conception'. Not only does *représentation* suggest the wrong German word, it is too passive, Berman argues, adopting the more direct *présentation*. The French *présentation* still coincides with *Vorstellung* in the sense that both can mean 'introduction' – introducing two people to one another (*Je vous présente ...*, Let me introduce) or introducing a new product onto a market – but *présentation* also contains the sense of active 'showing' or 'display' and captures more of *Darstellung*'s there-ness (you can *présenter* (show) your identity card in French; you can also *présenter* (present or show) a new fashion collection). These elements of showing or displaying are not as strong, nor as everyday, in the English 'presentation', but 'performance', with its connotations of (contingent and temporary) embodiment lends itself well to the translation of *Darstellung* and captures that aspect of translation that performs – but does not produce – pure language, 'by realising it in germinal or in concentrated form' (ibid.:12).

If translation is the *Darstellung* or performance of the text's *Bedeutung*, what exactly is it performing? The noun *Bedeutung* means 'meaning', but also 'significance' (in the sense of importance). Berman generally translates *Bedeutung* as *la signification*, which does mean 'meaning', although the French language also has the noun *sens* [sense/meaning] at its disposal. The French *signification* can also mean 'signification' in the sense used by Saussure, that is, the relationship between signifier and signified, the signifying process. It is impossible to read Berman's commentary without assuming that his *signification* points to 'meaning', 'significance' *and* 'signification'. The English 'meaning' is less polysemic. Benjamin can hardly be said to have intended a Saussurean 'signification' with *Bedeutung* but his usage does seem to anticipate a post-structuralist 'signification' – the text as a constantly shifting signifying entity. In my translation of Berman's commentary, *Bedeutung* has sometimes been rendered as 'meaning', sometimes as 'significance' and sometimes as 'signification'. Berman's *signification* – his translation of Benjamin's *Bedeutung* – has generally been rendered as 'signification'. Elsewhere in Benjamin's text – and this will be a topic of discussion as the commentary progresses – Benjamin uses the related verb *meinen* to talk about what the text wants to say or intends, and this further complicates the translation of *Bedeutung*.

The final sentence of paragraph four pronounces that the literary text reaches the 'latest' and 'most extensive' (*umfassendste*) stage of its 'development' (*Entfaltung*; literally, 'unfolding') via translation. This development is only one of many moments in the life of the text, a life that is characterised by constant 'renewal'. We have established that translation is the late fruit of the text. What remains to be seen is how translation constitutes the stage of the text's 'most extensive' development.

Paragraph five attempts to define the essence of this *Entfaltung*. Benjamin pronounces:

> Diese Entfaltung ist als die eines eigentümlichen und hohen Lebens durch eine eigentümliche und hohe Zweckmäßigkeit bestimmt.
>
> *(p. 11. para 5)*

> This development is that of a singular and elevated life and as such is determined by a singular and elevated purposefulness.

> Ce déploiement en tant que celui d'une vie originale (*eigentümlich*) et élevée (*hohe*) est déterminé par une finalité originale et élevée.
>
> *(Berman)*

[Literal translation of Berman's French translation:

> This unfolding as that of an original and elevated life is determined by an original and elevated purpose(fulness).]

At this juncture the concept of translation's purposefulness is introduced.

In a move which is characteristic of this text, or at the very least of those paragraphs we have discussed thus far, Benjamin immediately and systematically launches into a digression. This digression is of a philosophical nature and deals with the essence of life.

Benjamin himself said that there was no difference between the themes pursued by a text and digression. Each of his paragraphs digresses. In the third paragraph, if you remember, his digression was on the subject of the unforgettable; in the fourth paragraph, the essence of life; in the fifth, life and purposefulness.

In paragraph four Benjamin affirmed that life, of which the literary text is one of the most 'recognisable' forms, is at bottom historical:

> Daher entsteht dem Philosophen die Aufgabe, alles natürliche Leben aus dem umfassenderen der Geschichte zu verstehen.
>
> *(p. 11. para 4)*

> Therefore, the task arises for the philosopher of understanding all natural life in terms of the more extensive life of history.

> De là surgit pour le philosophe la tâche (*Aufgabe*) de comprendre toute vie naturelle à partir de la vie plus étendue (ou plus vaste: *umfassender*) de l'histoire.
>
> *(Berman)*

[Literal translation of Berman's French translation:

> From there arises for the philosopher the task of understanding all natural life in terms of the more extended (or more vast) life of history.]

We skipped this sentence and now is a good moment to return to it. This is the juncture in the text at which philosophy makes its first appearance and it will remain part of the text from this point on. Philosophy and translation are related in the sense that both are governed by the law of the *task*. Anything having to do with a task, as we have already established, has to do with the resolution of dissonance. We will see that resolving dissonance is the same for translation and for philosophy.

The historicity of life, which is characterised by mutations, by processes of engendering and maturation, is governed by purposefulness, by a goal. Life is all about purposefulness and purpose. Life is the sphere of existence where purposefulness resides. But in a curious manner. On the level of direct intuition, the 'purposeful' (*zweckmäßig*) nature of vital (or historical) phenomena is obvious. But on the level of objective knowledge (*Erkenntnis*), the sensual immediacy of life's purposefulness is elusive, because knowledge only ever establishes causal or, at best, functional relationships. 'Purpose' cannot be grasped by knowledge in the same way that 'cause' or 'function' can. Benjamin alludes to the famous pages of Kant's *Critique of Judgement* [*Kritik der Urteilskraft*] (1790) devoted to this problematic. There is an *interrelation* (*Zusammenhang*) between purposefulness and living matter that lies beyond the reach of objective knowledge. This *Zusammenhang* is of the same kind as that which links the original text and its translation: a mixture of intimacy and distance. All the purposefulness inherent in living beings points towards an 'end' which is not immanent in them but has to be sought outside life, *beyond* life and even above it. The purpose of life is *über* life.

This can be explained in the following manner: life is never an end in itself. Or rather: life is not an absolute value. Life sometimes has to be sacrificed in order for its 'sense' (or its 'purpose') to be realised – to *become apparent* even. This sense therefore constitutes life's most intimate meaning and essence *and* 'something' distinct from it. We might call this *the separation of life from its essence*. Life is dominated by a purposefulness which is simultaneously immanent in it and transcendent. This is what the German *über* expresses. The purpose of life lies beyond life and above it, but also *in* it (otherwise it would not belong to it).[1]

> Alle zweckmäßigen Lebenserscheinungen wie ihre Zweckmäßigkeit überhaupt sind letzten Endes zweckmäßig nicht für das Leben, sondern für den Ausdruck seines Wesens, für die Darstellung seiner Bedeutung.
>
> *(pp. 11–12. para 5)*

> All purposeful manifestations of life, just like their purposefulness as such, are ultimately not purposeful for life, but for the expression of its essence, for the performance of its meaning.

Tous les phénomènes vitaux doués de finalité, ainsi que leur finalité, possèdent au bout du compte une finalité non pour la vie, mais pour l'expression de son essence, pour la présentation de sa signification (*Darstellung seiner Bedeutung*).

(Berman)

[Literal translation of Berman's translation:

All vital phenomena endowed with purpose, like their purposefulness, ultimately possess a purpose not for life, but for the expression of its essence, for the presentation of its meaning.]

The purpose of life is the performance, *Darstellung*, of life's essence or meaning. This purpose has no meaning for life itself, even if it pertains to the most significant thing that life possesses.

Darstellung is a key term in German Romanticism. It is not 'répresentation', *Vorstellung*, as Gandillac's translation would suggest (Gandillac 1971:264) but the more direct 'présentation'.[2] The expressions of life that Benjamin speaks of above (the expressions that bear no meaning for life) are therefore performative acts. These performative acts reveal life's pure essence. But if life is history, this means that the purposefulness of life resides in the performance thereof. This purposefulness is never fully realised. If history is the history of 'life revealed (or revealing itself)', this history does not produce an absolute (definitive) 'performance' of life's essence. In other words, the 'meaning' of life is only revealed fragmentarily or through signs.

If we apply this to the relationship between the original text and its translation, we could say that the purpose of translation is to perform the pure signification which is immanent in the literary text and at the same time alien to it (a signification which the work does not fear and that the translation will 'bring to light' – this is one way in which one might translate *Darstellung*). This performance is realised (in part) via translation, whose purpose is to serve this end. Translation is one of the modes by which the signification that is immanent in the text is brought to light. It is not the only mode through which this occurs since elsewhere Benjamin insists that criticism plays exactly the same role.

The purpose of translation is the performance of the signification immanent in the original text. We will see in a moment why Benjamin does not pursue this line of thought. But we can develop it on his behalf.

The *Darstellung* of the original text that occurs through translation, and that ensures the text's *Überleben*, remains partial and fragmentary, a gesture towards *Darstellung* rather than the fulfilment thereof. Nonetheless – and this is key – a translation is, fundamentally, the *Darstellung* of the essence of a text, or of its *Bedeutung*.[3] Its performance of the text's signification is fragmentary, partial. There are two important points here: the fact that the translation is a performance of the pure signification of the work and that its performance thereof is fragmentary, unfinished or incomplete. It is unclear whether Benjamin was aware of this.

Translation is not the transmission of 'meaning' but a performance of the signifi-cation immanent in the text, of the way in which the original signifies (each text in its own distinct fashion), or rather *is* signification. Again, the concept of signification concerns the degree to which the work is signifiable in its entirety, independently of any of its empirically discoverable meanings. The literary text captures an infinite, unanalysable, unfathomable signification, *Bedeutung*. For a reason which – at this stage in the commentary – is not entirely clear, the text is incapable of freeing itself, of producing its signification by itself. A second event, which has to be external, is required for this signification to emerge, to be performed. For the Romantics, the events that liberate this signification in all of its purity are translation and, above all, criticism.

Hölderlin can help us understand this essence of translation. For Benjamin, Hölderlin the translator was a crucial reference point. But this is perhaps even more the case for us, if only because it appears that Benjamin didn't read Hölderlin's translation of Sophocles' *Antigone* very closely; rather he read his translations of Pindar, which do not exhibit the same characteristics.

What is key in Hölderlin's translation of Sophocles is that the translation does violence to the original text to force the emergence of its tragic truth, that is to say, of its original speaking power. It does this, for example, via the systematic replace-ment of the names of the gods by other termini (Zeus becomes 'the Father of the Earth', Ares 'the Spirit of War' etc.). Over the centuries, mythologising humanism had layered these names with significations that rendered them inaccessible. By expunging these, Hölderlin's translation offers a *Darstellung* of the tragic word. This *Darstellung* is, by necessity, violent.

Benjamin knew that translation and criticism are obliged to inflict violence on the original text to force the truth from it (and thus ensure its continued life or, in Goethean terms, its regeneration), as we can see here: 'That which smashes the work to pieces, breaks it into fragments of the real world, into the torso of a symbol, is what effects its completion' (Benjamin 1991d:181).[4]

In any case, in the paragraph that concerns us here, Benjamin is not yet exploring the relationship between the original and translation that takes the form of *Darstellung*. Rather, considering translation to be a vital phenomenon, he seeks to determine its purpose:

> So ist die Übersetzung zuletzt zweckmäßig für den Ausdruck des innersten Verhältnisses der Sprachen zueinander.
>
> *(p. 12. para 5)*

> Ultimately translation serves the purpose of expressing the innermost rela-tionship of languages.

> Ainsi la traduction a-t-elle en dernier ressort pour finalité l'expression du rapport les plus intérieur (*innersten*) entre les langues.
>
> *(Berman)*

[Literal translation of Berman's French translation:

> Thus translation has in the final instance as its purpose the expression of the most interior relationship between languages.]

This is an almost brutal shift: we are no longer discussing texts but languages. But it is a necessary shift since translation is the *Darstellung* of the truth of a text via interlinguistic transfer, and because this truth is inscribed in the text's relationship to (its) language.

What is meant by the innermost relationship between languages? And by the expression (*Ausdruck*) of this relationship? We know enough to understand that *Ausdruck* and *Darstellung* are being used synonymously here. Or more precisely that this expression is not, at bottom, an externalisation of something but rather the *performance* of something hidden.

The purpose of translation is therefore to reveal a relationship. A relationship between languages. Between the translated language and the translating language.

This means that translation is both the translation of texts (the *Darstellung* of a text's signification) *and* the translation of languages (the *Darstellung* of the relationship between two languages, of a relationship of intimacy – and therefore, following the law of *Innigkeit*, of distance – between two languages.)

Thinking about translation as the translation-of-a-text and as the translation-of-a-language is the crux of any theory of translation. It is not easy to think through these two things at the same time and we will therefore come back to this.

Benjamin continues:

> Sie kann dieses verborgene Verhältnis selbst unmöglich offenbaren, unmöglich herstellen; aber darstellen, indem sie es keimhaft oder intensiv verwirklicht, kann sie es.
>
> *(p. 12. para 5)*

It is impossible for translation to reveal, to produce, this hidden relationship; but it can perform it, by realising it in germinal or in concentrated form.

Elle ne peut pas elle-même révéler ce rapport caché, ne peut pas elle-même le produire (*herstellen*), mais le présenter, en le réalisant en germe (*keimhaft*) ou intensivement, elle le peut.

(Berman)

[Literal translation of Berman's French translation:

> [*Translation*] cannot itself reveal this hidden relationship, cannot itself produce it, but it can present it, by realising it in germinal form or intensively.]

Every word is significant here. Translation cannot reveal, nor produce this relationship of intimacy between languages, but it can 'perform' it or – if we take the term in its chemical sense – 'synthesise' it. Gandillac translates *herstellen* as 'restituer' [restore] (1971:264), but *herstellen* seems to me to signify 'produire' [produce, establish], since the hidden relationship between languages is not something that already exists – and there is a secret concordance between *herstellen* and *darstellen*.

Translation can therefore perform this relationship by 'realising' it (*verwirklichen*) either in germinal (*keimhaft*) or in concentrated form. *Keimhaft*, in germinal form, is reminiscent of another term that Benjamin uses to describe Goethe's vision of the literary text: *torsenhaft*, torsoesque, like a torso. And there is indeed a close relationship between the 'germ' and the 'fragment', as we can see in Novalis's collection *Blüthenstaub* [*Pollen and Fragments*] (1798). A fragment (or torso) is also a germ (or a grain of pollen). It conceals a reality that does not yet exist (and yet is already in existence). Every great translation is a germ with the potential to realise this intimate relationship between languages that does not yet exist. But this is the only mode via which translation is able to realise it – via the germ and the fragment. What this means for us is that translation is a fragment, a form of fragmentary writing, *l'écriture-torse* or *l'écriture-germe*. This of course is the basis of the Romantic passion for translation and of Benjamin's interest in it – even though neither Romanticism nor Benjamin succeeded in thinking through translation's fragmentary essence.

A thousand external signs point towards the fact that translation belongs in the realm of the 'fragmentary': firstly, its 'unfinished', 'approximate' nature; but also the great difficulty that one experiences, throughout the history of translation, of finding *complete* translations of a text, as if a complete translation would violate the sense of the act of translating, as if the concentrated translation of a fragment of text was worth more than the unconcentrated translation of the *whole* work. As if translating everything were a problem. The majority of Romantic translations are themselves fragmentary.[5] So it appears as though the very goal of translation (a goal that is hidden, moreover, from the translator) can only happen in a modus that is fragmentary, *torsenhaft* and/or *keimhaft*.

The concepts of concentratedness and the fragmentary intersect (without being identical of course). If translation is the performance/synthesis of the intimacy that holds between languages, it is only able to fulfil this role in a germinal and concentrated manner. In the modus of the 'fragment'. Every fragment is a fragment *of*, and as a fragment *of*, it points towards the fact that something other than itself, towards which it gestures, exists beyond its boundaries. It is a sign and a symbol *of*. Furthermore, the fragment itself is fundamentally multiple – *fragments* – and this is how it relates to translation, which only exists as translations, as a *multiplicity* of translations. We could even say that every translation is the fragment (germ) of an absolute translation that has never been realised but which is always present on the horizon of 'The Task of the

Translator'; translation is never undertaken from a perspective of relativity. This absolute translation would finally reveal the truth of the text and the intimacy of languages instead of these being performed as signs and symbols. In relation to this Translation, which exists as an Idea, real translations are 'fragments' or 'torsos'; more precisely, they are the germs of this Translation and they will always remain in germinal form.

If each translation is a 'germ', then this means that it plays an *annunciatory* role where the truth of the text and the intimacy of languages are concerned.

> Und zwar ist diese Darstellung eines Bedeuteten durch den Versuch, den Keim seiner Herstellung ein ganz eigentümlicher Darstellungsmodus, wie er im Bereich des nicht sprachlichen Lebens kaum angetroffen werden mag.
> *(p. 12. para 5)*

> And this performance of a signified via the attempt at – the germ of – its production, is an entirely singular mode of performance, such as is scarcely encountered in the field of non-linguistic life.

> Et certes cette présentation de quelque chose de signifié[6] par l'essai, le germe de sa production, est un mode de présentation tout à fait original, tel qu'on peut à peine le trouver dans le domaine de la vie non langagière.
> *(Berman)*

[Literal translation of Berman's French translation:

> And indeed this presentation of something signified by the attempt, the germ of its production, is a completely original mode of presentation, such that one can scarcely find it in the domain of non-linguistic life.]

In more modern language, we would say that translation is the *trace* of a relationship of intimacy between languages.

Versuch – attempt [*essai*] – is yet another Romantic term. In Novalis and Schlegel the *Versuch* is the essence of criticism and suggests *experimentation*. Criticism is always a form of experiment with a literary text as its starting point. In the Romantic cosmos, *attempt* and *experiment* are forms of fragmentary writing. It is fairly obvious, I believe, that the essay as a form is a fragment, a torso, a germ, and is only complete when it remains in this state. Translation is always an attempt and an experiment. But the translation experiment produces a *result*: this is why Benjamin talks about realisation, *Verwirklichung*, in relation to translation and its mode of performance. Translation is a fragmentary *incarnation* of the intimacy between languages – but it is an annunciatory incarnation, a 'not yet but yet already'. Translational *Darstellung* is a mode of signalling this intimacy without making it present. It gestures towards it as though to a future event, an *À-Venir* [Yet-to-Come]. This *À-Venir* is present in the translation.

This kind of performance – a temporally annunciatory performance in the sense of a sign of what is to come – does not feature in non-linguistic life.

Life that takes place in language is human life, life in history. Life that takes place outside language is natural life, in the broadest possible sense. Natural life also has its structures for the performance of signification. We know that Benjamin was very interested in 'sciences' like astrology and palmistry that decoded natural signs. The natural world (and natural man, immersed in the rhythms of this world) has 'other types of pointing-towards (*Hindeutung*) contained in analogies and signs' (Benjamin 1991a:12).[7] These signs and analogies form the decipherable and hermetic system that Foucault described in *The Order of Things* [*Les Mots et Les Choses*] (1966) with respect to the Renaissance. But the pointing-towards that characterises translation – and all linguistic and historical life – is of another kind: it is temporalising; it anticipates and announces. Analogies and natural signs suggest connections created by fate; these connections anticipate and announce the movement of history.

We can already identify two temporalities for translation.

Where the literary text is concerned, it is the lateness of translation in relation to the text's glory and the decline thereof. In the 'natural' time of the text, translation comes late and facilitates the text's accession to a higher stage of life. But where languages are concerned, translation's temporality is the announcement of an *À-Venir* in which the intimacy of languages will be revealed.

How can we think translation's two temporalities together?

We can do this by showing how the *Darstellung* of the intimacy that exists between languages permits, in turn, the *Darstellung* of the truth of the text – which is to say its passage to an *Überleben*, to a *Sur-Vie* [Above Life] in the strongest sense. It is the fact that translation 'saves' the text (and here, the connotation of 'saving' present in *Überleben* – survival – might come into play) from the finitude of its language so that it can accede to a higher language that ensures it (might ensure it) this *Sur-Vie*. In putting it this way, we are aligning Benjamin's thought with Romantic thought, which conceived of criticism and translation as ensuring the in-finitisation of the literary text. We will see if this interpretation is truly licit.

> Jenes gedachte, innerste Verhältnis der Sprachen ist aber das einer eigentümlichen Konvergenz.
>
> *(p. 12. para 5)*

> But this posited, innermost relationship of languages is one of a singular convergence.
>
> Mais ce rapport pensé et très intérieur des langues est celui d'une convergence originale.
>
> *(Berman)*

[Literal translation of Berman's French translation:

> But this thought and extremely inner relationship of languages is that of an original convergence.]

Singular/strange, *eigentümlich* [*original*]: the convergence here is a singular/strange one because it is not the same thing as a natural convergence, a relationship based on resemblance, for example. Two phenomena can be said to be convergent if they are like each other and enjoy a relationship of resemblance. But Benjamin is once again thinking of convergence in terms of difference (dis-semblance). The intimacy between languages springs from the very heart of their distance and difference from one another.

> Es besteht darin, daß die Sprachen einander nicht fremd, sondern a priori und von allen historischen Beziehungen abgesehen einander in dem verwandt sind, was sie sagen wollen.
>
> *(p. 12. para 5)*

> This relationship rests on the fact that languages are not alien to one another but are related to one another, *a priori* and irrespective of all historical relationships, in what they want to say.

> Elle consiste en ceci que les langues ne sont pas mutuellement étrangères, mais a priori, et indépendamment de toutes les relations historiques entre elles, sont parentes (*verwandt*) en ce qu'elles veulent dire.
>
> *(Berman)*

[Literal translation of Berman's French translation:

> It consists of the fact that languages are not mutually strange, but *a priori*, and independently of all historical relations between themselves, are related in what they want to say.]

Historically speaking – or rather empirically – languages are of course related, either by kinship or through contact. Even those languages that initially had nothing in common come to resemble one another, precisely because of the tremendous flow of exchange, borrowings and impositions. But Benjamin is saying that languages are related *a priori* – that is to say ontologically – even where no such historical ties exist. They are related in 'what they want to say'.

What does this mean? What does a language 'want to say'? Does a language 'want to say' anything? What does 'the kinship of languages' mean? 'The innermost relationship between languages' certainly signifies that they are kin. But what is 'kinship'? More precisely, other than 'natural' kinship, that is to say kinship founded in relationships of parentage, engendering or resemblance (everything that the empirical history of languages tells us), what kind of kinship is there?

The paragraph finishes on this seemingly enigmatic sentence. You will have noticed that every paragraph in 'The Task of the Translator' finishes on a sentence of this kind. At this juncture it might be useful to list the endings of the paragraphs we have already discussed:

§1 No poem pertains to the reader, no painting to the viewer, no symphony to the audience.

§2 If the original text does not exist for the benefit of the reader, how can translation possibly be understood in these terms?

§3 If translation is a form, then translatability has to be an essential feature of particular texts.

§4 In them the life of the original reaches its constantly renewed, latest and most extensive development.

§5 This relationship rests on the fact that languages are not alien to one another but are related to one another, *a priori* and irrespective of all historical relationships, in what they want to say.

The fact that each paragraph finishes on a sentence of this kind gives us some indication of the profound rhythm of the text – of the fact that it has a rhythm, that this intellectual text is also a poetic text. The manner in which each paragraph develops and digresses rides on this rhythm. The length of Benjamin's paragraphs is of great importance; they grow longer and longer as the text progresses. We will come back to the way in which each paragraph unfolds rhythmically and always has a different way of leading into the subsequent paragraph.

To be clear: paragraph six constitutes a break in the text. Thematically, paragraph seven follows on from and elucidates paragraph five. It is as though Benjamin could not immediately tackle the issue of the kinship of languages, as though he first had to explain the sphere in which this kinship plays out. He does this by clearing up an ambiguity.

This ambiguity is embedded in conventional theory. Translation theory sees in this ambiguity proof that translation embodies the kinship of languages. *Translation bears witness to this kinship and is simultaneously grounded in it.* It bears witness to it because it optimally demonstrates the fact that languages, whatever their formal dis-semblances, are fundamentally similar. Conventional theory comprehends the kinship of languages in terms of resemblance – this resemblance might be located in 'deep structures' or in the 'logos' which gives all languages their existence.

This is why Benjamin says:

> Wenn in den Übersetzungen die Verwandtschaft der Sprachen sich zu bewähren hat, wie könnte sie das anders als indem jene Form und Sinn des Originals möglichst genau übermitteln?

(p. 12. para 6)

If the kinship of language is to prove itself in translations, how could it do so other than by transmitting form and content as precisely as possible?

Si dans la traduction doit s'attester la parenté entre les langues, comment le pourrait-elle autrement qu'en transmettant (*übermitteln*) la forme et le sens de l'original le plus exactement possible?

(*Berman*)

[Literal translation of Berman's translation:

If the kinship of languages has to be attested to in translation, how could this be attested to otherwise than by transmitting the form and sense of the original in the most exact way possible?]

A transmission of this sort – both the possibility and the success thereof – would be proof of the similarity of languages. And translation would affirm this interlinguistic kinship by producing a *double* that resembles the original text. Translation, grounded in the 'resemblance' of languages, *would produce*, in turn, resemblance – a double resemblance of literary texts.

However, the accuracy (fidelity) of a translation that is committed to rendering 'form' and 'content' is difficult to define. We know that the concept of fidelity is vague and ambiguous. It is an unwieldy concept since it contradicts itself by looking to both form and content. Is an accurate translation one that results in a text whose content is similar to that of the original? Maybe, but then there is no longer a resemblance of form. And vice versa. Benjamin says that this way of thinking prevents us from grasping what is essential about translation.

In Wahrheit aber bezeugt sich die Verwandtschaft der Sprachen in einer Übersetzung weit tiefer und bestimmter als in der oberflächlichen und undefinierbaren Ähnlichkeiten zweier Dichtungen.

(*p. 12. para 6*)

In truth, however, the kinship of languages is much more profoundly and resolutely witnessed to in a translation than it is in the superficial and indefinable similarity of two literary texts.

En vérité, la parenté des langues s'atteste dans une traduction de manière beaucoup plus profonde et déterminée que dans la ressemblance superficielle et indéfinissable de deux œuvres littéraires (*Dichtungen*).

(*Berman*)

[Literal translation of Berman's French translation:

In truth, the kinship of languages is proven in a much deeper and resolute way in a translation than in an undefinable and superficial resemblance between two literary works.]

To show the inanity of the 'resemblance' school of translation theory, Benjamin digresses once again.

I will also digress: the critique of the 'resemblance' school of translation is all the more striking in Benjamin because of his passionate reflections on 'mimetic power' and subsequent development of a theory of resemblance.[8]

'The Task of the Translator' is heading towards a critique of resemblance. In the fragment from *One-Way Street* – a text written after this one – Benjamin appears to take translation into the domain of *mimesis*. Translation – he says – is to the original as 'mimesis' is to Nature. It is important to point out this oscillation in Benjamin's thought because it is difficult not to consider translation a mimetic act.

As the commentary progresses, we will see how the concept of a *less obvious resemblance* might correlate with what Benjamin discusses further on when he talks about *pure language*.

Notes

1 This is what the following lines from 'Critique of Violence' ['Zur Kritik der Gewalt'] (1921), a text written at least two years before 'The Task of the Translator', reference: 'Man is under no circumstances to be confused with his mere life nor with any other of his states and characteristics, not even with the singularity of his physical person. As sacred as man is (and also that life in him which is identical with his earthly life, death and continued life), his states, his physical life, vulnerable to his fellow man, are not' (1991b:201–202) ['Der Mensch fällt eben um keinen Preis zusammen mit dem bloßen Leben des Menschen, so wenig mit dem bloßen Leben in ihm wie mit irgendwelchen andern seiner Zustände und Eigenschaften, ja nicht einmal mit der Einzigkeit seiner leiblichen Person. So heilig der Mensch ist (oder auch dasjenige Leben in ihm, welches identisch in Erdenleben, Tod und Fortleben liegt), so wenig sind es seine Zustände, so wenig ist es sein leibliches, durch Mitmenschen verletzliches Leben.']

2 *Darstellung* means 'présentation' [presentation] or 'exposition' [exposition]. But it also a chemical term. Benjamin alludes to it in *The Concept of Criticism in German Romanticism*: 'Criticism is the performance [*Darstellung*] of the prosaic kernel in each text. The term *Darstellung* is to be understood in the chemical sense here, as the production of material via a particular process to which others are subject' (1991c:109) ['Kritik ist die Darstellung des prosaischen Kerns in jedem Werk. Dabei ist der Begriff «Darstellung» im Sinne der Chemie verstanden, als die Erzeugung eines Stoffes durch einen bestimmten Prozeß, welchem andere unterworfen werden.'] It is the synthesis of this material. This is what Schlegel meant when he said of *Wilhelm Meister* that the text 'not only judges itself, it also performs itself' (1926:12) ['es beurteilt sich nicht nur selbst, es stellt sich auch selbst dar']. *Darstellung* is a charged term in the history of German speculative terminology. It is both 'exposition' (for example in Hölderlin when he speaks of the 'clarity of exposition' in the Greeks) and 'synthesis'. In neither case can it be translated as 'réprésentation'.

3 Another Romantic term, and more specifically Schlegelian.

4 ['Dieses erst vollendet das Werk, welches es zum Stückwerk zerschlägt, zum Fragmente der wahren Welt, zum Torso eines Symbols.']

5 Wilhelm Schlegel declared that he did not know what the problem was with his translation of Shakespeare but he never seemed to be able to get round to finishing it. And in fact he never did. It was finished by another of the Romantics and the two translations, unsurprisingly, do not work well together.

6   *Bedeuteten,* here again Gandillac translates this as 'signifié' (1971:264), but for me the word 'signifié' is definitively annexed by the linguistic and Benjamin's thought is alien to the linguistic.

7   ['[kennt] in Analogien und Zeichen andere Typen der Hindeutung'.]

8   See Cahier 1, note 10.

Bibliography

Benjamin, W., 1991a [1923]. Die Aufgabe des Übersetzers. In: R. Tiedemann and H. Schweppenhäuser, eds. 1991. *Gesammelte Schriften.* IV.I. Frankfurt am Main: Suhrkamp. pp.9–21.]

Benjamin, W., 1991b [1921]. Zur Kritik der Gewalt. In: R. Tiedemann and H. Schweppenhäuser, eds. 1991. *Gesammelte Schriften.* II.I. Frankfurt am Main: Suhrkamp. pp.179–203.

Benjamin, W., 1991c [1920]. Der Begriff der Kunstkritik in der deutschen Romantik. In: R. Tiedemann and H. Schweppenhäuser, eds. 1991. Gesammelte Schriften. I.I. Frankfurt am Main: Suhrkamp. pp.7–122.

Benjamin, W., 1991d [1924–5]. *Goethes Wahlverwandtschaften.* In: R. Tiedemann and H. Schweppenhäuser, eds. 1991. *Gesammelte Schriften* I.I. Frankfurt am Main: Suhrkamp. pp.123–201.

Berman, A., 2008. *L'Âge de la traduction.* Paris: Presses Universitaires de Vincennes.

Foucault, M. 1966. *Les Mots et Les Choses.* Paris: Gallimard.

Gandillac, M. de, trans. 1971. La tâche du traducteur. In: *Œuvres I, Mythe et violence.* Paris: Denoël/Les Lettres Nouvelles. pp.261–275.

Kant, I., 1977 [1790]. *Kritik der Urteilskraft. Werkausgabe. Band 10.* Frankfurt am Main: Suhrkamp.

Novalis, 2016 [1798]. *Blüthenstaub.* Göttingen and Frankfurt am Main: Wallstein Verlag und Büchergilde Gutenberg.

Schlegel, F. 1926 [1798]. *Über Goethes Wilhelm Meister.* [e-book] Bielefeld and Leipzig: Verlag von Belhagen und Klasing. Available at: Deutsche Nationalbibliothek http://d-nb.info/1088439675 [Accessed 12 September 2017].

CAHIER 5

Problems surrounding the translation of words connected to meaning continue to be the focus of discussion in Cahier 5. The seventh paragraph of Benjamin's text introduces the verb *meinen*, which means 'to mean' in the sense of 'to intend' or 'to have an opinion, to think'. In its contemporary usage the related noun *Meinung* means 'opinion', but Benjamin uses it in 'The Task of the Translator' in the sense of 'meaning'.

> Vielmehr beruht alle überhistorische Verwandtschaft der Sprachen darin, daß in ihrer jeder als ganzer jeweils eines und zwar dasselbe *gemeint ist*, das dennoch keiner einzelnen von ihnen, sondern nur der Allheit ihrer einander ergänzenden Intentionen erreichbar ist: die reine Sprache.
>
> *(Benjamin 1991a:13, emphasis added)*

> Rather all supra-historical kinship of languages rests on the fact that in each language taken as a whole, one and indeed the same thing *is meant*; this is however unattainable by any single language, but rather is attainable only through the totality of their complementary intentions: pure language.

Meaning, as we have already seen, is a fraught concept in 'The Task of the Translator'. Benjamin rejects the restoration (or rendering) of meaning as a valid goal for translation, arguing instead for a focus on the letter. This, and the fact that the 'meaning' of Benjamin's text is at times deeply obscure, makes it difficult for the translator of his text to confidently use the word 'meaning' anywhere. There is a deep irony in the translator's desperate search for meaning within a text that advocates the letter as translation's primary focus.

The 'is meant' above could arguably also be rendered as 'is intended'. Gandillac translated 'eines und zwar das selber gemeint ist' as 'une chose est *visée, qui est la même* [one thing is *aimed* at, which is the same]. Berman moves away from this translation on the grounds that *visée* lies in the future – it is an intention that has not yet been realised – whereas Benjamin is discussing an aim that has been announced, that is already in motion. Berman therefore adopts a hyphenated *vouloir-dire*, an idiosyncratic version of the conventional compound verb that means 'mean' or 'want to say': 'une chose et certes la même est *voulue-dire*' 2008:114) [one thing and indeed the same thing is *wanted-to-say*]. He also goes on to use *vouloir-dire* as a noun to designate the *thing* that is meant or intended, the 'meaning' or 'intention'. At times, however, he goes back to Gandillac's *visée*. The decision as to how to translate *meinen* into English is complicated by the fact that it will subsequently appear in the text in various guises, for example, *das Gemeinte, Meinen, ihr Gemeintes*, and is clearly differentiated both from the noun *Intention* [intention] and from *Bedeutung* (see the introduction to Cahier 4). There is a need to differentiate, Benjamin says, 'in der Intention vom Gemeinten die Art des Meinens' (1991a:14). Benjamin's punctuation and syntax here are, as so often, idiosyncratic. The statement would be easier to parse if he had written 'in der Intention die Art des Meinens vom Gemeinten [zu unterscheiden]'. *Das Gemeinte* is the thing meant; *die Art des Meinens* is literally 'the way of meaning'; note that Benjamin nominalises the verb here. There is a need to differentiate, in the intention of a word, a text, a language, 'the way of meaning from what is meant'. At this juncture Berman returns to 'le mode de visée' [the mode of the aim] and 'le visé' [the past participle of the verb 'viser' meaning to aim, thus 'the [thing] aimed at'] (2008:122). My English translation of Berman's commentary also jumps between renderings depending on context and the desire to emphasise Benjamin's language or Berman's interpretation thereof – at times I had to decide whose 'letter' to follow.

We stopped at the beginning of paragraph six, analysing the problematic of resemblance. Benjamin writes: 'In truth, however, the kinship of languages is much more profoundly and resolutely witnessed to in translation than it is in the superficial and indefinable similarity of two literary texts (*Dichtungen*)' (Benjamin 1991a:12).

Further on he adds:

> so ist hier erweisbar, daß keine Übersetzung möglich wäre, wenn sie Ähnlichkeit mit dem Original ihrem letzten Wesen nach anstreben würde.
>
> *(p. 12. para 6)*

> here too one can demonstrate that no translation would be possible if translation strove, with all of its being, for similarity with the original.

> on peut démontrer ici qu'aucune traduction ne serait possible si elle s'efforçait, dans son essence ultime, à la ressemblance avec l'original.
>
> *(Berman)*

[Literal translation of Berman's French translation:

> one can establish here that no translation would be possible if it [*translation*] strove, in its ultimate essence, for resemblance with the original.]

Although Benjamin criticises the 'imitative' translation, it should be noted that a few years later, in *One-Way Street*, he would nonetheless go on to define translation as *mimesis*. Conceptualising translation as *mimesis* has a history, as we will see, that stretches from the sixteenth century to Romanticism. I will return to it briefly here, if only to show that conceptualising translation in terms of *mimesis* cannot be dismissed with a stroke of the pen as Benjamin does in this text but does *not* do in *One-Way Street*.

During the Renaissance, Péletier, a great rival of du Bellay, declared:

> Translation is the truest form of Imitation: because imitating is nothing more than wanting to do what somebody else does. This is true of the Translator, who not only submits to the Invention of another but also to his Disposition, and also to the author's Elocution.
>
> *(Naïs 1980:35)*[1]

For the seventeenth century, all writing was imitation and therefore *mimesis*. And translation is *mimesis* par excellence. From the mid-sixteenth century onwards, translation's mimetic essence meant that it met with rejection. This was when the great inquisition of the 'copy' in art began. Translation was its first victim. The rehabilitation of translational *mimesis* had to wait for Romanticism. We lack the time to go into this history but it is apparent that conceiving of translation in terms of *mimesis*, the production of resemblance, is very old. Translation is the very 'place' where mimetic activity appears in its pure form.

All translation ultimately wishes to reproduce the flesh of the text as well as to transmit its meaning: reproducing this flesh is the production of resemblance. It is probably the *immediacy* of translation's mimetic impulse that provoked the condemnation it encountered from the sixteenth century onwards. This mimetic impulse can clearly be observed in Charles Fontaine's 1555 introduction to his translation of Ovid, *Remèdes d'amour*. There are, Fontaine says,

> three things that a person who wishes to translate well has to observe:
>
> The first thing is that he retain and render the terms and diction of the author [...] what one might call the work's dress.
>
> The second is that he also render the text's meaning in its entirety throughout [...] what one might call the work's body.

The third is that he also render and naively express the natural grace, virtue, gentleness, elegance, dignity, strength and vivacity of the author that he wishes to translate [...] what one might call the spirit of the oratory.

(Horguelin 1981:62)[2]

The condemnation of translation-as-copy, translation-as-double, translation-as-mirror image, translation-as-calque – is this a condemnation of the *mimetic* essence of translation? Or is its mimetic essence one and the same as these various conceptualisations?

This is the question that Benjamin was doubtlessly contemplating in *One-Way Street*, he who was so fascinated by the problem of resemblance and mimesis.

The same question arises again with language. If language is not a simple system of arbitrary or conventional signs and if – at the same time – it is not primarily a mimicry of things, what is the nature of its resemblance to them?

Once again we encounter the problem of intimacy, of *Innigkeit*, with its two dimensions: distance and proximity. The intimacy of language with things is not imitation but it must rest on a more hidden *mimesis*. Benjamin thought that he had addressed this more hidden *mimesis* with the concept of 'intangible resemblance'. And this concept, in turn, is primordial for translation. Translation-as-calque (or translation-as-copy) is the naïve production of (or attempt at reproducing) a *tangible* resemblance. Criticising this translation-as-calque (as Meschonnic did) should not allow us to overlook the fact that translation pursues a more essential *mimesis*, of which Klossowski's translation of the *Énéide* is the best contemporary example. This is how 'literal' translation and translation grounded in intangible resemblance connect to one another.

'The Task of the Translator' is entirely focused on refuting the theory of translation-as-copy.

Refuting this theory is grounded, first of all, in a more general epistemological reflection borrowed from Kantianism: just as objective knowledge is not a passive copy of the real, so translation is not a passive copy of an original text. In the domain of knowledge, the theory of the copy presupposes a static real that we passively reproduce. But the real itself is not static and moreover the act of knowing is not passive perception, but an objectification, a construction. If knowing consisted of copying the real, there would be no knowledge. But does this mean, once again, that knowledge has no mimetic basis, no element of resemblance?

Before continuing with my commentary, I would like to cite another fragment from *One-Way Street* which, in its own way, sheds light on our problem. This is a fragment entitled 'Oriental Wares' ['Chinawaren']:

The power of a text also differs depending on whether one reads it or copies it down. [...] Only the text that is copied commandeers the soul of the person who engages with it; the mere reader never becomes cognisant of those new insights into his inner life that are paved by the text – that road through the inner jungle that continually closes in on itself – because the reader heeds the movement of the self through the open skies of reverie, whereas the copier allows it to be commandeered. Book transcription in China thus provided literary culture with incomparable surety, and the practice of copying is a key to that country's mysteries.

(Benjamin 1991b:90)[3]

This passage is striking because translation is also a 'copy' [*une copie*] – and doubly so. It is a copy of the original since translation usually aims to produce a text that resembles its source, but it is also a copy – materially speaking – because it 'transcribes' [*recopie*] the original line by line (in another language, of course). The copying described by Benjamin shares with the act of translating this manual, line-by-line rendering that distinguishes both of these acts from reading.

Translation is therefore a copy [*une copie*] (in the first of the senses described above) that comes about through transcription [*(re)copiage*]. And the fact of its being a copy is what gives it the ability to penetrate the text. The mimetic impulse of copy-transcribing the text (of – to a certain extent – re-submerging it in the writerly impulse where it began) is what gives it the ability to produce a revelatory resemblance. And this is precisely the point of translation orientated towards the production of intangible resemblance rather than passive reproduction of the petrified landscape of a text; this copying, this act of re-duplication reveals what Benjamin calls the 'power' of the text, the state of its originary impulse. The passive copy is a decoy (that of tangible resemblance), the active copy activates the impulse that relocates the text within its originary impulse.

The passages by Valéry and de Leyris that I cited earlier proclaim the same thing. Translation cannot proceed from the presupposition that the literary text is a being that has petrified in its fame like an unmoving aura. Translation is not a copy of a painting in the conventional sense. From this perspective Benjamin's investigation into the work of art and its reproduction (its reproducibility) is closely related – on a different level of course – to his investigation into the literary text and its translation. And we should re-read Benjamin's subsequent texts on the reproduction of the work of art, on cinema and on photography, in the light of 'The Task of the Translator' (and vice versa).

Let us return to the text:

Denn in seinem Fortleben, das so nicht heißen dürfte, wenn es nicht Wandlung und Erneuerung des Lebendigen wäre, ändert sich das Original.

(p. 12. para 6)

For in its continued life, which could not be called this were it not a transformation and renewal of living matter, the original undergoes change.

Car dans sa vie continuée, qui ne mériterait pas ce nom si elle n'était migration et renouveau du vivant, l'original se modifie.

(Berman)

[Literal translation of Berman's French translation:

> Because in its continued life, which would not deserve this name if it was not migration and renewal of living matter, the original changes.]

If the text is continual historicity, then translation cannot be a 'match' for that – if we adhere to the conventional definition of truth: 'a match between the intellect and the thing'.

What might the resemblance sought by the translator be based on *if the literary text does not resemble itself?* If the text continues to change, how can translation 'resemble' it?

Benjamin gives a series of examples of what change means in the literary text:

> Es gibt eine Nachreife auch der festgelegten Worte. Was zur Zeit eines Autors Tendenz seiner dichterischen Sprache gewesen sein mag, kann später erledigt sein, immanente Tendenzen vermögen neu aus dem Geformten sich zu erheben. Was damals jung, kann später abgebraucht, was damals gebräuchlich, später archaisch klingen.
>
> *(pp. 12–13. para 6)*

> Even words that appear fixed continue to mature. What might have been a tendency of the author's poetic language during his own epoch may later be exhausted; immanent tendencies can arise anew from the long-since formed. What had a youthful resonance can later sound worn, what was normal can come to sound archaic.

> Il y a un après-mûrissement aussi des mots fixés. Ce qui, du temps d'un auteur, a pu être une tendance de sa langue poétique, peut plus tard disparaître, des tendances immanentes peuvent ressortir d'une manière neuve de ce qui a été formé. Ce qui avait une résonance jeune peut paraître plus tard démodé, ce qui était courant peut sembler archaïque.
>
> *(Berman)*

[Literal translation of Berman's French translation:

> There is also an after-ripening of fixed words. What, in the time of the author, was perhaps a tendency of his poetic language, can disappear later on, immanent tendencies can re-emerge in a new manner from what has been formed. What had a youthful resonance can later appear out of fashion, what was current can appear archaic.]

There is nothing surprising in these remarks,[4] except – and Benjamin foresees this objection right away – these changes do not result from a corresponding change in our perception, but from the intimate life of the text and its language. The text undergoes change, and it is this change that brings with it the change in our perception. We have to pay attention to the verb used by Benjamin in the sentence that begins: '*Was damals jung*, what had a youthful resonance …', a verb that I have translated, with Gandillac, as 'paraître' [appear]. Because Benjamin says *klingen*, *résonner* [sound]. 'Paraître' is dangerous precisely because it subjectivises the transformation being studied and attributes it to fluctuations in our subjectivity. In truth, the text itself, in its ongoing life, changes its appearance, shows *us* that something that was new at the time of its emergence is now archaic. Attributing this transformation to the subjectivity of readers would, in Benjamin's words, not only confuse

> Grund und Wesen einer Sache
>
> *(p. 13. para 6)*

> cause and essence of the thing
>
> le fond et l'essence d'une chose
>
> *(Berman)*

[Literal translation of Berman's French translation:

> the basis and the essence of a thing]

it would also undermine

> einen der gewaltigsten und fruchtbarsten historischen Prozesse.
>
> *(p. 13. para 6)*

> one of the most awesome and fruitful historical processes.
>
> un des processus historiques les plus puissants et les plus féconds.
>
> *(Gandillac 1971:265–266)*

[Literal translation of Gandillac's French translation:

> one of the most powerful and the most fecund historical processes.]

This historical process – and I have said this before – is that of the life of texts: the life of texts as one of the most 'knowable' manifestations of life in general. We might say that, for Benjamin, the domain of texts is one of those privileged domains that allow us access to what life (and history) 'is'.

But the historicity of texts (and of languages) has nothing to do with the fact that these are caught up in the more general tide of what we call History. In a 1923 letter to Florens Christian Rang, Benjamin writes:

> I am preoccupied with reflection on how works of art relate to historical life. I take it as a given that there is no such thing as history of art. Whereas,

for example, the chain of temporal events carries with it more than what is causally essential for human life, but on the other hand human life would essentially not exist without being caught up in a chain of development, maturation, death and similar categories, this is very different for the work of art. The work of art is in its essence ahistorical. Attempts to position the work of art within historical life offer no insight into its innermost being [...]. The investigations carried out by contemporary history of art only ever result in a history of materials or of form, for which works of art furnish only examples or models; a history of the works of art themselves does not enter into consideration. There is nothing that connects works of art extensively or essentially [...]. The essential connection between works of art remains one of intensity.

(Benjamin 1978: 321–322)[5]

This letter – written immediately after the editing of *The Origin of German Tragic Drama* – will not be the subject of further comment here, but it does reveal an intuition that is fundamentally alien to aesthetics, whether they are an aesthetics of creation or of reception.

The text unfolds in its own history and its own temporality, which have nothing much to do with the 'historical time' of the historian. The text's 'intensive' time is not the 'extensive' time of history.

But even if we continued to assert that a text acquires its definitive shape at the point when the writer stops writing and that any transformation is therefore a transformation in the way we receive it, Benjamin argues that this cannot save the theory of translation-as-copy.

Denn wie Ton und Bedeutung der großen Dichtungen mit den Jahrhunderten sich völlig wandeln, so wandelt sich auch die Muttersprache des Übersetzers.

(p. 13. para 6)

Just as tone and meaning of the great literary works change completely over the centuries, so too does the translator's mother tongue.

Car, de même que la tonalité et la signification des grandes œuvres littéraires se modifient (*sich wandeln*) totalement avec les siècles, la langue maternelle du traducteur se modifie elle aussi.

(Gandillac 1971:266)

[Literal translation of Gandillac's French translation:

For, just as the tonality and meaning of the great literary works changes completely with the centuries, the mother tongue of the translator also changes.]

This immediately signifies that translation – the textual product – is itself caught up in the historicity of language. Any attempt at resemblance is therefore doubly pointless because the desired copy is no more fixed or stable than its model. Any attempt to grasp the truth of translation in an enterprise of this nature is just as senseless as attempting to grasp the truth of knowledge from the passive reproduction of the real – in both of these cases all the fixed points necessary for such an enterprise are missing. The real is fluid, the knowing subject too.

The essential point, however, can be found in what Benjamin utters immediately afterwards:

> Ja, während das Dichterwort in der seinigen überdauert, ist auch die größte Übersetzung bestimmt in das Wachstum ihrer Sprache ein-, in der erneuten unterzugehen.
>
> *(p. 13. para 6)*

> Indeed, whereas the poetic word endures in its language, even the greatest translation is destined to enter into the growth of its language and, in this renewed language, go under.

> Oui, tandis que la parole du poète perdure (*überdauert*) dans la sienne, la plus grande des traductions est vouée à s'effacer (*eingehen*) dans la croissance de sa langue, à sombrer (*untergehen*) dans cette langue renouvelée.
>
> *(Berman)*

[Literal translation of Berman's French translation:

> Yes, whereas the word of the poet endures in its [*language*], the greatest of translations is destined to disappear in the growth of its language, to drown in this renewed language.]

There are some key words in this sentence: a new verb with *über*, 'überdauern', [to endure, outlast] which Gandillac translates as 'survivre' [survive] (1971:266) and that I have translated as 'perdurer' [endure]; *eingehen*, 's'effacer' [to disappear]; and *untergehen*, 'sombrer' [drown, go under]. Then *Wachstum*, '*croissance*' [growth], which we will encounter again in a moment.

Why does the fact that the mother tongue undergoes growth and renewal imply an endurance [*sur-durée*, a lasting beyond], an ongoing life for the original text, but condemn translation to disappear, to sink beneath the waves?

This is the first question we have to ask.

The second question brings us to the distinction – which this commentary cannot fail to address – between a language's 'growth' and its 'renewal'.

With growth, translation *geht ein*. *Eingehen* is primarily 'entrer' [enter], then 'rétrécir' [shrink], 'cesser' [stop/cease], 'disparaître' [disappear], 'mourir' [die], 'se dissoudre' [dissolve]. When a publication *geht ein*, this means that it will cease to appear. Here, therefore, *eingehen* means a certain kind of disappearance, but in the sense of entering into the growth of the language, shrinking within it, dissolving in it and, consequently, ceasing to appear. In other words, with the growth of language, translation is reduced to the point of being erased. But what is the 'growth' of language? Its 'maturation', of course. But the question bounces back to us: what is the 'maturation' of language? The time to answer that has not yet arrived. What we are able to establish is that we are in the presence of two correlations:

Wachstum (*croissance*) [growth] → *eingehen*
Erneuerung (*renouveau*) [renewal] → *untergehen*

Untergehen means 'se coucher' [go down] (of a star), 'décliner' [decline/wane], 's'enfoncer' [sink], 'sombrer' [sink/fade], 'succomber' [succumb], 'couler' [pour/trickle away] … When the language to which a translation belongs is renewed, translation fades, goes under. *Eingehen* and *untergehen* therefore indicate two modes of disappearance. The difference between the two will need to be established by relating *eingehen* to the *growth* of language and *untergehen* to its *renewal*.

Benjamin continues:

> So weit ist sie entfernt, von zwei erstorbenen Sprachen die taube Gleichung zu sein, daß gerade unter allen Formen ihr als Eigenstes es zufällt, auf jene Nachreife des fremden Wortes, auf die Wehen des eigenen zu merken.
>
> *(p. 13. para 6)*

> Translation is so far removed from being the sterile equation of two dead languages, that of all forms it alone is fated to register that late maturation of the foreign word and the birth pangs of its own.

> Elle est si éloignée d'être la stérile égalisation de deux langues mortes que parmi toutes les formes il lui revient en propre d'indiquer cet après-mûrissement de la parole étrangère et les douleurs d'enfantement de la sienne.
>
> *(Berman)*

[Literal translation of Berman's French translation:

> It [*translation*] is so removed from being the sterile levelling of two dead languages that among all the forms it is proper to its nature to indicate this after-maturation of the foreign word and the birth pangs of its own.]

The language of the original text and the language of translation undergo change (*sich wandeln*).

This change has a double aspect: growth and renewal. But the relationship of the text to the 'maturation' or the 'change' of the language in which it is written is characterised by such intimacy that the growth and renewal of that language means that the text too grows and is renewed.

One cannot, in other words, separate the literary text from its language — and therefore from evolution [*devenir*]. *The text is its language.* We might call this the *Innigkeit* of the text and its language, which is infinite. The text is, from the beginning, so intimately connected to its language that no changes in its 'tone' and 'meaning' can ever affect its being, no more than changes in the language itself, which are never external to it.

The life of a literary text bears witness to the life of the language, and the life of the language bears witness to that of the literary text. And through the experience of the text, we enjoy the pure experience of the life of the language, which is composed of growth and renewal.

But if a language were only change – renewal – it would be difficult to see how a text written in phase X of that language could endure. Growth is a different matter, since it carries along with it everything that resides in the intimacy of that language.

If language were only pure change, texts would not endure. But language's change is such that phases of the 'past' remain alive within it and, furthermore, act as bearers of the future. None of our linguistic epochs is truly gone: everything lives on – in more or less tangible fashion – in the current linguistic epoch. And consequently, texts endure, even if their tone and their meaning have changed completely.

This is not the same for translation: the growth and becoming of its language brings aging and decline. It is well known that translations are mortal and texts (virtually) immortal. We still read Homer, Plato, Shakespeare – but not the translations of their texts from two centuries ago. Why do we find translations from the Renaissance or the classical age 'old' but not the original texts that were their contemporaries? If Homer or Virgil were well-translated in the sixteenth century, why don't we leave it at that, why do we persist in re-translating them or – at best – in 'adapting' existing translations of texts as Cassou did with translations of *Don Quixote*?

There is no easy answer to this question. But I would start by suggesting the following: the relationship between the translated text and its language (the translating language) is not one of *intimacy*. The translated text does not inhabit its language. Or rather it inhabits it only up to a certain point. As a consequence of this the linguistic impulse – growth and renewal – is external to it, and ultimately rejects it as though it were a foreign body. It is as though the linguistic impulse confines translation *to the precise point in history when it was created* while carrying original texts from the same epoch along with it. This is why translation shrinks to the point of disappearance when language supersedes the stage at which the translation came into being; this is why it trickles away and is swallowed up when language goes through a process of renewal, because the language of the translation neither grows nor is renewed; it is as though petrified in its bygone era. Diderot's language is still vitally alive, but the language of the translations of his era is inert and we cannot read them because they read like the pure past of our language – a past that we find strange, even unbearable, when presented thus.

I would also argue that because the text in its own language is perpetual renewal, translation, which captures only one aspect of the text, an aspect that will soon be over, will ultimately be anterior to the text and will have to be 'renewed': this 'renewal' happens via *re-translation*.

The text of the translation does not carry within it, therefore, the power of renewal, metamorphosis and growth. Since the end of the Romantic era, F.-V. Hugo's translation has been anterior to Shakespeare's text. This means that in and of itself it does not possess anything that can mature and metamorphose in a way that can match the evolution of Shakespeare in his own language.

That the translated text has no capacity to endure in its own language certainly stems from the fact that it is a text-in-translation with the insurmountable features of the *language* of this kind of text.

In a text composed in its mother tongue, the relationship of form and content, of the signifier to the signified, is one of absolute unity; moreover, each signifier in the text is both indissolubly tied to all other signifiers and to its own diachronic or historical aspect.

Translation does not work like this. The relationship between form and content is looser (because the same thing can be translated in several different ways); the relationship of the signifier to other signifiers has also become random (for example, it would be impossible for any translation to maintain the link between *eingehen* and *untergehen* that exists in Benjamin's sentence) and the signifier's link to its own diachrony is undone. We hear Novalis's *Aufgabe* behind the *Aufgabe* in 'The Task of the Translator', but there is *nothing* to hear behind *tâche* or 'task'. Separated from the way in which they signify and their own historicity, the words in the translation are condemned to signify only the meaning they have at a particular moment in the language, whereas the words of the original text carry both their earlier and their future meanings.

The perishability of translation is rooted in the fact that its language, through its very structure, is radically alien to the aspect that Benjamin calls *die Nachreife*, its ongoing maturation. Only a word that has an origin, a past, can mature. The words in a translation are rootless and therefore cannot mature.

Nonetheless, the translation's perishability is not a fault for which it should be maligned. Translation crystallises the positive and fecund impulses that provoke it. If translation is perishable because the language of the original changes and because its own language changes too, then there is no more transparent place for this to be revealed. The obsolescence of a translation bears witness to, signals, marks the 'post-maturation' of the translated language and the original text, just as it bears witness to, signals, marks the 'pangs' (*Wehen*) of its own language. As translation ages, we register that our language (and that of the original) have entered into another period of their history.

Let me sum up. If the essence of translation was about creating a copy that resembled the original, far from demonstrating the kinship of languages, this would demonstrate their gaping difference, and notably the difference between their respective epochs. The problematic translation of very old texts that were never contemporaneously translated – into French, for example – shows us that tangible resemblance is a decoy. This is the case with Dante, amongst others, but also with Shakespeare. Which epoch of the language should they be translated into? Into the language that was contemporaneous to them or into our language?

At different moments, both approaches have of course been attempted, notably by Pézard with Dante. Translating Dante's text into 'old French' – partially invented for the needs of the cause – is obviously an embrace of the most naïve form of the translation-as-copy, a translation that aims to establish a resemblance with the original. Not only is this a translation of Dante into an imaginary 'old French', but it forgets all the post-maturation of his text, a post-maturation that renders its translation into 'old French' an immediate anachronism because it does not respond to the changes in tone and meaning that Dante has accrued over the centuries. It is only ever actually possible to translate into the *present* state of the translating language despite the need to call upon all the diachronic layers of that language when translating classical texts.[6] Pézard's translation – its nobility and grandeur notwithstanding – is truly the 'sterile equation of two dead languages' (Benjamin 1991a:13).

This is the trap laid by tangible resemblance, the eternal trap against which the translator must be on her guard if, instead of a *copieur* [person who copies], she wishes to become the *copiste* [scribe, person who transcribes, copies down] responsible for revealing, line by line, the power of the text. The term 'power' [*force*] has to be taken seriously – perhaps in the light of Derrida's reflections (1967:7–49) on the term and on the relationship between power and the 'phenomenon'. This would give us a dual design for translation: one which orientates itself around power and one which orientates itself around the phenomenon. And correlatively, two forms of *mimesis*, one which reveals the power of the text (its original being-in-flux) and another that calques its phenomenal aspect. But the power of the text is nothing other than the power of the language within it, its dynamic vital energy. And here again we encounter Hölderlin who, piercing the phenomenal crust of the Sophoclean text, pushed into its burning kernel – the 'fire of heaven' – embodied in the 'murderous brutality' of the tragic word.

This brutal kernel of the text's language is without doubt always its *orality*.

Mimesis that is not based on resemblance is orientated towards synthesis (restitution), towards the *Darstellung* of the pure orality that lies beyond the written of the literary text. This kernel of pure orality can be found in all literary texts and the translational impulse is to synthesise it – to attempt to synthesise it because it is the origin of the text.

Does this 'oral' kernel of the work have anything to do with what – in the following paragraph – Benjamin will call *die reine Sprache*, pure language?

Formulated in this fashion, the question is far too obscure and will remain so for a while. But a later text attests to the fact that for Benjamin – fascinated though he may have been by writing and by the written – pure language had a profound relationship with orality (I will leave this concept undefined for the moment and return to it later):

> The Messianic world is the world of universal and integral timeliness. Universal history can only exist within it. What is called by this name today can only be a kind of Esperanto. Nothing can correspond to it before the

confusion stirred by the Tower of Babel has been settled. It presupposes a language into which all texts of all living and dead languages are to be translated undiminished. Or rather, it is this very language. *But not as a written language, rather as a festively enacted one.* This festive event has been purified of all festivity and has no songs of praise. Its language is the very idea of prose; it will be understood by all people in the way children born under a lucky star understand the language of birds.

(Benjamin 1991c:1239)[7]

I will now tackle the next paragraph:

Wenn in der Übersetzung die Verwandtschaft der Sprachen sich bekundet, so geschieht es anders als durch die vage Ähnlichkeit von Nachbildung und Original.

(p. 13. para 7)

If the kinship of languages announces itself in translation, this happens not through some vague similarity between imitation and original, but elsewhere.

Si dans la traduction la parenté des langues s'annonce, cela a lieu tout autrement que par la vague ressemblance de la reproduction (*Nachbildung*) et de l'original.

(Berman)

[Literal translation of Berman's French translation:

If in translation the kinship of languages is announced, this takes place completely differently than through the vague resemblance of the reproduction and the original.]

To this I will add, as Benjamin himself does further on – nor through any resemblance between the words of the two languages. Kinship is not resemblance.

Benjamin is dismissing two types of kinship here: kinship founded on resemblance and kinship founded on a common origin. Where languages are concerned, this would mean historical kinship, that of French and Latin for example – a kinship that necessarily also establishes a resemblance, a 'family trait'. Benjamin warns us – this is not the kinship I am thinking of, rather I am thinking of a supra-historical kinship – *überhistorische*.

Vielmehr beruht alle überhistorische Verwandtschaft der Sprachen darin, daß in ihrer jeder als ganzer jeweils eines und zwar dasselbe gemeint ist, das dennoch keiner einzelnen von ihnen, sondern nur der Allheit ihrer einander ergänzenden Intentionen erreichbar ist: die reine Sprache.

(p. 13. para 7)

Rather all supra-historical kinship of languages rests on the fact that in each language taken as a whole, one and indeed the same thing is meant; this is however unattainable by any single language, but rather is attainable only through the totality of their complementary intentions: pure language.

Bien plutôt toute parenté supra-historique des langues repose sur ceci qu'en chacune d'elles comme un tout, à chaque fois, une chose et certes la même est voulue-dire (*gemeint*) que néanmoins aucune d'elles isolément, mais seulement la totalité de leurs intentions qui se complètent mutuellement, ne peut atteindre: la pure langue.

(Berman)

[Literal translation of Berman's French translation:

Much rather all supra-historical kinship of languages rests in the fact that in each of them as a whole, every time, one thing and indeed the same thing is meant that nonetheless none of them in isolation, but only the totality of their intentions that mutually complete each other, can attain: pure language.]

We have now come to the central phrase of 'The Task of the Translator': pure language, *die reine Sprache*.

Pure language is what each language wants to say (*meint*), but it can only be reached through the complementary totality of what all languages want to say.

This summary requires some reflection.

Two points, first of all, concerning my re-translation. I have translated the verb *meinen* not as *visée* (aim, goal), but as *vouloir-dire* (literally, want-to-say; intention), thus following Yves Hersant's translation in Giorgio Agamben's extremely interesting text about Benjamin's thought, 'Langue et Histoire' (1986). *Meinen* does in fact mean *une visée*, but an aim that has been announced, put into words. *Damit habe ich gemeint, par là j'ai voulu dire*, 'what I meant by that', the German announces. *Meinung*, the corresponding noun, is the *visée*, an opinion, a *vouloir-dire*. Translating (in the wash of Husserlian language and its translation in France) *meinen* as *viser* is not wrong, especially because Benjamin immediately speaks – following Brentano and Husserl – of the *intention* immanent in each language, which is to say its intentionality and intentional aim. But that masks the linguistic impetus of *meinen*, and we are very much operating in the linguistic sphere here. And earlier on, Benjamin spoke of what languages 'want to say'.

Secondly (and still following Hersant), I have translated *die reine Sprache* as: 'la pure langue' and not as *le langage pur*.

Two considerations justify this, one relates to *rein* and the other to *Sprache*. By keeping *reine* in the same position in French (before *Sprache*), I am emphasising the *pur*, which reaches us first. By translating *Sprache* as *langue* and not as *langage*, I am making a choice that enlists our powers of interpretation.

Reine Sprache is not an abstract category; it is not the *langage* present in all *langues*. It is a language in its own right, as the fragment cited above makes clear. It is not an additional natural language, but the *langue* that each language wants to express but does not. It is not the *logos* underlying all languages and constituting their logical order,[8] but both the *langue* that was lost (that existed prior to the confusion of languages and their becoming multiple) and the *langue* which is coming. It is a language that people will speak: they will not speak it the way we speak at the moment, but they will speak it. The difference between *langage pur* – the strict equivalent of the Kantian *raison pure* [pure reason] – and *pure langue* is significant. The ambiguity of the German preserves the two meanings of the expression and Kant is too present in Benjamin's thought for us to disregard the signification of *langage pur*. But translation has a duty to draw attention to an element which is not, and which cannot be, present in the German text. So it has to proffer 'pure langue' because Benjamin's constant obsession was not the idea of a universal *logos* but the desire for a non-communicative and non-transitive *pure langue* which, in 'On Language as such and on the Language of Man' (1991d), he makes the original privilege of man – man before the fall into a type of language that was communicative and multiple.

This is a good moment to dwell a little longer on *rein*. The term is certainly of Kantian origin.[9] 'Pure', in Kant, signals everything that is not empirical (*a posteriori*), everything that is *a priori* in nature: the pure forms of intuition, the categories of understanding, the concepts of reason, all of this is *rein*. Metaphysical knowledge, were this possible for Kant, would be *pure* knowledge. For a project seeking to extend Kantianism – and this was Benjamin's project in the years 1916–1920 – pure reason would have to be rooted in the pure, categorical and syntactic forms of *langage*.

But Benjamin's *rein* has an additional source: Hölderlin,[10] whose poetic language is governed by *Reinheit*, by purity (although the poet could also have borrowed this from Kant whom he viewed as the 'Moses' of the German nation). *Rein*, for Hölderlin, is what connects us to the source. We have to be attentive to the echo, in Benjamin, of this Hölderlinian *rein*, which is felt in many of his poems in the sense I have indicated above. Poetic language – to the extent that poetry becomes language – is pure language, language which is 'pure song'. Benjamin's Messianic announcement of 'pure language' might secretly correspond to Hölderlin's prophetic *Bald sind wir Gesang* [Soon we shall be song].

If we return to the 1916 text 'On Language as such and on the Language of Man', we can see that pure language is the original language, the language of Adamic origin, and this is certainly closer to the Hölderlinian *rein* than the Kantian *rein*: the original language is not a universal *logos* that ontologically pre-exists all languages.

But *rein* also means empty, non-transitive. Pure language is language which is not the bearer of content, language which rests within itself, language which is not a means.

This is where the Kantian and the Hölderlinian meanings converge: the 'pure forms' of reason are 'empty' as long as they remain unfilled by the 'rhapsody of sensations', and poetry, when it turns into song, does not just sing any old tune: it is 'pure' song, intransitive song – contentless and with no aim outside itself.[11]

To grasp what is at stake in the expression 'pure language', we have to concede that from a certain point of view, this is a redundant expression because language is synonymous with purity. Or rather, pure language is only pure language because it is, first and foremost, 'language'. Language is the medium where 'pure', in general, is located. A comment of Benjamin's on Adalbert Stifter, an author who is often and quite justly described as having pure prose, seems to indicate this:

> The two entities to which we generally ascribe purity are nature and children. For nature the externally located condition of her purity is human language. Because Stifter does not feel *this conditionality that makes purity pure*, the beauty of his portrayal of nature is coincidental or, put differently, harmonically impossible.
>
> *(Benjamin 1978:206)*[12]

In an earlier letter to Scholem, from 1918, Benjamin said of Stifter: 'He is spiritually mute, which is to say that his being lacks that contact with the worldly and with language from which speech evolves' (ibid.:197).[13] In other words, pure language is not some vague ideal, is not a universal *logos*, but *language itself* – what Benjamin calls the 'dignity of its essence' (Benjamin 1978:127),[14] bearing in mind that all dignity and purity can only exist within the infinite medium of language. Benjamin celebrates, in all its facets, the fundamental dignity of language (in 'Critique of Violence', language is for example the medium of all peaceful relationships between men) – but for him it is primarily in literary texts, and in great literary texts, that it becomes, if not real, then at least perceptible. In literary texts, language draws closer to its essence of pure language. The language of the text is not pure language (*la pure langue*) itself, but it is a language that is pure (*une langue pure*). For the language of the text is always only *one* particular language and, as such, a language that has fallen into a communicative mode of signifying. And though the literary text certainly strains to tear *one* particular language away from this fate, what it produces is not pure language – but at best a purified language that gives 'a purer sense to the words of the tribe' (Mallarmé 1945:70).[15]

Pure langue et langue pure – voilà toute la question. [Pure language and language that is pure – that is the question.]

Language that is pure [*la langue pure*] is not (even if poetry sometimes creates this illusion) language itself, but pure language [*la pure langue*] *is*.[16]

With these provisional comments I have reached the still obscure statement that pure language is language itself and language in itself, in the 'dignity of its essence'.

Notes

1 ['La plus vraie espèce d'Imitation, c'est de traduire: car imiter n'est autre chose que de vouloir faire ce que fait un autre: ainsi que fait le Traducteur qui s'asservit non seulement à l'Invention d'autrui, mais aussi à la Disposition: et encore à l'Elocution de l'auteur.']

2 ['[...] trois choses, que doit observer un qui veult bien traduire: La premiere, c'est qu'il retienne et rende les termes et dictions de l'autheur [...] ce que l'on peult appeler la robbe. La seconde, qu'il rende aussi le sens partout entier [...] ce que l'on peult

appeller le corps. La tierce, c'est qu'il rende et exprime aussi naïvement la naturelle grace, vertu, energie, la doulceur, elegance, dignité, force et vivacité de son auteur qu'il veult traduire: […] ce que l'on peult appeller l'âme de l'oraison.']

3 ['So ist auch die Kraft eines Textes eine andere, ob einer ihn liest oder abschreibt. […] So kommandiert allein der abgeschriebene Text die Seele dessen, der mit ihm beschäftigt ist, während der bloße Leser die neuen Ansichten seines Innern nie kennen lernt, wie der Text, jene Straße durch den immer wieder sich verdichtenden inneren Urwald, sie bahnt: weil der Leser der Bewegung seines Ich im freien Luftbereich der Träumerei gehorcht, der Abschreiber aber sie kommandieren läßt. Das chinesische Bücherkopieren war daher die unvergleichliche Bürgschaft literarischer Kultur und die Abschrift ein Schlüssel zu Chinas Rätseln.']

4 Especially if we think of Borges's famous text on Pierre Menard's *Don Quixote*, which compares two identical passages from *Quixote*, one written by Cervantes, the other by Menard, and plays with various modes of continuing maturation, not only that of words but of literary languages.

5 From a letter dated 9 December 1923. It was necessary to cite this letter in its entirety. ['Mich beschäftigt nämlich der Gedanke, wie Kunstwerke sich zum geschichtlichen Leben verhalten. Dabei gilt mir als ausgemacht, daß es Kunstgeschichte nicht gibt. Während die Verkettung zeitlichen Geschehens für das Menschenleben beispielsweise nicht allein kausal Wesentliches mit sich führt, sondern ohne solche Verkettung in Entwicklung, Reife, Tod u. ä. Kategorien das Menschenleben wesentlich garnicht existieren würde, verhält sich dies mit dem Kunstwerk ganz anders. Es ist seinem Wesentlichen nach geschichtslos. Der Versuch das Kunstwerk in das geschichtliche Leben hineinzustellen eröffnet nicht Perspektiven, die in sein Innerstes führen […]. Es kommt bei den Untersuchungen der kurrenten Kunstgeschichte immer nur auf Stoff-Geschichte oder Form-Geschichte hinaus, für welche die Kunstwerke nur Beispiele, gleichsam Modelle, herleihen; eine Geschichte der Kunstwerke selbst kommt dabei garnicht in Frage. Sie haben nichts was sie zugleich extensiv und wesentlich verbindet […]. Die wesentliche Verbindung unter Kunstwerken bleibt intensiv.']

6 This happened with Klossowski's *Énéide*.

7 ['Die messianische Welt ist die Welt allseitiger und integraler Aktualität. Erst in ihr gibt es eine Universalgeschichte. Was sich heute so bezeichnet, kann immer nur eine Sorte Esperanto sein. Es kann ihr nichts entsprechen, eh die Verwirrung, die vom Turmbau zu Babel herrührt, geschlichtet ist. Sie setzt die Sprache voraus, in die jeder Text einer lebenden oder toten ungeschmälert zu übersetzen ist. Oder besser, sie ist diese Sprache selbst. *Aber nicht als geschriebene sondern vielmehr als die festlich begangene.* Dieses Fest ist gereinigt von aller Feier und er kennt keine Festgesänge. Seine Sprache ist die Idee der Prosa selbst, die von allen Menschen verstanden wird wie die Sprache der Vögel von Sonntagskindern.' The emphasis here is Berman's own.] This is one of the preparatory notes to the theses that Benjamin expounds in 'Theses on the Philosophy of History' ['Über den Begriff der Geschichte']. We will have to establish which relationship this purely vocal language – freed from the written – has with poetic language, or, at least, with the modern figure of poetry which asserts that it is a pure, empty word, like 'pure breath', as one of Rilke's *Sonnets to Orpheus* suggests [this appears to be a reference to 'ein Hauch um nichts' (1986:676), which literally translates as 'a breath for nothing']. Like Benjamin's pure language, this pure empty word is never 'realised' in the poem but is always announced – in the mode of a celebration that one might call programmatic. The pure poetic word and pure language are always 'yet to come' and yet already-present in the poem … and in translation.

8 The analyses of the Vienna School or those of Hermann Broch, contemporaries of Benjamin, engage with this. In a text he wrote about translation, Broch tries to show that if translation is possible it is because there is a *logos* in all languages made up of an ensemble X of syntactic, grammatical and categorical structures which constitutes languages as languages and pre-exists languages. If we translate 'reine Sprache' as 'langage pur', then we move in that direction. [Broch's text, which Berman does not identify, is 'Einige Bemerkungen zur Philosophie und Technik des Übersetzens' ['A Few Remarks on the Philosophy and Technique of Translating'] (1946). This text has not yet been translated into English.]

9 Benjamin had also read the theory of pure experience by the neo-Kantian Cohen.

10 The most superficial glance at Hölderlin's poems and speculative 'essays' immediately reveals the central role of the 'pure' and of 'purity' in his work. Here are a few examples.

The essay 'Reflexion' ['Reflection'] reads: 'Aus Freude musst du das Reine überhaupt [...] verstehen' (1961a:235) [literally: You have to understand Purity as such out of joy]. In the essay 'Über die Verfahrungsweise des poëtischen Geistes' ['On the Operations of the Poetic Spirit'], 'pure' is a fundamental concept: 'Das Reine in jeder besondern Stimmung begriffenes wiederstreitet dem Organ in dem es begriffen, es widerstreitet dem Reinen des andern Organs [...] Das Individuelle widerstreitet dem Reinen welches es begreift' (1961b:248) [literally: Purity as it is perceived in any special mood is in conflict with the organ through which it was perceived, it is in conflict with the Purity perceived by another organ [...] That which is individual is in conflict with the Purity that it perceives].

The ode 'Unter den Alpen gesungen' ['Sung under the Alps']:

> Heilige Unschuld, du der Menschen und der
> Götter liebste vertrauteste! [...]
> [...] doch staunet er, dem
> Wild gleich, oft zum Himmel, aber wie rein ist
> Reine, dir alles!
> *(Hölderlin 1951a:44)*

[literally: Holy innocence, you the most beloved and trusted by men and the gods! [...] yet he often looks up to heaven like the beasts, but how pure is Purity, all yours!]

The hymn 'An die Madonna' [To the Madonna']:

> Was kümmern sie dich
> O Gesang den Reinen, ich zwar
> Ich sterbe, doch du
> Gehst andere Bahn
> *(Hölderlin 1951b:215)*

[literally: What trouble are they to you, o song to Purities, I however, I am dying, yet you follow another path]

Benjamin was familiar with a good number of these texts and said of his life: 'For years Hölderlin's light has shone down on me out of this night' ['Seit Jahren strahlt mir aus dieser Nacht das Licht Hölderlins'] (Benjamin 1978:131). I cannot do a complete analysis here of the meaning of 'pure' in Hölderlin, but it is certainly something that relates on the one hand to an origin but on the other to the reign of differentiation ('Gott rein und mit Unterscheidung/ Bewahren' (Hölderlin 1951c:252) [God pure and with differentiation/Preserve]). His pure is the unadulterated. Hölderlin takes this up in a more speculative problematic; the dimension in which pure operates is the dimension that institutes difference. This problematic is also found in *langage*, the purity of languages requires that they are kept apart, otherwise there is what he calls the confusion of languages.

11 Rilke, again, in *Die Sonette an Orpheus [Sonnets to Orpheus]* (1922): '[…] singen […]/[…] Ein Wehn im Gott. Ein Wind' (1986:676). Contentless.

12 ['Die beiden Wesen, denen wir vor allem Reinheit zusprechen sind die Natur und die Kinder. Für die Natur ist die außerhalb ihrer selbst liegende Bedingung ihrer Reinheit die menschliche Sprache. Da Stifter *diese Bedingtheit welche die Reinheit erst zur Reinheit macht* nicht fühlt ist die Schönheit seiner Naturschilderung zufällig oder anders gesagt: harmonisch unmöglich.']

13 [This citation actually occurs in some notes on Stifter that Benjamin enclosed in a letter to Ernst Schoen, dated 17 June 1918, not in a letter to Scholem. 'Er ist seelisch stumm, das heißt es fehlt seinem Wesen derjenige Kontakt mit dem Weltwesen, der Sprache, aus dem das Sprechen hervorgeht.']

14 [This comes from a letter to Martin Buber, dated July 1916. Petitdemange's French translation of this letter is slightly misquoted by Berman as '[la] dignité de son essence' [the dignity of its essence] (Berman 2008:117) rather than Petitdemange's '[sa] dignité et son essence' (Benjamin 1979:117), which is the more accurate rendering of Benjamin's 'ihre[r] Würde und ihr[es] Wesen[s]', of its dignity and its essence.]

15 ['un sens plus pur aux mots de la tribu']

16 This is what we find in Valéry when he says that poetry is the translation of the language of men into the language of the gods. Pure language is not the language of the gods, it is a particular language that was created by a process of purification, it is a language that one can also define by traits that have much in common with Benjamin's pure language, which are the absence of content, non-communicability, emptiness – a series of predicates that appear to be the same. But at the same time, they are not the same thing. A further difference that will become apparent is that by definition the pure language of literature is a written language whereas the language of which Benjamin is thinking, pure language, is oral. It has been liberated from writing.

Bibliography

Agamben, G., 1986. Langue et histoire. Translated from Italian by Y. Hersant. In: H. Wismann, ed. 1986. *Walter Benjamin et Paris. Colloque international 27–29 June 1983*. Paris: Les Éditions du Cerf. pp.793–807.

Benjamin, W., 1978. *Briefe I und II. Herausgegeben und mit Anmerkungen versehen von Gershom Scholem und Theodor Wolfgang Adorno*. Frankfurt am Main: Suhrkamp.

Benjamin, W., 1979. *Correspondance 1929–1940*. Translated from German by G. Petitdemange. Paris: Aubier.

Benjamin, W., 1991a [1923]. Die Aufgabe des Übersetzers. In: R. Tiedemann and H. Schweppenhäuser, eds. 1991. *Gesammelte Schriften*. IV.I. Frankfurt am Main: Suhrkamp. pp.9–21.

Benjamin, W., 1991b [1928]. Einbahnstrasse. In: R. Tiedemann and H. Schweppenhäuser, eds. 1991. *Gesammelte Schriften*. IV.I. Frankfurt am Main: Suhrkamp. pp. 83–148.

Benjamin, W., 1991c. Notiz B14 zu den Thesen *Über den Begriff der Geschichte*. (Druckvorlage: Benjamin-Archiv, MS 441). In: R. Tiedemann and H. Schweppenhäuser, eds. 1991. *Gesammelte Schriften*. I.III. Frankfurt am Main: Suhrkamp. p.1239.

Benjamin, W., 1991d. Über Sprache überhaupt und über die Sprache des Menschen. In: R. Tiedemann and H. Schweppenhäuser, eds. 1991. *Gesammelte Schriften*. II.I. Frankfurt am Main: Suhrkamp. pp.140–157.

Berman, A., 2008. *L'Âge de la traduction*. Paris: Presses Universitaires de Vincennes.

Broch, H., 1975 [1946]. Einige Bemerkungen zur Philosophie und Technik des Übersetzens. In: P.M. Lützeler, ed. 1975. *Hermann Broch. Schriften zur Literatur 2: Theorie*. Band 9/2 der kommentierten Werkausgabe Hermann Broch. Frankfurt am Main: Suhrkamp. pp.61–86.

Derrida, J., 1967. *L'Écriture et La Différence*. Paris: Le Seuil.

Gandillac, M. de, trans. 1971. La tâche du traducteur. In: *Œuvres I, Mythe et violence*. Paris: Denoël/Les Lettres Nouvelles. pp. 261–275.

Hölderlin, F., 1951a. Unter den Alpen gesungen. In: F. Bessner, ed. 1951. *Gedichte nach 1800. Stuttgarter Hölderlin Ausgabe. Band 2. Hälfte 1*. Stuttgart: Verlag W. Kohlhammer. pp.44–45.

Hölderlin, F., 1951b. An die Madonna. In: F. Bessner, ed. 1951. *Gedichte nach 1800. Stuttgarter Hölderlin Ausgabe. Band 2. Hälfte 1*. Stuttgart: Verlag W. Kohlhammer. pp.211–216.

Hölderlin, F., 1951c. Der Vatikan. In: F. Bessner, ed. 1951. *Gedichte nach 1800. Stuttgarter Hölderlin Ausgabe. Band 2. Hälfte 1*. Stuttgart: Verlag W. Kohlhammer. pp.252–253.

Hölderlin, F., 1961a. Reflexion. In: F. Bessner, ed. 1961. *Der Tod des Empedokles, Aufsätze. Stuttgarter Hölderlin Ausgabe. Band 4. Hälfte 1*. Stuttgart: Verlag W. Kohlhammer. pp.233–236.

Hölderlin, F., 1961b. Über die Verfahrungsweise des poëtischen Geistes. In: F. Bessner, ed. 1961. *Der Tod des Empedokles, Aufsätze. Stuttgarter Hölderlin Ausgabe. Band 4. Hälfte 1*. Stuttgart: Verlag W. Kohlhammer. pp.241–265.

Horguelin, P., 1981. *Anthologie de la manière de traduire. Domaine français*. Montréal: Linguatech.

Klossowski, P., 1964. *Virgile. L'Énéide*. Paris: Gallimard.

Mallarmé, S., 1945. Le tombeau d'Edgar Poe. In: S. Mallarmé, *Œuvres complètes*. Paris: Gallimard. p.70.

Naïs, H., 1980. Traduction et imitation chez quelques poètes du XVIe siècle. *Revue des sciences humaines*, 180, pp.33–49.

Rilke, R.M., 1986 [1922]. Die Sonette an Orpheus. In: *Die Gedichte*. Frankfurt am Main: Insel Verlag. pp. 671–717.

CAHIER 6

In his essay 'Translation and the Trials of the Foreign' (trans. Venuti 2000), Antoine Berman outlines his negative analytic, a list of twelve deforming tendencies, unconsciously practised by translators, that give rise to target texts which fail to respect the foreign-ness of the original text. Just as the problematic of meaning in 'The Task of the Translator' makes the translator's relationship with words connected to meaning in Benjamin's text somewhat inhibited, so too does Berman's unforgiving critique make the translator nervous about approaching *his* commentary. But the Antoine Berman of *The Age of Translation* is a more forgiving critic, a human critic; one might even say that he is a translator's translator. In the very first cahier of his commentary, he acknowledges the longstanding criticisms of Gandillac's translation of 'The Task of the Translator' but argues that French readers should nonetheless acknowledge the 'gift' that Gandillac made them in the sixties when he introduced Benjamin's texts into France (2008:20). The many revisions to Gandillac's 'La tâche du traducteur' that were made both by the translator himself and by subsequent editors point to the complexity of Benjamin's text and the humility of the translator in the face of this complexity. It is against this background that Berman's introduction, in a footnote, of the concept of the translational *défaillance*, which I have translated as 'default', should be understood.

> *There is no translation without translation default.* The location of defaults can vary, but they always exist. Re-translation highlights them, but is not free of them. Further re-translation will also detect them.
>
> *(ibid.:78)*

In Cahier 6, there are two defaults in Berman's translation of the following passage from Benjamin, defaults that I would not have noticed had I not

attempted my own translation of the German, a translation that is indebted –
as are all my translations of passages from 'Task' – to Gandillac's and Berman's
versions.

> Damit ist allerdings zugestanden, daß alle Übersetzung nur eine
> irgendwie vorläufige Art ist, sich mit der Fremdheit der Sprachen
> auseinanderzusetzen. Eine andere als zeitliche und vorläufige Lösung
> dieser Fremdheit, *eine augenblickliche und endgültige*, bleibt den
> Menschen *versagt* oder ist jedenfalls unmittelbar nicht anzustreben.
> (Benjamin 1991:14, emphasis added)

> Here one must admit that all translation is only a provisional way of
> engaging with the foreignness of languages. A solution to this foreign-
> ness that is other than temporary and intermediate, *a solution that is an
> immediate and definitive solution*, remains *but a promise* to humankind or
> in any case is not immediately accessible.

> C'est là concéder que toute traduction n'est qu'un mode relativement
> provisoire de s'expliquer (*auseinandersetzen*) avec l'étrangeté des
> langues. Une solution de cette étrangeté qui soit autre que temporelle
> et provisoire, *instantanée et définitive*, voilà qui est *refusé* à l'homme ou,
> du moins, vers quoi il ne peut tendre immédiatement.

The second sentence in the above citation lists four adjectives in two sets of
pairs and appears at first glance to be an example of syntactic parallelism. In the
parallel clause 'eine augenblickliche und endgültige', Benjamin elides the noun
Lösung [solution] that appears in the preceding clause. The gender of the indefinite article and the endings of the adjectives in the parallel clause tell us that
the noun that is being qualified is the same. This elision may be the reason why
we are tempted to erroneously read the parallel clause as a repetition of the first
clause with different adjectives, that is, 'a solution to this foreignness that is other
than immediate and definitive' rather than its opposite, 'a solution that *is* an
immediate and definitive solution'. Berman falls into this trap, perhaps because
the adjectives *zeitlich* and *augenblicklich* appear at first glance to be synonymous. For Berman's reading to be correct, however, the Benjaminian sentence
would need to repeat 'eine andere als' [a ... that is other], which it does not.
Furthermore, the incompatibility of *vorläufig* and *endgültig* rule out this reading.
Interestingly, Gandillac does not make this mistake: 'une solution qui soit plus
que temporelle et provisoire, qui soit instantanée et définitive' (1971:267).

There is a further default in the sentence, but one which is almost impossible
to 'resolve'. A solution to the foreignness of languages 'bleibt den Menschen
versagt'. Both Gandillac and Berman translate this as *refusé* [refused, deprived].
This is correct, but the German verb *versagen* from which the participle here
is derived can mean both 'fail, refuse' but also 'promise', and both meanings

are hinted at. There is no obvious solution to the foreignness of languages, but Benjamin will argue that translation contains the 'promise' of pure language, a language beyond foreignness. There is no one English or French equivalent for *versagen* that contains these two opposite meanings and Berman's translation may be less an example of a 'default' than sheer resignation. My own solution errs more on the side of promise than refusal, suggesting a counterpoint to Berman's and Gandillac's readings.

Pure language is language itself and in itself; this is the contention at which we have arrived. Each language is driven by a meaning, an intention, something it wants to say [*un vouloir-dire*] that is fundamentally directed towards this pure language. Each language means, or intends [*veut-dire*, wants to say], pure language, language itself, but it does not *say* it.

Pure language is the *unsaid* [the *non-dit*] par excellence of 'natural' languages.

Benjamin makes another claim here: it is the *totality* of these intentions that results in pure language. Natural languages are mutually exclusive but, on another level, they are cumulative, they 'complete' each other. And when they 'complete' each other like this, pure language emerges.

This is obviously the reason why translation has (*can* have) a central role to play, because with each translation a unique language is formed out of two languages. In his letter to Scholem on the subject of Hölderlin's translations, Benjamin claimed that in these translations, Greek and German become one language, born of the love that the translator felt for both languages in equal measure. In the terminology of 'The Task of the Translator', these two languages, far from being mutually exclusive, are brought into harmony. And this harmony gives a performance – *Darstellung* – of pure language where it is both present and absent in the manner that we discussed earlier.

Admittedly these contentions remain obscure at the present time.

What also remains obscure is *how* this pure language which, for Benjamin, is language itself – this pure language which is non-transitive, non-communicative and non-signifying – is proclaimed in translation.

Languages are related in that it is their fundamental nature to intend pure language. Translation bears witness to their kinship. Reveals it. Why, and how?

There can be no doubt that translation is a trial of the gulf that separates languages but it is no less a trial of the gulf that unites them.

But how can translation be said to bear witness to something other than an empirically or rationally verifiable resemblance between two languages? We have already dismissed the assertion – the assertion that dominates conventional translation theory – that presents the self-evident factuality of this resemblance as proof of the unity of languages, and the act of translating as a victory over Babel. But this same presupposition can be found in Benjamin: that Babel – in other words, the multiplicity of languages – is a negative state of affairs that the passage of History will overcome. Benjamin's thought is in line with tradition here, and the Mallarmé text that is cited at a later stage bears witness to this. In brief: for

Mallarmé, the pure language of poetry 'redeems' the 'shortcoming of languages' (their multiplicity); for Benjamin, that pure language that issues from translation is the 'resolution' (*Lösung, Auflösung*) of this shortcoming. We can therefore say that Benjamin's thinking operates in the same sphere as conventional theory, but in a manner which reinterprets it and, in reinterpreting it, opens it up to something else.

In this manner the multiplicity of languages emerges as fragment(ation). Each language is a *Bruchstück*, a fragment. And each language thus points us towards an All, towards a 'bigger' language. The sum total of these fragments of languages (languages-as-fragments) results – will result – in pure language, which will no longer be fragmentary. This is where the metaphor of the amphora or vase (which is mapped onto the relationship between translation and original) comes into play further on in the text. Each language is a fragment, a piece of the larger language. As individual pieces, the fragments of this large vase of language do not, of course, resemble one another. But because of their nature as fragments of this vase, they can complete each other and (re)constitute the vase as an integral whole. From this perspective, attempting to establish a resemblance between fragments of language is completely futile but by contrast, attempting to put them together to (re)constitute the whole of which they are fragments is not. And this will be the task of translation: to work towards the integration of fragmentary languages in order to reveal, if not the intact plenitude of the larger language, then at least the shadow that it casts.

Our concept of pure language requires some refinement: pure language is the *larger language*, the intact language composed of the totalising reunion of those fragments of language that are natural languages.

Thinking the multiplicity of languages as fragment(ation) is something peculiar to Benjamin. The traditional pathos that surrounds the 'ghost of the multitude of languages' is therefore completely transformed. There is none of this pathos in Benjamin. There is not even the idea that this multitude is purely negative in itself, an idea that always leads to positing either one particular natural language or an artificial language as a potential means of overcoming this in the future. 'Pure language' is not an authoritarian means of overcoming natural languages. It is the reunion of these languages within a 'larger language' and not some kind of Esperanto. From the conventional perspective, translation's only role is to demonstrate the unity of languages, languages that will disappear one day to make way for a single language – English or Esperanto, for example. Once this language has been established, all translation will of course be superfluous.

From Benjamin's perspective, it is the task of translation to ripen language itself within natural languages and to do this by bringing these languages together as one would bring fragments back together. Of course this does not mean that this unification will be purely and simply accomplished in the translated text. No – rather this reunifying operation is announced in translation and – as we will see – in a manner which is itself fragmentary. We might therefore say that we find fragments of non-fragmentary language in translation. Translation contributes – in a particular manner – to reconstituting the great broken vase of pure language. This is the imposing metaphor that Benjamin offers us for the task of the translator.

We will have to re-think this metaphor, both on its own terms and in terms of how it relates to the other metaphors for translation that proliferate in 'The Task of the Translator'. We will need to examine the global image drawn or woven by these metaphors and the way in which they break with an entire tradition of negative metaphors for translation.

Let us return now to our paragraph, and to an ambiguity that it is impossible to overlook. It concerns the scope and nature of 'intention' (*meinen, vouloir-dire*). Fundamentally, this 'intention' is, in each language, the intention of pure language. But Benjamin, in order to explain the fact that,

> diese Sprachen [ergänzen] sich in ihren Intentionen selbst
>
> *(p. 14. para 7)*

> these languages complete each other in their intentions
>
> ces langues se complètent dans leurs intentions mêmes
>
> *(Berman)*

[Literal translation of Berman's French translation:

> these languages complete each other in their very intentions],

says something quite different:

> Dieses Gesetz, eines der grundlegenden der Sprachphilosophie, genau zu fassen, ist in der Intention vom Gemeinten die Art des Meinens zu unterscheiden.
>
> *(p. 14. para 7)*

> To precisely grasp this, one of the fundamental laws of the philosophy of language, we have to distinguish, with regards to the intention, between what is meant and the way of meaning.

> Pour saisir exactement cette loi, l'une des lois fondamentales de la philosophie du langage, il faut distinguer dans l'intention le mode de visée du visé lui-même.
>
> *(Berman)*

[Literal translation of Berman's French translation:

> To precisely grasp this law, one of the fundamental laws of the philosophy of language, one has to distinguish within the intention the manner of the aim from what is aimed at.]

(I have returned to Gandillac's translation here (cf. Gandillac 1971:266), in order to remain in the Husserlian sphere signalled by the use of *Intention*. But we should not forget here that this 'visée' is above all a 'vouloir-dire'.)[1]

> In »Brot« und »pain« ist das Gemeinte zwar dasselbe, die Art, es zu meinen, dagegen nicht.
>
> *(p. 14. para 7)*

> The same thing is meant by *Brot* and *pain*, but the way in which it is meant is not.

> Dans «Brot» et «pain» le visé est certes le même, mais le mode de visée, par contre, ne l'est pas.
>
> *(Berman)*

[Literal translation of Berman's French translation:

> In *Brot* and *pain* what is intended is indeed the same, but the mode of the intention, by contrast, is not.]

Benjamin uses a concrete example here, something which is quite rare in his writing.

The two modes of intention implicit in *pain* and *Brot* are different and are not at all interchangeable for people from France or Germany. But their signified, their referent is the same. If Benjamin's comment went no further than this, it would do nothing more than reformulate, in phenomenological language, what linguistics has to say about the relationship between signifier, signified and referent. But this is an entirely alien plane for Benjamin, because it concerns the way in which a language signifies reality. And what is more, Benjamin strenuously rejects the 'intentional' nature of language (its nature as a set of signs).

However, this concrete example does indeed bring us back to the plane of the intentionality or referentiality of language. And in a manner so ambiguous one can of course object – with Humboldt – that not only does each language's mode of intention[2] differ but simultaneously *what is intended*. We can clearly say, to take another example, that 'porte', 'puerta' and 'Tür' are three ways of intending the same intended, the same 'real'. But if this leads us to say that, where 'words' are concerned, what distinguishes one language from another is that there are different signifiers for the same signifieds, then it is obvious that this is not how things work and that this is a fundamentally dubious suggestion that can only be true for particular limited designatory planes. The distinction between the mode of intention and what is intended is, to a certain extent, artificial and Benjamin goes on to say this (in paragraph ten):

> Treue in der Übersetzung des einzelnen Wortes kann fast nie den Sinn voll wiedergeben, den es im Original hat. Denn dieser erschöpft sich nach seiner dichterischen Bedeutung fürs Original nicht in dem Gemeinten, sondern gewinnt diese gerade dadurch, wie das Gemeinte an die Art des Meinens

in dem bestimmten Worte gebunden ist. Man pflegt dies in der Formel auszudrücken, daß die Worte einen Gefühlston mit sich führen.

(p. 17. para 10)

Fidelity in the translation of the individual word can almost never fully render the sense that the word has in the original text. This is because this sense, in its poetic significance for the original, is not exhausted in what is meant but achieves this significance precisely in how what is meant and the way of meaning are tied together in a particular word. This is normally expressed by saying that words carry an emotional tone.

La fidelité dans la traduction du mot isolé ne peut presque jamais rendre pleinement le sens qu'il a dans l'original. Car celui-ci ne s'épuise pas dans sa signification littéraire pour l'original dans ce qui est visé, mais acquiert justement cette signification du fait que le visé est lié au mode de visée dans le mot déterminé. On a coutume d'exprimer cela dans la formule selon laquelle les mots portent avec eux une tonalité affective.

(Berman)

[Literal translation of Berman's French translation:

Fidelity in the translation of an isolated word can almost never fully render the sense that it has in the original. Because this is not exhausted in its literary signification for the original in what is intended, but rather acquires that signification from the fact that what is intended is linked to the mode of intention in the particular word. This tends to be expressed in the saying that words carry with them an emotional tonality.]

The distinction between the mode of intention and what is intended is arbitrary on the plane where Benjamin formulates it – the linguistic plane. This plane seems to be unconnected to the fact that each individual language intends pure language, language without intention.

We can therefore identify, within any one language, *two intentions*: natural language as a whole (a fragmentary whole) intends pure language. But, in its specific elements – Benjamin lists words, sentences, the 'interrelationships between foreign languages' (Benjamin 1991:13–14) (larger syntactic groupings) – intention simply signifies the intention of established signifieds (referents). It is in the unique way in which, in each language, signifieds and, in the final analysis, the real, are intended, that that *other* intention is hidden, the intention of pure language, within which the other intention (will) no longer exist(s).

Benjamin is therefore attempting – fairly clumsily – to think these two planes together:

Während dergestalt die Art des Meinens in diesen beiden Wörtern einander widerstrebt, ergänzt sie sich in den beiden Sprachen, denen sie entstammen.

Und zwar ergänzt sich in ihnen die Art des Meinens zum Gemeinten. Bei den einzelnen, den unergänzten Sprachen nämlich ist ihr Gemeintes niemals in relativer Selbständigkeit anzutreffen, wie bei den einzelnen Wörtern oder Sätzen, sondern vielmehr in stetem Wandel begriffen, bis es aus der Harmonie all jener Arten des Meinens als die reine Sprache herauszutreten vermag.

(p. 14. para 7)

Thus whereas the mode of intention in these two words is at odds, this mode of intention is completed in the two languages from which they hail. And indeed in these languages the mode of intention becomes the thing intended. When languages are left in isolation, incomplete, what they intend is never encountered in relative independence, as it is in individual words or sentences, but rather is caught up in continual change until it is able to step out from the harmony of all these modes of intention as pure language.

Tandis que de la sorte le mode de visée est en opposition dans ces deux mots, il se complète dans les deux langues dont ils proviennent. Et certes se complète en elles le mode de visée du visé. Dans les langues prises une à une et incomplétées, en effet, le visé ne peut jamais être atteint dans une relative autonomie, comme dans les mots ou les propositions particulières, mais il est plutôt pris dans un changement continuel, jusqu'à ce qu'il puisse surgir (*hervortreten*) de l'harmonie de tous ces modes de visée comme la pure langue.

(Berman)

[Literal translation of Berman's French translation:

Whereas the mode of intention is thus in opposition in these two words, it is completed in the two languages from which they stem. And indeed the mode of intention is completed in them from what is intended. In languages taken one by one and incomplete, in effect, what is intended can never be achieved in relative autonomy, as it is in words or particular sentences, but rather it is taken up in continual change, until it can emerge from the harmony of all these modes of intention as pure language.]

Words and sentences taken in isolation express the pure difference between the modes of intention. But when each language is taken as a whole, its mode of intention does not exclude other languages' modes of intention: rather its mode is realised by these other modes.

These two planes of thought have clearly been amalgamated rather than thought alongside each other.

For Benjamin, a language's mode of intention is realised at the level of the entire language. This is more than a fundamental principle of the philosophy of language, it is a raw metaphysical conviction. It is even, as we will see, a *religious* conviction (but this term has to be thought). This conviction, and let me emphasise this again, is that each language, far from being simply a closed system of modes of intending reality, is a fragment of a 'larger language'. Whereas fragments can complete one another and only ever acquire their true meaning when they do so, by contrast closed linguistic systems do not complete each other in the slightest: they only present, like monads, one way of intending the real, *ad infinitum*.

Pure language emerges from the 'harmony' of all the different modes of intention and this harmony is achieved via a process of *harmonisation*, of *Auflösung*: until this harmonisation takes place, pure language, the true 'intention' of each language's intention, remains 'hidden' (*verborgen*) (Benjamin 1991:14) within natural languages.

We might say that each language is a unique mode of referential intention that carries within it, hidden, *another* intention, that of a language which no longer has a referential intention of this kind. The latter is not a static entity. On the contrary, it is in continual change, but once again this change – a trajectory of life – is not simply diachronic, nor a simple process of 'renewal': it is maturation, growth [*Wachstum*]. Pure language is what ripens and continues to ripen within each language. Once more we find ourselves face to face with a fundamental statement of belief.

> Wenn aber diese derart bis ans messianische Ende ihrer Geschichte wachsen, so ist es die Übersetzung, welche am ewigen Fortleben der Werke und am unendlichen Aufleben der Sprachen sich entzündet, immer von neuem die Probe auf jenes heilige Wachstum der Sprachen zu machen.
>
> *(p.14. para 7)*

> But when languages grow all the way to the Messianic end of their histories in this fashion, then translation, sparked by the eternal continuing life of literary texts and by the neverending coming-alive of languages, must constantly test this holy growth of languages anew.

> Mais lorsque, de la sorte, elles [les langues] croissent jusqu'au terme messianique de leur histoire, c'est à la traduction, qui s'enflamme de l'éternelle vie continuée des œuvres (*Fortleben der Werke*) et de l'infinie renaissance [*Aufleben*] des langues, qu'il appartient toujours à nouveau de faire l'épreuve de cette sainte croissance des langues.
>
> *(Berman)*

[Literal translation of Berman's French translation:

> But when, in this manner, they [languages] grow until the Messianic end of their history, it is translation, which catches fire from the eternal continued life of literary texts and the infinite rebirth of languages, that must constantly test this sacred growth of languages.]

These are key lines.

Translation is sparked (*entzündet sich*) by the *Fortleben* of texts and the *Aufleben* of languages.[3] This continual renaissance of linguistic life finds its first expression in the *Fortleben* of literary texts. More precisely, this *Fortleben* and *Aufleben* are indistinguishable, intermingled. And yet – I will come back to this – the life of the literary text and the life of languages are not identical. The difficulty of thinking the essence of translation stems from the fact that translation is faced with and is a trial for both the *Fortleben* of literary texts and the *Aufleben* of languages. And yet *Aufleben* is growth, *Wachstum*. And this, Benjamin says, is *heilig*, holy or sacred.

Heilig is an adjective that of course primarily belongs to the sphere of organised religion. But it is also one of the key terms in Hölderlin's poetry. *Das Heilige sei mein Wort* [May the sacred be my word], Hölderlin sings in a hymn (1951:118). 'Pure' language ripens in the 'holy' growth of languages. All things 'pure' (*rein*) are also 'sacred' (*heilig*). In Hölderlin the nexus of the 'pure' and the 'sacred' is patent, and connects to something that has features of the religious. And religion is just about to raise its head.

Translation tries – puts on trial – the 'holy' growth of languages. Translation measures

> wie weit ihr Verborgenes von der Offenbarung entfernt sei, wie gegenwärtig es im Wissen um diese Entfernung werden mag.
>
> *(p. 14. para 7)*

> how far what is hidden is removed from revelation, how present it can become with knowledge of this distance.

> combien ce qu'elle cache est éloigné de la révélation, comment elle peut devenir présente [la croissance] dans le savoir de cette distance.
>
> *(Berman)*

[Literal translation of Berman's French translation:

> how much what it hides is removed from revelation, how it [growth] can become present in the knowledge of this distance.]

These lines can only be illuminated at a later stage. But this much is certain: to the extent that translation is a trial of and for the *Aufleben* of languages (not only the *Fortleben* of texts), it carries within it knowledge, knowledge of the proximity (of the coming) and of the distance of the pure language that is ripening within natural languages. How? That remains to be seen.

> Damit ist allerdings zugestanden, daß alle Übersetzung nur eine irgendwie vorläufige Art ist, sich mit der Fremdheit der Sprachen auseinanderzusetzen. Eine andere als zeitliche und vorläufige Lösung dieser Fremdheit, eine augenblickliche und endgültige, bleibt den Menschen versagt oder ist

jedenfalls unmittelbar nicht anzustreben. Mittelbar aber ist es das Wachstum der Religionen, welches in den Sprachen den verhüllten Samen einer höhern reift.

(p. 14. para 8)

Here one must admit that all translation is only a provisional way of engaging with the foreignness of languages. A solution to this foreignness that is other than temporary and intermediate, a solution that is an immediate and definitive solution, remains but a promise to humankind or in any case is not immediately accessible. More immediately it is the growth of religions that ripens the hidden seed of a higher language within languages.

C'est là concéder que toute traduction n'est qu'un mode relativement provisoire de s'expliquer (*auseinandersetzen*) avec l'étrangeté des langues. Une solution de cette étrangeté qui soit autre que temporelle et provisoire, instantanée et définitive, voilà qui est refusé à l'homme ou, du moins, vers quoi il ne peut tendre immédiatement. Mais médiatement, c'est la croissance des religions qui fait mûrir dans les langues la semence voilée d'une langue plus haute.

(Berman)

[Literal translation of Berman's French translation:

This is to concede that all translation is only a relatively provisional mode of coming to terms (*auseinandersetzen*) with the strangeness of languages. A solution to this strangeness that is other than temporal and provisional, momentary and definitive, this is refused to man or, at least, something towards which he cannot immediately reach. But in the meantime, it is the growth of religions that ripens within languages the veiled seed of a higher language.]

For the moment I will leave aside the first two sentences, which proclaim the following: that translation does not undo languages' foreignness towards one another; that man cannot undo this strangeness by himself, that is to say without mediation.

What is important is that the 'holy' growth of languages to which translation will bear witness is mediated by *another* growth, that of religions. And this is where we get to the very heart of Benjamin's convictions, convictions that he never developed precisely because of their centrality. 'Religion' here evidently means *a religion of revelation*, whether this be Christianity, Judaism or Islam. In religions of revelation, human language experiences a decisive 'mutation' because *revelation takes place through human language*. Language's destiny is therefore linked to the development of religion. Even the growth of languages is only 'holy' to the extent that it is linked to the growth of religions; without this it would be nothing more than pure change.

However, I will invert this proposition and say that the growth of religions is linked to the growth of that higher language whose veiled germination religions mediate. And this, in turn, happens via translation. The life of religion is so intimately linked to translation that one cannot conceive of religion without it, and the life of translation is so intimately linked to that of religion that *all 'great' translations have a religious foundation.* In saying this, I am of course talking about the Bible, but also, although in a different manner, about the Qur'an. The act of translating sacred texts is a fundamental act and, for the texts themselves, it is a question of their very being. Although the desire for translation and the refusal of translation – the two elements that we discussed earlier – hold true for every text, they could not be more true in the case of sacred texts. It does not matter if we have a religious connection to these texts or not; they remain sacred even if we do not 'believe' in them. In their sacredness, they both wish to be translated and not to be translated. If we adopt the metaphor of the vase, then we can say that language is the vase that receives the word of Revelation. On the one hand, this vase is too small to contain the word all by itself because the word requires the totality of languages; and only this totality (ideally an infinite one) can accommodate its infinity. The word of revelation is absolutely unable to inhabit a single language and this is why it has to be translated: only thus can it extensively realise its infinity. The word of revelation must be poly-translated or poly-re-translated in order to have its effects. And in this never-ending poly-re-translation, language – each language – continues to ripen and reach a 'higher' level.

For every natural language, translating a sacred text initiates its transformation into a receptacle for the word of revelation. This transformation is of course never complete because translation has no way of definitively establishing the word of revelation in one language. This is why the Bible is the one text that constantly undergoes re-translation. It is the most translated text on earth and the only text (ultimately) to be translated into all of the earth's languages. We cannot differentiate here between the growth of religions, the growth of languages and the growth (indefinite renewal) of translations. Translation is so truly the sanction of the growth of languages that Louis-Lazare Zamenhof, the creator of Esperanto, made it a priority to translate the Bible into this new language. For whom? That didn't matter. Why? So that Esperanto could reach a 'higher' level of language. But the sacred text is also the text that resists translation the most. For the link that is established between a language and the word of Revelation is absolutely sacrosanct and unique.

Paradoxically, the sacred text is therefore maximally translatable – it is from the sacred text that the ordinance for translation emanates in fact – and maximally untranslatable. Thus, with respect to the Bible and the Qur'an, two equally valid commandments converge:

Thou shalt translate
Thou shalt not translate

But higher language grows and matures similarly either way, because two forms of maturation offer themselves in resolution of this conflict: *maturation through translation or maturation in veneration of the letter, of the sole language that is consecrated the vase of the Word of Revelation.* In the former, language matures via translation, *re- and polytranslation* (the Christian path), and in the latter it matures via *commentary*, which has the same infinite essence as translation but is intensive rather than extensive (the Jewish tradition). In both cases, language matures and slowly climbs towards its essentiality. This is why translation and commentary *are* the life of the tree of the sacred text.

These relationships are mysterious but this much is certain: all the great Western translations have a religious foundation, are religious texts; and this goes far beyond translations of the Bible. Hölderlin's translations of Pindar and Sophocles are religious. So too is the French translation of Milton's *Paradise Lost* by Chateaubriand, or George's translation of Baudelaire. Religion has to be understood in a very broad sense here, as anything that links man to the world as a whole. In the sense that every great text, sacred or profane, expresses and establishes this link, in the sense that every great text is 'religious', the act of translating such a text is religious too. There is a trace of this in the concept of *fidelity*, hackneyed though it is.

There will always be two touchstones (Classicist Germany knew this, Goethe above all) in Western thought on translation and in how we think this link between the religious and translation that Benjamin expresses only in the form of an intuitive conviction: these are translation of the Greeks (poetry, theatre and philosophy)[4] and translation of the Bible. Even when we are translating something that appears to be completely unrelated – Latin American novelists, Freud, a Japanese or Chinese poet – we cannot forget or leave aside the fact that for us the meaning and purpose of translation is *decided* in the act of translating the Bible and the Greeks.

One thing unites all of the great sacred texts – those written by the Prophets, the Evangelists or the tragic playwrights of Greece – and that is *poetics.* A literary text is only religious in so far as it is poetic. There is *religiosity* in a text's most profane-seeming poetics. Poeticity of this kind does not exclude prose. On the contrary, one of the laws governing poetry of the most intense, most sacred, kind, is – and Benjamin never tired of repeating it – its prosaicness. I refer you here to what Pasternak said about the 'translational tension' of prose.[5]

With all of these – still unexplored – correlations in mind, we should re-read Benjamin's sentence:

> More immediately it is the growth of religions that ripens the hidden seed of a higher language within languages.
>
> *(1991:14)*

For me, the growth of religions is nothing other than the growth of the Revealed Word in natural languages via translation or non-translation (commentary). The growth of religions can only be the *Fortleben* of the sacred text which lies at their heart and, through and in this *Fortleben*, the *Aufleben* of languages.

The essence of commentary (non-translation) and translation is religious. This is not to say that the translator has religious convictions of a dogmatic or orthodox nature, but that in her task, she engages with the *letter* of the text. Through the translation of the letter of the sacred text, the translator's own language undergoes a decisive mutation which takes it beyond itself, to a point of non-return to what was *before*. In the life of a language, the translation of the foreign 'sacred' text marks a caesura. In other words: the translating language becomes religious. Or rather the foreign letter, the receptacle of the 'sacred', imprints itself upon it; it leaves behind an impression. Through translation the translating language becomes the vase and receptacle of a word which is both entirely contained within its language of origin and ceaselessly strives to move beyond it.

We would have to think the concept of 'religiosity' quite precisely for it to encompass works such as those by Kafka, Broch, Proust, Rilke, George, Freud or Guimarães Rosa, or Tolstoy or Dostoevsky, or Racine, Diderot, Rousseau,[6] Goethe etc. If we could achieve this, then we would arrive at the conclusion that translating, translating great texts, is always a religious act[7] through which language matures. Not only is language expanded, enriched and refined (profane categories), it penetrates further into the secret of its own life and its most profound *oral* life. What we can sense when we read the great French texts of the sixteenth century, from Rabelais to Montaigne, is that through the act of total writing we call translating, language matures in its orality, fulfils its oral truth, a truth that goes beyond that of orality tied to its natural life – since this trickles away like water. Let us not forget that these great literary texts were only possible because translations course through them.

We would sense that the more a language – through writing, through translation – nears its oral truth, the more it nears what Benjamin calls 'pure language', and that this – bringing a language back to its oral truth – is the religious essence of translation. Orality – and I will finish on this note – is always religious, and the great 'religious' text is always oral.

Notes

1 [Gandillac's translation includes a footnote on his decision to translate *Meinung* as *visée* (cf. Gandillac 1971:272).]
2 ['mode de visée' is Berman's translation of Benjamin's *die Art des Meinens*, which I have rendered in my translation of Benjamin's passage as 'way of meaning'.]
3 *Aufleben*: *renaître à la vie, se réanimer, revivre, s'épanouir* [revive, flourish, blossom, recover, come back to life].
4 But the theatre above all.
5 [In the footnote that occurs at this juncture, Berman's commentary gives a heavily abridged citation from Pasternak's 1934 speech to the First All-Union Congress of Soviet Writers, in Catherine Perrel's French translation: 'Qu'est-ce qu la poésie […]? La poésie, c'est la prose […], la prose elle-même, la voix de la prose, la prose en acte et non en

paraphrase littéraire. [...] c'est justement cela, c'est-à-dire, la prose pure dans sa tension originelle, qu'est la poésie' (1990:1553). Perrel translates the Russian *напряженность* as 'tension' [tension]. In Angela Livingstone's English translation, *напряженность* is rendered as 'intensity'. Both 'tension' and 'intensity' come close to the Russian word, which is is an abstract substantive derived from the past passive participle of the verb *напрячь*, meaning something like 'burden/stress/strain'. The root is related to verbs for harnessing (e.g. horses). Livingstone's translation of this passage is given in full here for context: 'What is poetry, comrades, if we are seeing its birth before our very eyes? Poetry is prose, prose not in the sense of the aggregate of someone or other's prose works, but prose itself, the voice of prose; prose in action, not in literary narration. Poetry is the language of organic fact, that is to say of fact which has living consequences. And, like everything else in the world, it may of course be good or bad, depending on whether we preserve it undistorted or contrive to spoil it. In any case, comrades, precisely like this – pure prose in its primal intensity – is poetry' (Pasternak 2008:218). In his footnote Berman points out that Armand Robin suggests an important variation on Perrel's translation: 'la prose pure dans sa tension traductive, voilà ce qu'est la poésie' (Bourdon 1981:71). According to Berman, Perrel's 'tension originelle' [original tension] becomes 'tension traductive' [translational tension] in Robin's version, but Robin actually used the expression 'tension traductrice'. This has the same meaning as 'tension traductive' but introduces a feminised aspect – with echoes of the adage *traduttore traditore* – by using the French noun for a female translator in adjectival form. The Russian word *первородный*, which finds such different renderings in Perrel's and Robin's versions, is very rare. It literally means 'first [*перво*] born [*род*]', as in born before everything else. Its most common collocation is *первородный грех* [original sin], and that is what Pasternak's usage conjures. The English 'primal' does not carry this biblical subtext.

6   For Hölderlin, it was natural to think Rousseau in religious terms.

7   And this religious translational act, strangely, happens in three languages, not two. In essential translation, the passage from one language to another is mediated by a third. See Berman 1994:198–214. [The equivalent reference for the English translation of this text is 2009:169–184.]

Bibliography

Benjamin, W., 1991 [1923]. Die Aufgabe des Übersetzers. In: R. Tiedemann and H. Schweppenhäuser, eds. 1991. *Gesammelte Schriften*. IV.I. Frankfurt am Main: Suhrkamp. pp.9–21.

Berman, A., 1994. *Pour une critique des traductions: John Donne*. Paris: Gallimard.

Berman, A., 2000 [1985]. Translation and the Trials of the Foreign. Translated from French by L. Venuti. In: L. Venuti, ed. 2000. *The Translation Studies Reader*. 1st ed. New York: Routledge. pp.284–297.

Berman, A., 2008. *L'Âge de la traduction*. Paris: Presses Universitaires de Vincennes.

Berman, A., 2009. *Towards a Translation Criticism: John Donne*. Kent, Ohio: Kent State University Press.

Bourdon, A., 1981. *Armand Robin ou La Passion du verbe*. Paris: Seghers.

Gandillac, M. de, trans. 1971. La tâche du traducteur. In: *Œuvres I, Mythe et violence*. Paris: Denoël/Les Lettres Nouvelles. pp. 261–275.

Hölderlin, F., 1951. Wie wenn am Feiertage ... In: F. Bessner, ed. 1951. *Gedichte nach 1800. Stuttgarter Hölderlin Ausgabe. Band 2. Hälfte 1*. Stuttgart: Verlag W. Kohlhammer. pp.118–120.

Pasternak, B.L., 1990 [1934]. Discours au Premier Congrès des Écrivains Soviétiques. Translated from Russian by C. Perrel. In: M. Aucouturier, ed. 1990. *Œuvres*. Paris: Gallimard. pp.1552–1554.

Pasternak, B.L., 2008 [1934]. Speech at the First All-Union Congress of Soviet Writers. Translated from Russian by A. Livingstone. In: A. Livingstone, ed. 2008. *The Marsh of Gold: Pasternak's Writings on Inspiration and Creation*. Boston: Academic Studies Press. pp.217–218.

CAHIER 7

When Benjamin announces in his eighth paragraph that 'das Verhältnis des Gehalts zur Sprache [ist] völlig verschieden in Original und Übersetzung' (1991:15) [the relationship of the substance of the text to its language is completely different in the original text and in the translation], he introduces the noun *Gehalt* into his text, a noun that Berman translates as *teneur* [which is related to the verb *tenir*, meaning 'to hold' or 'to keep']. *Gehalt* would normally be translated as 'content' or 'contents', and implies content(s) of an intellectual or conceptual nature, or content(s) in the sense of the percentual or proportional content of a material substance. Like *teneur*, *Gehalt* is related to a verb that means 'to hold', *halten*. Translating *Gehalt* in this context as either 'content' or 'contents' would be problematic, however, since one of these words must serve to translate 'Inhalt'. It is clear from Benjamin's statements that *Gehalt* is precisely not *Inhalt* [content, as contrasted with form], that is, it is not 'content' in the sense of a message. Rather it is 'that aspect of translation that goes beyond the delivery of a message', it is the text's 'essential kernel' (Benjamin 1991:15). *Gehalt* has therefore been rendered as 'substance', a word that suggests an essential if undefined presence both within philosophical thought and in everyday life, and that simultaneously escapes the form vs. content binary.

I have attempted to explain – in broad strokes – the link between religion (the religions of revelation), language and translation. This link will only truly become clear at the end of 'The Task of the Translator', when sacred texts are discussed.

Benjamin, in any case, is convinced that the growth of religions 'ripens' the seed (*Samen*) of a 'higher' language that exists within natural languages.

Is this 'higher' language pure language? And in what sense is it 'higher', *höher*? Benjamin continues:

> Übersetzung also, wiewohl sie auf Dauer ihrer Gebilde nicht Anspruch erheben kann und hierin unähnlich der Kunst, verleugnet nicht ihre Richtung auf ein letztes, endgültiges und entscheidendes Stadium aller Sprachfügung.
>
> *(p. 14. para 8)*

> Although translation – unlike art – cannot lay claim to the longevity of its products, it does not refute its orientation towards a final, ultimate and decisive stage of all linguistic structure.

> La traduction, encore qu'elle ne puisse prétendre à la durée de ses ouvrages (*Gebilde*), et en cela dissemblable de l'art, ne renonce pas à s'orienter vers un stade ultime, définitif et décisif de tout édifice de langue (*Sprachfügung*).
>
> *(Berman)*

[Literal translation of Berman's French translation:

> Translation, while it cannot pretend to the longevity of its works, and in this it is unlike art, does not step back from orientating itself towards an ultimate, definitive and decisive stage of all linguistic construction.]

Gandillac's translation commits a significant misinterpretation when it translates *unähnlich* [dissimilar, unlike] as its opposite:

> und hierin unähnlich der Kunst.
>
> *(p. 14. para 8)*

> and in this it is unlike art.

> et en cela elle n'est pas sans ressemblance avec l'art.
>
> *(Gandillac 1971:267)*

[Literal translation of Gandillac's French translation:

> and in this it is not without resemblance to art.]

This is a major misinterpretation, because we have seen that Benjamin contrasts the perishability of translations with the 'eternity' of original texts.
But the perishability of translation has another angle:

> In ihr wächst das Original in einen gleichsam höheren und reineren Luftkreis der Sprache hinauf, in welchem es freilich nicht auf die Dauer zu leben vermag, wie es ihn auch bei weitem nicht in allen Teilen seiner Gestalt

erreicht, auf den es aber dennoch in einer wunderbar eindringlichen Weise wenigstens hindeutet als auf den vorbestimmten, versagten Versöhnungs- und Erfüllungsbereich der Sprachen.

(pp. 14–15. para 8)

In translation the original text grows upwards into a, as it were, higher, purer, aerial dimension of language. The text cannot live there permanently of course, just as not all parts of its form have a chance of reaching this dimension, but it nonetheless points towards it in a wonderfully insistent way as the predetermined, promised domain of linguistic reconciliation and fulfilment.

En elle croît (*wächst*) l'original dans une atmosphère de langue pour ainsi dire plus haute et plus pure, dans laquelle, il est vrai, il ne peut vivre à la longue, de même qu'il ne l'atteint pas, tant s'en faut, dans toutes les parties de sa structure (*Gestalt*), mais vers laquelle cependant il fait au moins signe sur un mode étonnamment insistant, comme le domaine prédéterminé et refusé de la réconciliation et de l'accomplissement des langues.

(Berman)

[Literal translation of Berman's French translation:

In it [*translation*] the original grows in a linguistic atmosphere that one might describe as higher and more pure, in which, it is true, it cannot live long-term, just as it cannot reach it, far from it, in all parts of its structure, but towards which nonetheless it at least gestures in a fashion that is surprisingly insistent, as the predetermined and refused domain of the reconciliation and accomplishment of languages.]

This one sentence speaks volumes – as does the entire paragraph.

How, one might ask oneself first of all, does the original text grow in translation into an aerial dimension of higher, purer language? Secondly, why can't the text stay there, why is it only able to reach it in part?

To shed some light on these questions, we need to listen to the language in this first part of the sentence: *Luftkreis der Sprache, höher, reiner.*

This is indisputably Platonic language. The *logos* upon which philosophy, in its Platonic form, sets its sights is higher, purer and, shall we say, more aerial than natural language.

But philosophy is not alone in setting its sights upon this language: poetry – resolutely Platonic poetry – also has it in its sights. At this juncture I must bring in two authors who, curiously, were contemporaries without knowing one another: Novalis and Joubert. Both thought (the text's) poetic language in terms of a higher and purer aerial milieu (purer in all the senses of the term that we have discussed: unadulterated, luminous, empty, non-transitive). Novalis writes, for example: 'The spirit only ever appears in strange, aerial form' (Novalis 1965:428).[1]

And Joubert spent his entire life trying to capture the 'emptiness' of the milieu of poetic language: 'The diaphanous transparency, the lack of concrete materiality, the magic; the imitation of the divine who made all things out of so little, out of nothing, really: this is one of the essential characteristics of poetry' (Joubert 1989:317).[2]

It is obvious that this goes beyond the *purified* poetic language that Valéry was thinking of, to something more radical and certainly something closer to Benjamin's pure language.

But why should the text come closer, in translation, to this more aerial, more transparent, more unfettered language that obsessed Novalis and Joubert?

Let me remind you of what I have argued elsewhere on the subject of translation's Platonism:[3] that translation, because it liberates meaning, produces a different relationship between signifiers and signifieds in the translating language, a relationship where the ideality of meaning is allowed to dominate.

Let me remind you of what Nietzsche said about Schopenhauer: that he was both 'lighter' and closer to his 'truth' in French translation. Let me remind you also of Novalis's memorable statement that the German Shakespeare is superior to Shakespeare in English.

We extracted a hidden historical truth – belonging to Platonic thought – which sees the essence of translation as clarifying, illuminating, enriching and embellishing. This tradition has never properly been articulated or systematised, of course, but Benjamin's argument is not operating in an entirely different sphere.

This raises the question of whether Benjamin is simply reformulating, in his own fashion, the Platonic conviction that the language of translation is superior to (purer, higher, more aerial, more luminous than) the language of the original, which is mired in the depths of its natural language. Clearly the answer to this is both yes and no.

Yes, in so far as Benjamin always adopts the claims of the Platonic tradition. I have said that pure language could *also* be the Platonic *logos*. However, if it was no more than this, the remainder of Benjamin's sentence would be incomprehensible. And the remainder of the sentence states that translation is unable to sustain the original text within this purer language and that it does not even succeed in positioning the *totality* of the original within it. If the aerial dimension of Benjamin's purer and higher language was *merely* the Platonic language of translation where the liberated ideality of signification reigns, this assertion would make no sense. In the Platonic tradition, it is the *totality* of the text that is liberated by translation. For Benjamin, the original text only reaches a purer language in covert and fragmentary fashion.

We should ponder this. Translation is never a definitive and complete *accomplishment*. We therefore cannot interpret Benjamin's thought within the framework of the traditional Platonic theory of translation.

But how then are we to interpret the statement that translation makes the original grow within a higher and purer linguistic medium? Particularly given that the key thing for Benjamin is absolutely not the liberation or capture of meaning (the entire 'Task of the Translator' bears this out)? And that the mode of translation preached by Benjamin (if we can talk of a mode of translation) is one that is diametrically opposed to the restitution of meaning, i.e. that his is a literal mode that is of course the enemy of the entire Platonic tradition that I have been discussing? How therefore – according to what criteria – are we to locate those moments where the original text 'moves' into a purer and higher language in translation? These are not the moments where meaning is most visibly liberated but those where the language of the original and the language of the translation move into one another in the translation. It is through literalness that the translated text gestures towards (*hindeutet*) the 'promised domain of linguistic reconciliation and fulfilment'.

Reconciliation (*Versöhnung*) and fulfilment (*Erfüllung*) are two words that indisputably bring us back to the religious sphere, to the 'Messianic end' of the history of languages. For Benjamin, translation is a proclamation (anticipation) of this end. At certain points (but never to any greater degree than this) translation manages to reconcile languages, not through any common ideality of meaning, but through the element which separates them *a priori*: the very letter of the text. And this sporadic reconciliation is, in turn, a sign of the fulfilment of languages, a fulfilment that can be nothing other than the coming of pure language.

Can we locate precisely where and when, in a great translation, a reconciliation of this kind takes place? Let us take the example – with all the risks and dangers that this entails – that I have already cited several times, the line from Sophocles' *Antigone* (line 21)[4] in Hölderlin's translation, the verse where Ismene addresses Antigone as follows:

Τι δ εστι; ζηλοις γαρ τι καλκαινουσ εποσ

(Soph. Ant. 20)[5]

Attempting to pin down the precise point in a translation where the reconciliation of languages is proclaimed is, of course, more than risky. Such a point may well exist in a great translation but it is difficult to pinpoint it to one example. The above verse is, nonetheless, a verse that has provoked quite considerable reactions, reactions that history has documented, most notably the ridicule of Voss (Voss, the son of the Homer translator and himself an experienced translator of Shakespeare) and Schiller, and, by contrast, Goethe's silence, a striking silence that says much more than the ridicule of his contemporaries.

Hölderlin's translation is more or less literal if we compare it with more traditional translations such as Mazon and Grosjean's translations into French: Mazon:

De quoi s'agit-il donc? Quelque propos te tourmente, c'est clair.

(Mazon 1964)[6]

[Literal translation: What's the matter? Some subject troubles you, that is apparent.]

Grosjean:

> Qu'y-a-t-il ? quelqu'histoire *t'assombrit*, je le vois.
>
> *(Grosjean 1967)*

[Literal translation: What's the matter? Some story *clouds* you, I see it.]

Here Hölderlin translates the verb καλκαινα[7] in accordance with its primary meaning, which is 'to be the colour crimson' rather than in its figurative sense of 'to be sombre, tormented'. In German this reads:

> Was ist's, du scheinst ein rotes Wort zu färben.
>
> *(Hölderlin 1969:738)*

Literally:

> What's the matter, you seem to colour/dye a red word.

Lacoue-Labarthe suggests:

> Qu'y-a-t-il ? Tu sembles *broyer un pourpre dessein*.
>
> *(Lacoue-Labarthe 1998)*[8]

[What's the matter? You seem *to crush a crimson design/drawing*.][9]

The Hölderlinian translation is almost supra-literal because it translates the Greek verb καλκαινα in its literal sense rather than in its figurative, more abstract sense. We know that this translation is deliberate and that it cannot be attributed to philological naïvety on Hölderlin's part (he definitely did not have a *philological* knowledge of Greek)[10] but instead to a very specific interpretation of the tragic Word. The 'red word' is the word that he defines, in his prefatory 'Remarks on Oedipus' and 'Remarks on Antigone' ['Anmerkungen zum Oedipus' and 'Anmerkungen zur Antigonae'], as *tödtlichfactisch* [deathly efficacious, factically deadening, deadly-factual], as contrasted with *tödtendfactisch* (1974:270) [deadly efficacious, factically deadly, killing-factual]. In *Antigone*, the word is *tödtlichfactisch*.

But the key thing is that in the verse translated by Hölderlin, which certainly pushes conventional German aside, the Greek language speaks. The German verse remains German, but Greek and German are *infinitely* united within it, one language moving endlessly into the other. This is why Goethe failed to laugh: he must have recognised some capacity of translation with which he was extremely familiar (because he was, alongside Hölderlin, the greatest translation thinker of his era), even if he failed to put this to the test in his own translational activity (although he did try it once).

In the example that I have chosen, the two languages have indeed entered into perfect harmony, to the complete detriment of meaning. This is why Schiller and Voss laughed: because the translation is indifferent to meaning, the meaning that is present in all the other translations, a meaning that there is no reason to reject. Hölderlin is not suggesting a different meaning. There is no other meaning, just the fusion of the letter of the two languages.

The languages have only entered into harmony at this *one* point. Not in the totality of the translation which, in order to achieve its goal – which is to liberate the violence within the tragic Word – uses, has to use, other means, notably the *transformation* of the original text (which does not concern us here). The harmony of the two languages that are brought together in translation can only be sporadic. But at this one point the translation produces a *third* language that gestures towards the (absent) domain where languages are reconciled and complete each other. I will call those points where translation fully unites two languages its 'miraculous' points. This has nothing to do with the manner in which a translation 'happily renders' (words that we so often hear) the spirit and the form of an original, that achievement for which it is most often praised by the critics. Rather it has to do with those points – which are imperceptible to the translator – where this feat transcends itself to produce something that we can only call the silent harmony of two languages, within and around a text. Everything intriguing about translation is concentrated and encapsulated here. The points where translation makes one language move into another, fully, are also the points where, in the translating language, the truth of the original text is *revealed*.

Steiner has given us another example of this: Celan's translation of a poem by Supervielle.[11] In this translation, the original text *truly* ascends to a purer and higher language – a deeper language, in fact, though height and depth are of course one and the same thing. The truth of Supervielle's poem, what it *is*, is revealed in this translation. Unlike Hölderlin's translation, it is not literal. Rather it *condenses* what remains loose and poetically poorly expressed in Supervielle's text. Steiner, who compares the original and the translation, sees in it an example of 'magnifying transfiguration',[12] the perfection of which erases the original. Without challenging this judgement at all, I see something more essential at work here. Whereas the original poem never realises, in effect, its own poetic and linguistic fulfilment because, despite its finesse, it is imprisoned by poetic or rhetorical cliché;

> Et le soupir de la Terre
> Dans le silence infini

> [And the sigh of the Earth
> In the infinite silence]

its translation confidently reassembles the poem around *its* Word and fully unfurls it in the (poetic) language that could have been its own:

das Seufzen dieser Erde
im Raum, der sie umschweigt

[The sigh[ing] of this earth
in the space that wraps its silence around it]

In other areas of his oeuvre, Supervielle succeeded in taking hold of his own Word and his own language; this is why his poetry – despite its fundamental unevenness – is close to that of the late Rilke and, via Rilke, to Celan. One would in fact do justice to the German version by describing the extreme condensation of its verse as Rilkean. Supervielle was only rarely able to attain the level of condensation where natural language suddenly becomes invested with a greater urgency. Rilke himself only achieved it quite late in the day.

The essential thing about Celan's translation is the transmutation, word by word, of the poem. This brings it closer to its own intimacy, which is precisely the Word of the Intimacy of Things that we have encountered as *Innigkeit*. This Word of the Intimacy of Things is the true intention of Supervielle's poetry. In fulfilling this intention more radically than Supervielle, Celan's translation reveals not only Supervielle's 'poetic default' or the greater rigour of the poet-translator – it reveals translation's inherent *capacity* to express the truth of a text by transmuting it into purer language, language which has always been its intention. One might say that translation is always *double*: it is the translation of one language into another and translation of the language peculiar to the original into a purer language.

These two planes are difficult to tell apart, but in order to understand 'The Task of the Translator' we have to be able to tell them apart and bring them together. It is because translation makes two languages move into one another and produces – in the translating language – a 'higher' language, that Benjamin's statements make sense. The translating language, *per se*, is obviously neither higher nor purer. It only gives the appearance of this (for Nietzsche this is the case with the French translation of Schopenhauer, for example) simply because translation produces, *via* interlinguistic movement, another form of movement. The language of translation is purer and higher because it plunges the translated text into another medium. At the same time this purer medium only comes about because of the movement of two languages into one another.

German and French move into one another in Celan's translation, not by the literal path, as is the case with Hölderlin, but by a more subtle path, where German blossoms to liberate the poetic intention immanent in the original.

When we re-read the passage where Derrida defines what, for me, is the Platonic essence of translation, 'A verbal body does not allow itself to be translated or transported into another language. It is the very thing that translation abandons. Abandonment of the body is the essential energy of translation' (Derrida 1967:312),[13] we can see that translation escapes this essence by going to work on the signifier. Far from liberating the meaning of Supervielle's poem, Celan actually liberates its letter, *accentuating* its signifying density.

Benjamin continues:

Den erreicht es nicht mit Stumpf und Stiel, aber in ihm steht dasjenige, was an einer Übersetzung mehr ist als Mitteilung. Genauer läßt sich dieser wesenhafte Kern als dasjenige bestimmen, was an ihr selbst nicht wiederum übersetzbar ist. Man mag nämlich an Mitteilung aus ihr entnehmen, soviel man kann und dies übersetzen, so bleibt dennoch dasjenige unberührbar zurück, worauf die Arbeit des wahren Übersetzers sich richtete. Es ist nicht übertragbar wie das Dichterwort des Originals, weil das Verhältnis des Gehalts zur Sprache völlig verschieden ist in Original und Übersetzung. Bilden nämlich diese im ersten eine gewisse Einheit wie Frucht und Schale, so umgibt die Sprache der Übersetzung ihren Gehalt wie ein Königsmantel in weiten Falten. Denn sie bedeutet eine höhere Sprache als sie ist und bleibt dadurch ihrem eigenen Gehalt gegenüber unangemessen, gewaltig und fremd.

(p. 15. para 8)

It does not fully reach this domain, but that aspect of translation that goes beyond the delivery of a message can be found there. This essential kernel can be more precisely defined as that which is not in turn translatable. One can extract as much of a message as one can from it and translate this message, but the thing towards which the work of the true translator was directed will remain untouchable. It is not transmittable like the poetic word of the original text because the relationship of the substance of the text to its language is completely different in the original text and in the translation. Whereas in the original the text's substance and its language constitute a particular unit like a fruit and its peel, in the translation, language envelops its substance like a royal robe with generous folds. This is because this language signals a higher language than itself and therefore has an inappropriate, formidable, foreign relationship to its own substance.

Celui-ci [ce royaume], il ne l'atteint pas complètement, mais en lui réside ce qui dans une traduction est plus que de la communication. Précisément ce noyau essentiel se laisse déterminer comme ce qui, en elle [la traduction], n'est pas à nouveau traduisible. Si l'on peut en effet extraire d'elle de la communication et la traduire, ce vers quoi le travail du vrai traducteur s'orientait reste néanmoins intouchable. Cela n'est pas transmissible (*übertragbar*) comme la parole poétique (*Dichterwort*) de l'original, parce que le rapport de la teneur (*Gehalt*) à la langue est tout à fait différent dans l'original et dans la traduction. Si celles-ci forment dans le premier une certaine unité comme le fruit et sa peau, la langue de la traduction enveloppe (*umgibt*) sa teneur comme un manteau royal aux larges plis. Car elle signifie une langue plus haute qu'elle-même et reste par là, face à sa propre teneur, inappropriée, forcée et étrangère.

(Berman)

[Literal translation of Berman's French translation:

> This [this kingdom], it does not attain it fully, but in it resides what in a translation is more than communication. Precisely this essential kernel can be determined as that within it [translation] which cannot be translated again. If one can, in effect, extract communication from it and translate it, the verse towards which the work of the true translator orientates itself remains nonetheless untouchable. This is not transmittable (*übertragbar*) like the poetic word of the original, because the relationship of the substance (*Gehalt*) to the language is completely different in the original and in translation. If, in the first of these two, these form a certain unity like a fruit and its skin, the language of the translation envelops (*umgibt*) its substance like a royal coat in wide folds. Because it means a higher language than itself and remains, faced with its own substance, inappropriate, forced and strange.]

Those aspects of a translation that go beyond the communication of meaning are what Benjamin calls its 'substance' (*Gehalt; teneur*). They, in turn, are not translatable (transferable, transmissible).

This is a difficult section to think.

What translation has sometimes achieved is a fragment of higher and purer language which – without being *reine Sprache* – gestures towards it. The production of this type of language, though fragmentary, is the aspect of translation that goes beyond communication (of meaning). This is the essential kernel of translation. This kernel (which is therefore a seed of pure language) is itself untranslatable.

It is possible, if one so desires, to translate a translation. We can translate the poetry of Hölderlinian Sophocles or Celan's Supervielle. When we do this, we view these translations as original texts and carry out a further transfer of meaning. But Benjamin says that what the true translator aims for in his or her work remains untouched by this. In other words, the language that translation occasionally manages to reach cannot itself be translated. Translations are untranslatable.

But why? Our intuition tells us that this is true, but why? Benjamin replies in a completely paradoxical manner by saying that the relationship of the text's substance (*teneur*) to its language is different in the original and in translation. Benjamin does not say: content (*contenu*) and form. 'Contenu' [content] would be *Inhalt* [substance] and 'teneur' translates as *Gehalt*. The language itself relates to its 'Word' in a different manner in each case. In the original, Benjamin writes, the language forms a 'particular unit' with its substance: that of a fruit and its peel. This is the first metaphor. In translation, language envelops its substance like a 'royal robe with generous folds'. A second, more puzzling, metaphor.

Language and the substance of the text are one in the original, not absolutely, but intimately so, precisely in keeping with a fruit and its peel – so far so good. In the original text, this is how the language encompasses the text's substance. Translation comes along and 'peels', 'removes the rind from' the text, takes off its casing. And this is precisely what convention, using quite different images drawn from the natural sphere, has long considered impossible.

What Benjamin wants to say is that the unity of language and substance is *natural*. The attraction of the 'domestic' text is located precisely in the naturalness of the relationship between its language and its substance. This is particularly true in classical texts where, over time, the peel of the language has tightened around the substance in such a manner that the effect of distance or strangeness that the text once had has vanished. Reading Montaigne has this effect, for instance. The language of a translation, by contrast, has a different relationship to the substance of the text.

We can say with confidence that language is essentially external to the text's substance in the translated text because this substance did not 'grow' within it. Once again, Benjamin touches on conventional ways of thinking before sweeping them aside. At this juncture an unusual image appears, an image that is not at all 'natural', that of the royal robe with generous folds thrown over the substance of the text. Whereas a fruit is encased in its peel, the royal robe scarcely grazes the royal body.

A king's robe is always large and (by comparison) his body small. Whereas a fruit and its peel are in intimate union, the relationship of any given king to the royal robe is devoid of intimacy. The royal robe is not the king's robe – but one of the symbols, along with the sceptre, the crown etc., that makes the king the king. The royal robe signifies royalty. Just as the fruit/peel relationship belongs to the *natural* order, so the relationship between the royal robe and the royal person belongs to the – fundamentally different – *symbolic* order.

Benjamin's image is, I believe, wholly unique within the rich chain of images that 'define' translation. It is really an *allegory* of translation. Let me try and probe it some more.

The royal robe is always beautiful and large and generous. It adorns, flows, billows: in a word, it is *more* than the person that it adorns. But how can one say that the language of translation envelops the text's substance in this fashion? Who would dispute that this language is not – by definition – tailored to the measure of its substance? Surely to argue that it has a royal essence goes against conventional wisdom? Though we can accept the first metaphor – on the grounds that the literary text is perceived as an organic whole – we have difficulty accepting the second metaphor because translations have never been described as royal. But translation does have a splendour that is reflected, for example, in its critical appreciation. Certain translations do give the impression of having achieved something unique, almost unheard of, notwithstanding the inevitable defaults that they harbour. It is the translating language that finds itself magnified, more so than that of the original text. Thomas Mann was engulfed by this feeling with respect to Ludwig Tieck's translation (c.1800) of *Don Quixote*, a translation which – from a Hispanicist's perspective – is full of defaults, given that at least three thousand errors have been corrected. And nonetheless Thomas Mann felt that the German language shone in the text with an almost unparalleled brilliance.

There is therefore – sometimes – something royal about translation or more precisely about the *language* of translation, of the translated text. This language *is magnified* all the more because it no longer envelops its substance in the way a fruit is enveloped by its peel, its 'robe'.

But what is the *nature* of this magnification? This royalness of the translating language?

Just as the royal robe is a symbol of the royal personage (we could say that it is a symbol par excellence of that symbolic thing, the Royal, the Royal Principal), in the same way the royal language of translation, for Benjamin, has also become a symbol:

> Denn sie bedeutet eine höhere Sprache als sie ist und bleibt dadurch ihrem eigenen Gehalt gegenüber unangemessen, gewaltig und fremd. Diese Gebrochenheit verhindert jede Übertragung, wie sie sie zugleich erübrigt.
>
> *(p. 15. para 8)*

This is because this language signals a higher language than itself and therefore has an inappropriate, formidable and foreign relationship to its own substance. This brokenness prevents any transposition, just as it renders it superfluous.

> Car elle signifie une langue plus haute qu'elle, et reste ainsi, par rapport à sa teneur, inappropriée, forcée et étrangère.[14] Cet être-brisé (*Gebrochenheit*) interdit une transmission qui, en même temps, est inutile.
>
> *(Berman)*

[Literal translation of Berman's French translation:

> Because it means a higher language than itself and remains, faced with its own substance, inappropriate, forced and strange. This broken-being (*Gebrochenheit*) prevents a transmission that, at the same time, is useless.]

Perhaps the best way to understand the nature of the language of translation is through the realisation that it is itself untranslatable.

Every literary text, as we have seen over and over again, displays the principle of translatability and the desire for translation. The hermetic unity of the fruit and its peel alludes to the text's resistance to translation and its desire for it. Every fruit wishes to be tasted.

Translation – and by this I mean the translated text – on the other hand, displays no such principle and harbours no desire of this kind. It does not resist translation (there is always enjoyment to be had from translating a translation) but in this non-resistance there is an infinite indifference to translation. The translation has escaped from the domain of the translatable. It is untranslatable in the sense that a translation thereof is meaning-less.

Whereas the destiny of an original text is its translation, the destiny of a transla-tion is to be supplanted by another translation. And this has something to do with the royal robe of the translating language. It 'signals', Benjamin says, another, higher language. But precisely because it exhausts itself in doing this – because it signals this higher language (and therefore magnifies itself) and because it is the seed of pure language which is the end of all languages – it cannot, in turn, be translated. If translating involves moving from the hermetic unity of the fruit and its peel to the loose unity of the royal robe and the mortal body of the King, this latter unity leaves nothing for translation to ground itself in.

Let us return to our image. Benjamin says that the language of the translation remains 'inappropriate', 'formidable' and 'foreign' in relation to the text's substance. There is nothing surprising about that. What is surprising is that this language *should be simultaneously* characterised as royal. But it is precisely because it is royal, because it is pure symbol, that it is all of these things. The king – the real person of the king – never lives up to the pomp of the robe that clothes him. This robe is always too large for him. The more royal the language of the translation is, there-fore – a language magnified to become a symbol of *the* language – the less intimacy it has with the text's substance and the more it is 'inappropriate', 'formidable' and 'foreign' in its relationship to them. It is of a different nature to this substance, or rather, it is no longer natural in any way.

This is the source, says Benjamin, of an incredible irony. Translation is more per-ishable than the original text and transplants the original text into more definitive terrain, more definitive in the sense that once it has been installed there, the text cannot be further uprooted via translation. The irony here is that the perishable is, in one sense, more definitive than the imperishable. The *natural* grandeur of the original text (fruit and peel/robe) contrasts with the *unnatural* grandeur of the translation (royal robe).

A question arises as one probes Benjamin's images more closely. If the fruit corresponds to the text's substance and the fruit's peel to the language of the orig-inal text, then the royal robe corresponds to the language of translation, but is there an image to represent its substance? The answer is obviously no. The royal robe 'girds' the King, but Benjamin does not say this. And if we follow through on Benjamin's imagery, we are left without knowing what the substance of translation is. I believe we can say that the magnification of language that occurs in translation is accompanied by the destruction or relativisation of the text's substance. This will come to be echoed in the distinction drawn between the task of the translator and that of the creator, and in the lower status ascribed to meaning. Because the text's substance is unavoidably linked to meaning.

The language of a translation is more important than its substance. The sub-stance is either desperately mistreated or treated as inessential. This is another irony and in this context Benjamin inevitably goes on to discuss the Romantics and their theory of form. The relativisation of the text's substance or content is the very point of Romantic irony. This relativisation of the text's substance is, at the same time, an absolutisation of form. Benjamin's statement that translation is a 'form' should be re-read in this light – in light of the Romantics rather than of Goethe. From the Romantic perspective, the form of the text, that which is erected on the ruins of ironised content, is symbolic. It is *Bedeutung*, signifying something higher than itself, and for the Romantics, it is the Idea of Art as an *analogon* of the 'infinite games of Nature'.[15]

Translation is a *form* because the text's substance is destroyed there, leaving only the royal robe of language as a signifier of pure language. Translation frees the text from what Novalis called the 'tyranny of content'. And undoubtedly, the royal language that remains, which has an inappropriate, formidable and foreign relationship to the text's substance and a tendency to move away from content, is *truly* the symbol of pure language, language without intention, language that no longer signifies. Pure language is *not* the royal language of translation, but the latter is in its image and therefore brings us closer to it.

We can now see *why* this royal language is close to the aerial language that is the intent of philosophy and poetry in Platonism, and of Novalis and Joubert. The ironic destruction of content, of meaning, of substance, features in both their work. The text, through translation, enters a higher and purer aerial dimension of language because its language, in translation, has become a royal robe, a pure symbol.

Benjamin has adopted this conceptual development – and this is borne out by the rest of the passage – from the Romantics, even though he questions their ability to construct a systematic theory of translation. A question arises, however: can translation be both a form in the Goethean sense of a living metamorphosis of the original text and a form in the Romantic sense of the destruction of the text's substance for the purposes of attaining a purer language – purer because it is without content and is uncoupled from the empirical burden of substance? Isn't Benjamin caught between two incompatible thoughts, that of translation as the sur-vival of the text and that of translation as the death of the text? We will finish today on that question.

Notes

1 ['Der Geist erscheint immer nur in fremder, luftiger Gestalt.']
2 ['La transparence, le diaphane, le peu de pâte, le magique; l'imitation du divin qui a fait toutes choses avec peu et, pour ainsi dire, avec rien: voilà l'un des caractères essentiels de la poésie.']
3 See Berman 1986.
4 This is actually line 20.
5 [There are some errors in the commentary's rendering of the Greek here. It should read: τί δ' ἔστι; δηλοῖς γάρ τι καλχαίνουσ' ἔπος.]
6 [Berman's commentary gives no page references for the various French translations.]
7 [Correctly rendered, this should read καλχαίνω.]

8   I have italicised anything that relates to the verb καλκαινα.
9   The French verb 'broyer' literally means 'to crush' or 'to grind'. The idiom 'broyer du noir' means 'to be pessimistic or depressive', literally 'to grind black'. The expression 'broyer des couleurs' refers to the grinding action by which painters mix their colours. Lacoue-Labarthe is obviously playing with these expressions in his translation.
10 Sic. The inclusion of the word 'not' is probably a transcription error in the French source text.
11 See Steiner 1998:425–426.

Supervielle's poem	Celan's translation
Jésus tu sais chaque feuille	Jesus, du kennst sie alle:
Qui verdira la fôret,	das Blatt, das Wald grün bringt,
Les racines qui recueillent	die Wurzel, die ihr Tiefstes
Et dévoilent leur secret,	aufsammelt und vertrinkt
La terreur de l'éphémère	die Angst des Tagesschöpfes,
À l'approche de la nuit,	wenn es sich nachthin neigt,
Et le soupir de la Terre	das Seufzen dieser Erde
Dans le silence infini.	im Raum, der sie umschweigt.
Tu peux suivre les poissons	Du kannst den Fische begleiten,
Tourmentant les profondeurs,	dich wühlen abgrundwärts
Quand ils tournent et retournent	und mit ihm schwimmen, unten,
Et si s'arrête leur cœur …	und länger als sein Herz …

12 [Steiner uses the terms 'magnification' (1998:317) and 'transfiguration' (ibid.:314) whereas Berman's 'surtraduction positive' seems to combine these two terms into one.]
13 ['Un corps verbal ne se laisse pas traduire ou transporter dans une autre langue. Il est cela même que la traduction laisse tomber. Laisser tomber le corps, telle est l'énergie essentielle de la traduction.']
14 [Berman's translation here differs in minor details from his earlier translation of this same sentence.]
15 [Berman attributes this to Schlegel in-text but gives no reference.]

Bibliography

Benjamin, W., 1991 [1923]. Die Aufgabe des Übersetzers. In: R. Tiedemann and H. Schweppenhäuser, eds. 1991. *Gesammelte Schriften*. IV.I. Frankfurt am Main: Suhrkamp. pp.9–21.

Berman, A., 1986. L'essence platonicienne de la traduction, *Revue d'Esthéthique*, 12, pp.63–73.

Berman, A., 2008. *L'Âge de la traduction*. Paris: Presses Universitaires de Vincennes.

Derrida, J., 1967. *L'Écriture et La Différence*. Paris: Le Seuil.

Gandillac, M. de, trans. 1971. La tâche du traducteur. In: *Œuvres I, Mythe et violence*. Paris: Denoël/Les Lettres Nouvelles. pp.261–275.

Grosjean, J., 1967. *Tragiques grecs: Eschyle, Sophocle*. Paris: Gallimard.

Hölderlin, F., 1969. *Werke und Briefe. Band II*. Frankfurt am Main: Insel-Verlag.

Hölderlin, F., 1974. Anmerkungen zu Antigonae. In: *Sämtliche Werke*. Stuttgart: Verlag W. Kohlhammer. pp.263–272.

Jebb, R.C., 1900. *Sophocles. The Plays and Fragments. Part III: The Antigone*. Cambridge: Cambridge University Press.

Joubert, J., 1989. *Pensées, jugements et notations*. Paris: José Corti.

Lacoue-Labarthe, P., 1998 [1978]. *Les Tragédies de Sophocle*. Paris: Christian Bourgois.

Mazon, P., 1964. *Sophocle: Tragédies*. Paris: Les Belles Lettres.

Novalis, 1965. *Schriften. Band 2. Das philosophische Werk*. Stuttgart: Verlag W. Kohlhammer.

Steiner, G., 1998 [1975]. *After Babel*. Oxford: Oxford University Press.

CAHIER 8

Of the three extended metaphors for translations that feature in Benjamin's text – the royal robe that is the translating language; natural languages as fragments of the vessel of 'pure language'; and the relative positions of original and translation within the mountain forest of language – the metaphor of the mountain forest is the most puzzling, not only in terms of its imagery, but also linguistically.

> Sie besteht darin, diejenige Intention auf die Sprache, in die übersetzt wird, zu finden, von der aus in ihr das Echo des Originals erweckt wird. Hierin liegt ein vom Dichtwerk durchaus unterscheidender Zug der Übersetzung, weil dessen Intention niemals auf die Sprache als solche, ihre Totalität, geht, sondern allein unmittelbar auf bestimmte sprachliche Gehaltszusammenhänge. Die Übersetzung aber sieht sich nicht wie die Dichtung gleichsam im innern Bergwald der Sprache selbst, sondern außerhalb desselben, ihm gegenüber und ohne ihn zu betreten ruft sie das Original hinein, an demjenigen einzigen Orte hinein, wo jeweils das Echo in der eigenen den Widerhall eines Werkes der fremden Sprache zu geben vermag.
>
> *(Benjamin 1991a:16)*

The task of the translator consists of finding that intention towards the translating language from whence the echo of the original is roused. This is a characteristic of translation that clearly differentiates it from poetry, because poetry's intention is never towards language as such – the totality thereof – but is simply directed at specific *interrelations* of linguistic content. Translation, however, unlike poetry, does not see itself

> in the inner mountain forest of language itself, as it were, but outside it. Without entering this forest, standing across from it, translation calls to the original text, from the only place where, in each case, the echo in the translating language is able to render the reverberation of the foreign-language text.

The original text inhabits the centre of its mountain forest (the source language in which it was created). Translation, by contrast, resides outside the forest, on the periphery. It is unclear whether all languages are one forest or whether we must conceive of separate forests. Berman sees translation as inhabiting some sort of plain that lies adjacent to the mountain forest. Alternatively, translation could be inhabiting the edge of its own mountain forest (that of the translating language), a forest that sits across from the mountain forest of the source language. Benjamin's metaphor is sufficiently lacking in detail to allow for both interpretations. There are several linguistic oddities in the metaphor. Firstly, translation calls the original text 'hinein' [into]. This particle is an unusual choice, since directionally it would normally signal movement away from the person or thing doing the calling (here: translation) rather than towards. Secondly, in German, when movement occurs, one normally expects to find the accusative case. Instead we have a dative case, implying a fixed position, so that rather than being called to a particular place, the original text is being called from a particular position, the position of translation ('an demjenigen einzigen Orte', from the only place), where 'the echo in the translating language is able to render the reverberation of the foreign-language text'. It is worth stressing that Benjamin's grammar and prepositional choices here are idiosyncratic in the extreme; it is as though his own text were a translation that is paying tribute to the 'letter' of some hidden source text.

Finally, *Echo* and *Widerhall* are close synonyms of 'echo' – they mean the same thing. The translating language has an echo [*Echo*] and the source text has an echo [*Widerhall*, but Benjamin also uses the word *Echo* for the source text]. The translation is an echo of an echo. There are two problems with Berman's interpretation of this complex metaphor. The first is that by rendering *Echo* and *Widerhall* as *écho* and *résonance* respectively, Berman suggests a difference in sonic quality that does not exist in the German. *Résonance* sounds weightier, richer than *écho* and is closer to the German *Resonanz*. But it is far from clear that Benjamin is making such a qualitative distinction; rather it might be said that *Echo* and *Widerhall* echo each other (they are the same but not the same). The second problem is that Berman sees the call of translation as echoing at a particular point in the source language – this is suggested by his commentary (2008:150) rather than his translation of the above passage – but within Benjamin's broader argumentation this cannot be the case since translation is of no importance to the source text. Rather the source text echoes in its own language and this echo echoes in the translating language.

Berman goes on, in Cahier 8, to discuss Benjamin's attempt to differentiate between the intention of the poet and that of the translator, a difference that Benjamin summarises in six adjectives. 'Die [Intention] des Dichters ist *naive, erste, anschauliche*, die des Übersetzers *abgeleitete, letzte, ideenhafte* Intention' (1991a:16). Berman renders this as: 'celle du poète est *naïve, première, intuitive*, celle du traducteur *dérivée, dernière, idéelle*' (2008:153), using the same adjectives as Gandillac. These six adjectives are infinitely challenging. Although I have chosen six words, this is nonetheless an occasion when translation has to give way to or be supplemented by commentary, as Berman argues elsewhere (Berman 2008:73).

What does it mean to describe the poet's and the translator's intentions in these terms? *Naiv* suggests that poetry – which we can take as standing for literature more broadly – has an innocence or childishness about it; it must create its own experience out of nothing. This contrasts with the translator's *abgeleitete* intention, an intention which is derived from or follows on from the intention of an other, but *abgeleitete* also has the sense of being sent in another direction, redirected.

Erste and *letzte* appear to be a clear and obvious pair of opposites, 'first' and 'last', but their satisfying simplicity in German does not produce the same satisfaction in English. This may have something to do with that drive, discussed elsewhere, towards using a different lexis and higher register for philosophical texts in English. *Erste* pushes towards 'primary' rather than 'first' in English; *letzte* towards 'final'. But 'final' is problematic, because *letzte* in German can also mean 'most recent' and the entire sense of translation that we gain from 'The Task of the Translator' is that translation is provisional, multiple, that it can and should be superseded by further translations, that its language gestures towards pure language, performing it rather than producing it. None of this is 'final'. And all translators know that there is nothing final about the texts they produce.

The final pair, *anschaulich* and *ideenhaft*, are more nebulous. *Anschaulich* can mean many things; the related verb *anschauen* means 'to look at'. Something *anschaulich* can be rich in images, pictorial; it can be lively, expressive, descriptive. Paired with *naiv*, it suggests that the poet works with images, intuition and instinct, rather than with the intellect, and indeed Berman and Gandillac have opted for *intuitive*, which is the same as 'intuitive' in English. *Ideenhaft* literally means 'like ideas, of ideas' – the more usual adjective *ideenreich* means 'rich in ideas', but Benjamin does not use this. Berman and Gandillac have translated *ideenhaft* as *idéelle*, which contains the French word for 'idea', *idée*, and means 'of ideas, conceptual'. The translator's task occurs at a remove, *abgeleitet*, and this distance means that the translator's task is more intellectual than that of the poet.

In choosing English words for these six adjectives, one also has to think about the words that Benjamin did *not* use. He did not use *original* and *sekundär*, for example. I chose 'naïve', 'immediate', 'expressive' for the poet's intention, and 'derived', 'current', 'conceptual' for the translator's. 'Immediate' complements 'naïve'; 'derived' does not have the value-laden (negative) connotations of 'derivative'. The list of words I considered but abandoned includes 'primary', 'primal', 'originary', 'vivid', 'derivative', 'redirected', 'inferred'. What is striking, of course, is that Benjamin upholds the value of the derived and the conceptual against an idealisation of the immediate: it is translation that gestures towards pure language, not the first act of inspired creation.

We paused on this question: is it possible, in Goethe's wake, to posit translation as metamorphosis, as the continued life of the text, but also to posit it, in the wake of Romanticism, as the ironic destruction of the same? Benjamin acknowledges his debt to the Romantics and their 'feeling for' (but not their theory of) translation. The Romantics, he says, had 'a feeling for the essence and the dignity of the form' (Benjamin 1991a:15), even though they failed to systematise this feeling and devoted their energies to constructing a theory of criticism instead. Globally speaking, this is accurate, and one can almost read 'The Task of the Translator' as the conceptualisation of Romantic intuitions about translation. Especially, according to Benjamin, because Romantic thought – that of Friedrich Schlegel and Novalis – is 'Messianic' in nature.

The following lines mark, as is customary, a shift that announces the next paragraph:

> Diese Gefühl – darauf deutet alles hin – braucht nicht notwendig im Dichter am stärksten zu sein; ja es hat in ihm als Dichter vielleicht am wenigsten Raum.
>
> *(p. 15. para 8)*

> This feeling – everything suggests this – is not necessarily strongest in the poet; indeed it has perhaps the least space in the poet qua poet.

> Ce sentiment – tout l'indique – n'a pas besoin nécessairement d'être le plus fort chez le poète; oui, il a en lui, en tant que poète, le moins d'espace.
>
> *(Berman)*

[Literal translation of Berman's French translation:

> This feeling – everything indicates this – does not necessarily need to be the strongest in the poet; yes, it has in him [the poet], as poet, the least space.]

This sentence, and those that follow, are important in two respects. Firstly, because they counter the still dominant prejudice that the translation of poetry is the preserve of poets. Secondly, this is the premise on which Benjamin attempts to distinguish between the task of the poet and that of the translator.

Why is a feeling for the essence and the dignity of the form unable to find space in the poet? History has certainly known poets who have been great translators – I have already mentioned their names. Benjamin cites two, Hölderlin and George, and I can cite plenty of others, particularly in the twentieth century (Ungaretti, Celan etc.). Nonetheless it is generally true that the truly great translators have never been great poets – and vice versa. The examples Benjamin gives are revealing: in the German tradition Luther, Voss and W. Schlegel were greater translators than they were writers. This historical evidence raises a more significant issue: the difference between the poet's and the translator's *intention*. Those who claim that poetry can only be translated by poets (like Kenneth White, for example) have never *thought about* the difference in intention between the poetic act and the translational act. For them, the translation of poetry, of *Dichtung*, is *Nachdichtung*, re-creation. Translation belongs to the sphere of the *Nach-*; it is a post-poetry, which is to say a sub-poetry.

For Benjamin, translation has its own *identity*; it is more of an *Überdichtung* than a *Nachdichtung* since it facilitates the work's accession to an 'aerial dimension of language that is higher and more pure'. Translation does not operate under the sign of *nach*, of the mere after, but of *über*, the movement beyond. It is governed by a different *law* than that of poetry. The poet is therefore poorly placed to feel the essence of translation unless he is governed by a *double law*, in other words unless he is something else in addition to being a poet. Hölderlin and George fell into this category for Benjamin because of their link to the religious, because of the tie that binds together poetry, ethics and the religious in their work. To which one might add – going beyond Benjamin – that ever since Romanticism, poetry and translation have been bound by an essential link. This explains the fact that from Goethe to Nerval, from Mallarmé to Valéry and Stefan George, from Celan to Jouve, Bonnefoy, Deguy, Ungaretti etc. etc., the majority of *modern* poets have also been translators. The modern poet is therefore naturally governed by this double law that I have mentioned. Why? The answer would go beyond the framework of this commentary. The question points towards the hidden role of translation not only in the sphere of modern poetry but also in modern philosophy, ethnology and psychoanalysis. We now find ourselves in the age of translation.

Benjamin's concern is now to define the law and the task of translation as distinct from the law and the task of poetry.

Wie nämlich die Übersetzung eine eigene Form ist, so läßt sich auch die Aufgabe des Übersetzers als eine eigene fassen und genau von der des Dichters unterscheiden.

(p. 16. para 8)

Just as translation is its own form, the task of the translator can also be understood as its own task, clearly distinguishable from that of the poet.

Comme, en effet, la traduction est une forme propre, la tâche du traducteur se laisse également distinguer de celle du poète, très exactement, comme une tâche propre.

(Berman)

[Literal translation of Berman's French translation:

Because, in effect, translation is its own form, the task of the translator can also be distinguished from that of the poet, very precisely, as its own task.]

The task of the translator is a distinct task because it derives from the distinct form that is translation. Not only is translation a form, but this form is that form which is, *par excellence*, exalted at the expense of substance.

Sie besteht darin, diejenige Intention auf die Sprache, in die übersetzt wird, zu finden, von der aus in ihr das Echo des Originals erweckt wird. Hierin liegt ein vom Dichtwerk durchaus unterscheidender Zug der Übersetzung, weil dessen Intention niemals auf die Sprache als solche, ihre Totalität, geht, sondern allein unmittelbar auf bestimmte sprachliche Gehaltszusammenhänge. Die Übersetzung aber sieht sich nicht wie die Dichtung gleichsam im innern Bergwald der Sprache selbst, sondern außerhalb desselben, ihm gegenüber und ohne ihn zu betreten ruft sie das Original hinein, an demjenigen einzigen Orte hinein, wo jeweils das Echo in der eigenen den Widerhall eines Werkes der fremden Sprache zu geben vermag.

(p. 16. para 9)

The task of the translator consists of finding that intention towards the translating language from whence the echo of the original is roused. This is a characteristic of translation that clearly differentiates it from poetry, because poetry's intention is never towards language as such – the totality thereof – but is simply directed at specific *interrelations* of linguistic content. Translation, however, unlike poetry, does not see itself in the inner mountain forest of language itself, as it were, but outside it. Without entering this forest, standing across from it, translation calls to the original text, from the only place where, in each case, the echo in the translating language is able to render the reverberation of the foreign-language text.

Elle [la tâche du traducteur] consiste à trouver dans la langue où il est traduit cette intention à partir de laquelle, en celle-ci, est éveillé l'écho de l'original. C'est là un trait de la traduction la distinguant décisivement de l'œuvre poétique, parce que l'intention de celle-ci ne va jamais vers la langue même et sa totalité, mais seulement et immédiatement vers des corrélations de teneur langagière déterminées. La traduction ne se voit pas, comme la poésie, pour ainsi dire, à l'intérieur du massif forestier de la langue elle-même, mais hors de celui-ci, face à lui, et sans y pénétrer, elle appelle l'original, en cet unique lieu où, à chaque fois, l'écho dans sa propre langue peut donner la résonance d'une œuvre de la langue étrangère.

(Berman)

[Literal translation of Berman's French translation:

It [the task of the translator] consists of finding in the language into which it is translated that intention from which, in it (that language), is awoken the echo of the original. This is a trait of translation distinguishing it decisively from the poetic work because the intention of this (the poetic work) never goes towards the language itself and its totality, but only and immediately towards the correlations of the determined linguistic contents. Translation does not see itself, as poetry does, so to speak, inside the wooded massif of language itself, but outside it, across from it, and without entering it, it calls the original, in that unique place where, each time, the echo in its own language can give the resonance of a text in the foreign language.]

Awakening the *echo* of the original in the translating language: that is the task of the translator. Or rather grasping that *place* in the translating language where the foreign text can unfold its *resonance*. These dense lines say two things: translation and poetry have different intentions, and the original and the translated text inhabit different places.

It is not that the original text and the translation inhabit different places because they each inhabit their own language. Rather, each has a different topological relationship *to language itself.* The original text and the translation inhabit language in different ways. Strictly speaking, only the original text inhabits its language, the heart of its language, the centre of its language, whereas translation operates (as we will see) at the periphery of its language, in a position that allows it to see the other language.

To explain this state of affairs, Benjamin follows both a conceptual and a metaphorical thought process. The two are in fact interwoven. The metaphorical thought process is structured like a web around the image of the *Bergwald*, which should be translated as 'massif forestier' [mountain forest] rather than 'fôret' [forest]. Translating it as 'fôret' prevents our understanding of the metaphorical web.

> *Bergwald (massif forestier,* mountain forest)
> *Echo (écho;* echo)   *Widerhall (résonance;* resonance or echo)
>   *Ort (lieu;* place)

In order for the call that the translator launches at the original text to echo, there has to be a place where the sound of this call can bounce back and return to the translator enriched by the resonance of the original text. This cannot be the dense and opaque space of a mere forest, but must be the space of a *mountain forest*, full of rocky recesses, slopes, inclines, rock faces. The verisimilitude of the image derives entirely from the fact that language is not simply a wooded mass, but a *mountain* forest.

A mountain is characterised by inherent topological irregularity, which is typical of all *natural* language. The original text is located at the heart (*innern*) of the mountain. Translation cannot penetrate this space. For translation, language is not a mountain forest. Rather, the language of translation is the open and even periphery of the translating language from where one can observe the mountain of the foreign language. One cannot observe a mountain from another mountain.[1] If translation inhabited its language in the same way that the original text inhabited its language, such observation would be impossible. The original text is buried within its own language, whereas translation is exposed. This exposed linguistic space within which translation operates is necessarily the translating language's *edge*. Every language has a centre and an edge. From this edge, translation calls the original text, which is hidden within its own language, into that unique place, *Ort*, of the translating language in which the translating language can echo the resonance of the foreign work.

For us this means that *translation (the translated text) is an echo*. An echo both of the resonance (*Widerhall*) that the foreign text has within its own language, and of the foreign language itself. Translation-as-echo can only be an echo of the foreign language as it resonates in a literary text. The translator leaves the original text in its mountain forest, but has it resonate as an echo in the translating language. We might say that *through translation, one language resonates within another*.

As is the case with all original metaphors, Benjamin's dwindles away into the unanalysable. But for me, it captures something essential about the original–translation–foreign language relationship. Translation is that call to the original text that creates an echo. The echo is not the resonance, *Widerhall*, of the text on its own linguistic mountain. It is a purified form of it. It is the trace of the foreign language in the most aerial medium of the translating language, a trace that *imprints itself* in *that* place within the translating language where this is permissible. Benjamin tells us that this place is unique.

This place that creates an echo exists for any text. In the translation of an Argentinian novel by Roberto Arlt, *Les sept fous* [*Los Siete locos*], that I did with my wife Isabelle Berman – a novel in which the writing, which is extremely complex, is rooted in the linguistic mountain of the Argentinian language, and whose contents are inseparable from this wooded space – we looked for what we called the 'weak points' in the French language, the points where French would be able to accept the inscription of the original text's language – and echo it.

Echoicity is a fundamental characteristic of translation. It is a structure of reference where the translating language allows the translated language to appear *indirectly* (absent/present). Borges cites a translation by Ezra Pound where one can see very clearly how the translation becomes an echo of the original:

> This is how he [Ezra Pound] translated, for example, the beginning of the Anglo-Saxon elegy *The Seafarer*:
>
> *May I for my own sake song's truth reckon*
> *Journeys Jargon*

Gordon translates literally:
I can utter a true song about myself
tell of my travels.

This is absolutely transparent and correct, but the poem says:

Maeg iebemie sylfum sothgied wrecan
Siehas secgan.[2]

Borges contrasts Gordon's translational philology, where there is only room for meaning, with Pound's translation-echo.

The translator can only achieve this echo phenomenon through a kind of *free literality* on the syntactic and the phonic level. Literality is an echo.[3]

Let us now return to the beginning of the paragraph and the particular concept it wants to articulate. Whereas the poet's intention relates solely to particular '*interrelations* of linguistic content', the translator's intention concerns the *totality* of language. The latter implies being *across from* language, whereas a concern with particular '*interrelations* of linguistic content' means being *in* language. This was Jean Paul's claim: translation's true domain is language [*langue*], not the text's contents or content. That is why the poet, immersed in the mountain forest of his or her *own* language, finds it difficult to perceive the 'being-outside-of-one's-language' that is exclusive to the translator. The translator is between-languages, on the *border* of languages. To allow the original text to resonate in the translating language, the translator has to occupy the border of that language – the exposed, diaphanous area where he is not at home (home = *Bergwald*) – standing across from the dense and stony obscurity of the foreign language. It is because the translator is positioned almost *outside* his language (or at its extreme edge) that he or she is able to make the voice of the original text resonate within it. This is something that the poet, while occupying the role of poet, cannot do.

Ihre Intention geht nicht allein auf etwas anderes als die der Dichtung, nämlich auf eine Sprache im ganzem von einem einzelnen Kunstwerk in einer fremden aus, sondern sie ist auch selbst eine andere: die des Dichters ist naive, erste, anschauliche, die des Übersetzers abgeleitete, letzte, ideenhafte Intention. Denn das große Motiv einer Integration der vielen Sprachen zur einen wahren erfüllt seine Arbeit.

(p.16. para 9)

It is not only that the intention of translation aims at something different than the intention of poetry, namely at the totality of language beginning from a single work of art located in a foreign language, but the intention itself is a different one: the intention of the poet is naïve, immediate, expressive, the translator's intention is derived, current, conceptual. For the translator's work is replete with the great motive of integrating the many languages into one true language.

> Son intention ne se dirige pas seulement vers quelque chose d'entièrement autre que celle de la poésie, c'est-à-dire vers une langue en totalité d'une œuvre d'art particulière dans une langue étrangère, mais elle est elle-même autre: celle du poète est naïve, première, intuitive, celle du traducteur dérivée, dernière, idéelle. Car le grand motif de l'intégration des langues multiples dans une langue vraie emplit son travail.
>
> *(Berman)*

[Literal translation of Berman's French translation:

> Its intention is not only directed towards something entirely different to that of poetry, that is to say towards a language in totality from a particular work of art in a foreign language, but it is itself a different intention: that of the poet is naïve, primary, intuitive, that of the translator derived, final, conceptual. For the great motive of the integration of multiple languages into one true language fills [the translator's] work.]

The poet's intention is naïve, immediate and expressive where the language and its substance are concerned. This intention resides at the very heart of language's mountain. Conversely the translator's aim is derived, current and conceptual. This is because translation is secondary and reflexive. But this difference – which empirically speaking is quite apparent – is based on something deeper that radically separates poetry (creation) and translation: the 'integration' of multiple languages into a (single) 'true language'.

The poet's domain is the creation of a 'higher', 'purer' language. The domain of the translator is the reunion of those fragments that are languages to produce a seed of true language. And this is another way of defining pure language: as 'true' language, the 'language of truth', *die wahre Sprache, die Sprache der Wahrheit*.

The implication is that some languages are 'true' and others are not. But this is imprecise: language [*la langue*] itself is the language of truth. Empirical languages are not 'language itself' [*la langue même*] and this is why they are not true. They have become mere systems of referential signs, chopped up into infinite pieces. The multiplicity of languages signifies two things: their turning-into-signs and their fragmentation. For Benjamin, the two things are linked. Translation, by bringing two languages together to form a single language, gestures towards true language [*la langue vraie*].

It is not that Benjamin thinks that if there were only one language, this would be true language. Rather he thinks that translation, by making the echo of language Y resonate in language X, foreshadows this language in which all empirical languages will come together and return to the pure being of language, to a language that is no longer sign and communication. The language of truth is hidden in languages and translation makes it gleam and shine for an instant.

Wenn anders es aber eine Sprache der Wahrheit gibt, in welcher die letzten Geheimnisse, um die alles Denken sich müht, spannungslos und selbst schweigend aufbewahrt sind, so ist diese Sprache der Wahrheit – die wahre Sprache. Und eben diese, in deren Ahnung und Beschreibung die einzige Vollkommenheit liegt, welche der Philosoph sich erhoffen kann, sie ist intensiv in den Übersetzungen verborgen.

(p. 16. para 9)

But if there is a language of truth, an effortless and even silent repository for the final secrets towards which all thought strives, then this language of truth is – the true language. And it is this language, whose anticipation and description contains the only perfection for which the philosopher can hope, that is concealed in concentrated form within translation.

Mais s'il existe une langue de la vérité, dans laquelle les ultimes secrets auxquels s'efforce toute pensée sont conservés sans tension et même en silence, cette langue de la vérité est – la vraie langue. Et précisément celle-ci, dont le pressentiment et la description sont la seule perfection que le philo-sophe peut espérer, est intensivement cachée dans les traductions.

(Berman)

[Literal translation of Berman's French translation:

But if a language of truth exists, in which the last secrets towards which all thought strives are preserved without tension and even in silence, this language of truth is – the true language. And precisely that [language], whose foreshadowing and description are the only perfection that the philosopher can hope for, is intensively hidden within translations.]

Let me emphasise something: this language does not appear in translations, it is hidden there, *verborgen*. Hidden in concentrated form [*intensiv*], Benjamin says. His adverb only serves to underline the extent to which translations (the language of translated texts) conceal the language of truth, that language that silently and effort-lessly acts as a repository for the secrets, the mysteries – of the world, of Being. Once more we find ourselves confronted with the link between translation–language–truth that constitutes the mystery of Benjamin's text and through which philosophy and translation are 'related'. What philosophy desires is hidden in translation.

We approached the problematic of truth from the point of view of the original text, by positing translation as a revelation of the truth of the text, but also from the point of view of language, positing translation as a magnification of language. These correlations are admittedly still obscure. We will leave them to their obscurity and move on.

Es gibt keine Muse der Philosophie, es gibt auch keine Muse der Übersetzung. Banausisch aber, wie sentimentale Artisten sie wissen wollen, sind sie nicht.

Denn es gibt ein philosophisches Ingenium, dessen eigenstes die Sehnsucht nach jener Sprache ist, welche in der Übersetzung sich bekundet.

(pp. 16–17. para 9)

There is no muse of philosophy, nor is there a muse of translation. But philosophy and translation are not servile, as sentimental artistes would have them. For there exists a philosophical ingenium, at the heart of which is the longing for that language that announces itself in translation.

Il n'y a pas de Muse de la philosophie, il n'y a également aucune Muse de la traduction. Mais elles ne sont pas, commes des artistes sentimentaux veulent le faire accroître, banausiques. Car il y a un ingenium philosophique, dont le plus propre est la nostalgie de cette langue, qui s'annonce dans la traduction.

(Berman)[4]

[Literal translation of Berman's French translation:

There is no Muse of philosophy, there is also no Muse of translation. But they are not, as sentimental artists would lead one to believe, banausic. For there exists a philosophical ingenium whose most essential (feature) is longing for that language that makes itself felt in translation.]

There is indeed no muse of philosophy, nor of translation, in the Greek cosmos. Where philosophy is concerned, not only is there no muse, but if we read Plato, a muse of philosophy would be a contradiction. Because philosophical *logos* cannot be determined, dominated, by a principle such as the Muse, which belongs exclusively to the arts. Philosophy is not governed by the inspiration implied by the word 'muse' (among others), nor is translation. Because both are 'derived, current, conceptual'. This explains the proximity of their two essences.

But what is the Muse? Or rather, what is it for Benjamin? At the end of his dissertation *The Concept of Criticism in German Romanticism*, when discussing Goethe, Benjamin discusses the Muses. The passage in which he does so is so difficult that it would require its very own commentary. Benjamin distinguishes between the Romantic vision of Art, determined by the primacy of form – of the Idea – and Goethe's vision, determined by the primacy of the text's contents (or of content: this text shows that Benjamin does not distinguish between the two) – of the Ideal. I will cite from this opaque text:

The Ideal, too, is a conceptual unit, that of substance. Its function is therefore entirely different to that of the Idea. It is not a medium that contains the interrelationship of forms within itself and forms them from its fabric, but a different kind of unit(y). It can only be grasped in a limited multiplicity of pure content(s), into which it is segmented. The Ideal therefore manifests itself in a limited, harmonious discontinuum of pure contents. In this insight,

Goethe and the Greeks are in close proximity. Interpreted from the perspective of the philosophy of art, the idea of the Muses under the glory of Apollo is an idea of the pure contents of all art. The Greeks considered there to be nine such contents and certainly neither their form nor their number were determined at random. The very concept of pure contents, the ideal of art, can therefore be described as Musean. Just as the inner structure of the Ideal is unstable in contrast to the Idea, so too is the interrelationship of this ideal with art not given in a single medium, but is characterised by a discontinuity. Pure contents as such thus cannot be found in any individual work. Goethe calls these pure contents *Urbilder* [primal images]. Individual works of art cannot reach those invisible – but concrete – *Urbilder* whose protectors the Greeks knew as the Muses – they can only resemble them to one degree or another.

(Benjamin 1991b:111)[5]

Thus 'the Musean' relates to the *content* of art, to poetry for example. Inspiration is the vehicle via which the Muses allow creation, the relationship to a content – a pure content, in the sense that the essential content is determined *a priori* for each art form. Translation and philosophy (translated texts and philosophical texts) are not governed by this law, which means, of course, that they evade both substance and content.

Philosophy's longing is for pure language without content; the essence of translation is to announce-and-hide this pure language within itself.

Notes

1 [The forest seems to be implied here, since there is no reason why one could not observe a mountain from another mountain. The next sentence corroborates this reading.]
2 [Berman does not give a reference for this citation from Borges.]
3 We can see this at work in another example, the translation of fragments of Sappho by Michel Deguy in *Actes*. See Berman 1999:80–84.
4 Two terms require explanation here: *banausique* [banausic] (translated as 'futilités' [things that are pointless, without value] by Gandillac (1971:270)); and *ingenium* (which he translates as 'genie' [genius] (ibid.)). *Banausic* is a term of Greek origin, found in Plato and subsequently in Aristotle, meaning 'servile'. In Aristotle's *Politics* artisanal activities are *servile*. In the Greek language 'banausic' does have a meaning derived from 'futilité' but here Benjamin is using it in its primary sense: banausic activities are servile activities that contrast with noble activities presided over by a Muse. As for *ingenium*, this is an old term that comes from the Latin philosophical tradition – we find it in the Stoics, in Scholasticism and again in Descartes. It comes from the Latin *ingenere*, that which is innate to the individual. In eighteenth-century Germany *ingenium* gave birth to the term *genius*. Gandillac's translation is therefore based on an actual historical relation. Nonetheless, in a more literal translation, *ingenium* should be left as it is. All the more so because Benjamin devoted a number of texts to the notion of genius, even though this is otherwise not a term that forms part of his vocabulary.
5 ['Auch das Ideal ist eine höchste begriffliche Einheit, die des Gehalts. Seine Funktion ist also eine völlig andere als die der Idee. Es ist nicht ein Medium, welches den Zusammenhang

der Formen in sich birgt und aus sich bildet, sondern eine Einheit anderer Art. Erfaßbar ist es allein in einer begrenzten Vielheit reiner Inhalte, in die es sich zerlegt. In einem begrenzten, harmonischen Diskontinuum reiner Inhalte also manifestiert sich das Ideal. In dieser Auffassung berührt sich Goethe mit den Griechen. Die Idee der Musen unter der Hoheit Apollons ist von der Kunstphilosophie aus gedeutet die der reinen Inhalte aller Kunst. Die Griechen zählten solcher Inhalte neun und gewiß war weder deren Art noch Zahl willkürlich bestimmt. Der Inbegriff der reinen Inhalte, das Ideal der Kunst, läßt sich also als das Musische bezeichnen. Wie die innere Struktur des Ideals eine unstetige im Gegensatz zur Idee ist, so ist auch der Zusammenhang dieses Ideals mit der Kunst nicht in einem Medium gegeben, sondern durch eine Brechung bezeichnet. Die reinen Inhalte als solche sind in keinem Werk zu finden. Goethe nennt sie die Urbilder. Die Werke können jene unsichtbaren – aber anschaulichen – Urbilder, deren Hüterinnen die Griechen unter dem Namen der Musen kannten, nicht erreichen, sie vermögen nur in mehr oder weniger hohem Grad ihnen zu gleichen.']

Bibliography

Arlt, R., 1981 [1929]. *Les Sept fous*. Translated from French by A. Berman and I. Berman. Paris: P. Belfond.

Benjamin, W., 1991a [1923]. Die Aufgabe des Übersetzers. In: R. Tiedemann and H. Schweppenhäuser, eds. 1991. *Gesammelte Schriften*. IV.I. Frankfurt am Main: Suhrkamp. pp.9–21.

Benjamin, W., 1991b [1920]. Der Begriff der Kunstkritik in der deutschen Romantik. In: R. Tiedemann and H. Schweppenhäuser, eds. 1991. *Gesammelte Schriften*. I.I. Frankfurt am Main: Suhrkamp. pp.7–122.

Berman, A. 1999. *La Traduction et La Lettre ou L'Auberge du lointain*. Paris: Éditions du Seuil.

Berman, A., 2008. *L'Âge de la traduction*. Paris: Presses Universitaires de Vincennes.

Gandillac, M. de, trans. 1971. La tâche du traducteur. In: *Œuvres I, Mythe et violence*. Paris: Denoël/Les Lettres Nouvelles. pp.261–275.

CAHIER 9

The tenth paragraph of Benjamin's text contains a sentence that is 'absolutely essential, almost historic, for translation' (Berman 2008:168).

> Die wahre Übersetzung ist *durchscheinend*, sie verdeckt nicht das Original, steht ihm nicht im Licht, sondern läßt die reine Sprache, wie verstärkt durch ihr eigenes Medium, nur um so voller aufs Original fallen.
> *(Benjamin 1991a:18, emphasis added)*

> True translation is *translucent*, translation does not cover the original text, does not block its light, but allows pure language to fall on the original all the more fully, as though strengthened by its own medium.

Three out of Benjamin's four sets of Anglophone translators have rendered the adjective *durchscheinend* as 'transparent' in English. Gandillac too translated it as *transparente*. But Berman argues quite forcefully that *durchscheinend* (literally, 'shining through') should rather be interpreted as *translucide* (translucent, or in Hynd and Valk's invented term, 'translucid' (2006:305)). 'Transparent' has the unfortunate consequence of resonating with those metaphors that would view translation as a window or a pane of glass (see, for example, Sayers Peden 1989:13 and Shapiro as cited in Venuti 2008:1). Typically, when translators and writers talk about translation in these terms, they are subscribing to the idea that fluency is the ideal quality of a translation and clarity of meaning paramount; this is certainly Shapiro's belief. Translating *durchscheinend* as 'transparent' bolsters the dominance of 'instrumentalism' in Anglophone translation thought (the term is Lawrence Venuti's and describes the belief that translation is concerned with the reproduction of an invariant source text (2012:3)). However, what is designated by a 'transparent' translation may be less stable than is commonly assumed. Jean Boase-Beier argues that transparency in translation could also be understood as the desire to give the reader a literal sense of the source text by adhering closely to the 'obvious lexical, syntactic and phonetic properties of the original', an approach that would actually correlate with neglect of meaning (Boase-Beier 2011:80).

Translating *durchscheinend* as 'translucent', in any case, references something like *washi*, the paper that is used for room dividers in traditional Japanese houses – thus suggesting that translation is and/or reveals a silhouette, a palimpsest, an imprint. A translucent translation, Berman argues, 'allows the light from the original to pass through, it does not place itself in between the original and language' (2008:168) as is the case with transparent translation. A translucent translation will look and read like a translation rather than denying its status as a translation; and it achieves this via literality.

Let us now turn to the Mallarmé citation which, at this juncture in Benjamin's text, sheds light on what he is saying about the philosophical *ingenium*.

> Les langues imparfaites en cela que plusieurs, manque la suprême: penser étant écrire sans accessoires, ni chuchotement mais tacite encore l'immortelle parole, la diversité, sur terre, des idiomes empêche personne de proférer les mots qui, sinon se trouveraient, par une frappe unique, elle-même matériellement la vérité.
>
> *(Mallarmé 1945:363–364)*

There is a lot that one might say about this citation and the fact that it comes from a poet rather than a philosopher.

Curiously the citation is truncated, censored, because this is what Mallarmé goes on to say immediately afterwards:

> Cette prohibition sévit expresse, dans la nature (on s'y bute avec un sourire) qui ne vaille de raison pour se considérer Dieu; mais, sur l'heure, tourné à de l'esthétique, mon sens regrette que le discours défaille à exprimer les objets par des touches y répondant en coloris ou en allure, lesquelles existent dans l'instrument de la voix, parmi les langages et quelquefois chez un. À côté d'*ombre*, *ténèbres* se fonce peu; quelle déception, devant la perversité conférant à *jour* comme à *nuit*, contradictoirement, des timbres obscur ici, là clair. Le souhait d'un terme de splendeur brillant, ou qu'il s'éteigne, inverse; quant à des alternatives lumineuses simples – *Seulement*, sachons *n'existerait pas le vers*: lui, philosophiquement rémunère le défaut des langues, complément supérieur.
>
> *(ibid.:364)*[1]

It is verse – poetry – that compensates for what languages are lacking and that closes in on those words that are 'materially the truth' ['matériellement la vérité']. Benjamin has censored this, and I know, or at least I suspect, why: pure language [*pure langue*] – heralded by and concealed in translations – is not the purity of language [*la langue pure*] of which Mallarmé dreams. Pure language is 'materially the truth'.

Materially: an essential word, meaning *in its letter*. Pure language is language where letter and meaning are now one. We will come back to this.

Benjamin harnesses Mallarmé, the master of pure poetic language, and he does this in a text that prefaces a translation of Baudelaire, about whom Benjamin will go on to say that he is the master of a new poetic word, an impure word.[2]

The Mallarmé citation is truncated and presented to us in its original language, French. Benjamin, who translates Baudelaire, does not translate Mallarmé's text. *He leaves it in French.* Why?

Derrida, in his commentary on 'The Task of the Translator', says that this Mallarméan text is 'untranslatable' (1985:176). But is this true? Linguistically, and even literarily, no. Derrida touches on something nonetheless: Benjamin, in a text about translation, leaves a citation *untranslated*. A citation that happens to deal with the imperfection of languages – their multiplicity, in other words – and therefore the very thing that constitutes both the necessity and the impossibility of translation. Mallarmé's French is a French that is articulated in a strange manner, in which syntactic structure is, if not absent, then at least peculiarly rarefied, as the first sentence of the citation shows. This matches, moreover, the middle section of the passage – which Benjamin does not cite – where the issue is that of the mimological truth (or falsity, rather) of *words*. The entire problem of translation is at stake here: syntax and the word. He will soon go on to discuss this.

Benjamin therefore does not translate the seminal text that (tacitly) posits the problem of syntax and the word in translation, just prior, or almost prior to, thematic engagement with the problem of syntactic literality and what German calls *Wörtlichkeit*.

What is also striking is that this citation is followed shortly afterwards by another citation, in German this time, from Rudolf Pannwitz's *Die Krisis der europäischen Kultur* [The Crisis of European Culture] (1917). Pannwitz's statement also abuses the syntactic element of the sentence – not to mention that it does not use, in the manner of Jakob Grimm or Stefan George, German capital letters for proper nouns.

The two citations are therefore related, not thematically (Mallarmé does not talk about translation) but *formally*; a relationship which happens to make them both, in very different ways, untranslatable. Mallarmé cannot be translated into German because of the absence of syntactic linkage, Pannwitz cannot be translated into French because translation cannot restore the effect of strangeness created by the absence of capital letters in German.

Benjamin cites from two texts that have at least two points of untranslatability. The most curious thing of all, according to Alain, is that Mallarmé's work of syntactic redaction stems from his experience of literal translation from the English, where the syntactic structures are weaker, in his opinion, than those of French (Alain 1964:57). This literal translation appears to be of the kind that is lauded by Pannwitz. The two citations are therefore connected by all sorts of subterranean threads and if we are tempted to assume that Benjamin was unaware of this, there remains the fact that these are the only two citations in 'The Task of the Translator' and that, for Benjamin, citation was already the object of a specific practice and reflection; this would only become more and more the case. We cannot linger on this point but it is important to signal this link between translation and citation. Citation introduces a 'foreign' text into a 'self-same'[3] text; translation introduces into its 'self-same' language a foreign text and, indirectly, its language. The formal structure of these two is therefore the same and this raises the question of whether citations should be translated. In 'The Task of the Translator', the Mallarmé citation introduces a strand of untranslatability into the text, since the effect of the contrast between the French and the original text *cannot* be reproduced. Conversely, Gandillac translates the Pannwitz citation, but *its letter* (not its meaning) remains untranslatable.

Benjamin's citations – such as they are – gesture towards the enigma of translation, not only in their content, but in their form – *their letter*. And the letter will be the sole focus of the remainder of the text.

Benjamin concludes:

> die Übersetzung mitten zwischen Dichtung und der Lehre. Ihr Werk steht an Ausprägung diesen nach, doch es prägt sich nicht weniger tief ein in die Geschichte.
>
> *(p. 17. para 9)*

> translation stands right in the middle of poetry and teaching. The work of translation has left less of an impression than these two, but it is no less imprinted in history.

> la traduction se tient juste au milieu entre la poésie et la doctrine. Son œuvre a moins d'empreinte que celles-ci, mais elle ne s'imprime pas moins dans l'histoire.
>
> *(Berman)*

[Literal translation of Berman's French translation:

> Translation stands right in the middle between poetry and doctrine. Its work has less of an imprint than these, but it imprints itself no less in history.]

I will leave to one side, so as not to fall into a commentative infinity, the term 'teaching' [*Lehre*]. For Benjamin philosophy's form is teaching, *Lehre*. I will also leave aside the implied relationship between poetic and intellectual texts, and history. Suffice it to say that Benjamin's assertion here is that translation is *imprinted* in history, and is therefore historical, a bearer and creator of historicity, just like poetic and intellectual texts, but in a less obvious manner. The stamp of its action is simply less *visible*. Translation has a peculiar *active invisibility*. Does this stem from translation's *status* in Western history, from its ancillary condition, or from its most intimate being? This question remains to be answered. But there is no doubt that for Benjamin, like Heidegger, translation 'belongs at the heart of the movement of history' (Heidegger 1978:164).[4] For Benjamin this means, in so far as it engenders the seeds of pure language.

We have come full circle with these assertions. What remains to be asked is how translation engenders these seeds. And in paragraph ten, Benjamin must be asking himself the same question (the paragraph that follows does not really offer a response to this question either).

Paragraph ten begins with:

> Erscheint die Aufgabe des Übersetzers in solchem Licht, so drohen die Wege ihrer Lösung sich um so undurchdringlicher zu verfinstern. Ja, diese Aufgabe: in der Übersetzung den Samen reiner Sprache zur Reife zu bringen, scheint niemals lösbar, in keiner Lösung bestimmbar.
>
> *(p. 17. para 10)*

> Once the task of the translator appears in this light, the paths to its resolution are threatened by all the more impenetrable darkness. Yes, this task – of ripening the seed of pure language in translation – appears forever unresolvable, unresponsive to any solution.

> Si la tâche du traducteur apparaît sous cette lumière, les chemins de sa solution (*Lösung*)[5] risquent de s'obscurcir de façon d'autant plus impénétrable. Disons plus: de cette tâche qui consiste dans la traduction à faire mûrir la semence d'une pure langue, il semble impossible de jamais s'acquitter, il semble qu'aucune solution ne permette de la définir.
>
> *(Gandillac 1971:270)*[6]

[Literal translation of Gandillac's translation:

> If the task of the translator appears under this light, the ways of its solution (*Lösung*) risk darkening in a manner all the more impenetrable. Let us say this: of this task that consists of ripening the seed of a pure language in translation, it seems impossible to ever free oneself, it seems that no solution allows for its definition.]

The problem is knowing how the translator faced with the task of producing the seeds of pure language should proceed. Unfortunately, there can be no hope of a set method and Benjamin gives no clues. We are completely in the dark. Translation is in the dark because, traditionally, in its theoretical determination, translation can be only one thing: the restitution of meaning. This is why Benjamin says:

> Denn wird einer solchen nicht der Boden entzogen, wenn die Wiedergabe des Sinnes aufhört, maßgebend zu sein?
>
> *(p. 17. para 10)*

> But isn't the rug pulled out from underneath translation if reproduction of meaning ceases to be its measure?

> Ne la prive-t-on pas de toute base si rendre le sens cesse d'être l'étalon?
>
> *(Berman)*

[Literal translation of Berman's French translation:

> Does one not deprive it of its entire basis when rendering meaning ceases to be the normal measure?]

Benjamin will return to this: the restitution of meaning is the fundamental determinant of conventional theories of translation. It is even the fundamental determinant of translation theory in general – theory as distinct from reflection upon translation. This is I why I said at the beginning of the commentary that Benjamin's text was not a *theory* of translation.

Benjamin says:

> Und nicht anderes ist ja – negativ gewendet – die Meinung alles Vorstehenden.
>
> *(p. 17. para 10)*

> The meaning of everything said above is after all nothing other than this – merely inverted.

> Et certes tel est bien – transcrit en négatif – le sens de tout ce qu'on vient de dire.
>
> *(Berman)*

[Literal translation of Berman's French translation:

> And indeed such is – negatively transcribed – the meaning of everything that we have just said.]

If the purpose of translation is the production of pure language, this no longer has anything to do with the restitution of meaning, especially because pure language is aligned, to return to Mallarmé, with the materially revisited letter, and not with meaning.

Benjamin then reflects extensively on the antinomy inherent in the two concepts that are fundamental to any theory of translation: fidelity and freedom. A *translation theory* aims to address all of the processes involved in translation. But the body of potential source texts for translation is completely heterogeneous. The only element they have in common is meaning. Formally and otherwise, they are not related. As soon as one brings up meaning, however, one finds oneself confronted with the fidelity/freedom antinomy.

In the history of translation, the concept of fidelity has traditionally focused on the letter. Being faithful to a contract means being faithful to the 'terms' of the contract, not to its 'spirit'. Benjamin says this further on: 'fidelity to the word' (1991a:17). The 'bad translator', to borrow Benjamin's language, characteristically operates on a playing field – to put it truly unfaithfully – that consists of wishing to be 'faithful to the spirit of the text and not to its letter'.

In contrast, the *freedom* claimed by the translator in order not to be considered a slave to the letter, operates within the sphere of meaning.

The translator can either be free or faithful. And this opens up an interminable discussion: fidelity to the letter or freedom from this letter so that meaning can be more optimally restored. The limitations of these concepts of freedom and fidelity become apparent when they are presented as a choice. When the translator says: I have freed myself from the letter so that I can be faithful to the meaning, this is a sign that the translation has lost its footing and no longer holds to any principles. Benjamin says:

> Zwar sieht ihre herkömmliche Verwendung diese Begriffe stets in einem unauflöslichen Zwiespalt. Denn was kann gerade die Treue für die Wiedergabe des Sinnes eigentlich leisten?
>
> *(p. 17. para 10)*

> The conventional usage of these terms always places them into unresolvable conflict. For how can fidelity serve the reproduction of meaning?

> Assurément leur application traditionnelle envisage toujours ces concepts dans une incessante dissociation. Car à quoi peut proprement servir la fidélité pour la restitution du sens?
>
> *(Berman)*

[Literal translation of Berman's French translation:

> Of course their traditional application always envisages these concepts in an unending dissociation. Because what can fidelity properly deliver for the restitution of meaning?]

Effectively, it cannot. Because the translator who is faithful to the letter is not a free translator and the free translator has nothing to do with the letter of the text.

For once Benjamin's text goes in a direction that is fairly straightforward: if the translator focuses on the letter, the restitution of meaning is immediately threatened. Benjamin cites Hölderlin's translations from the Greek as an example. There are certain places in the text where meaning collapses. Literality is therefore a threat to meaning. But, and let me be clear here, this is not only the case for translation, but also for the original text. The letter always reigns to the detriment of meaning. In an extremely elegant text published in the journal *Recueil*, Jean-Paul Goux demonstrates – through various examples – the antinomy or contradiction between meaning and literality, and notably syntactic literality, that exists in the literary text.

> the rough formula for what appears to be an essential and self-evident law concerning the relationship of syntax and meaning – a law that is nonetheless never clearly expressed – is as follows: the closer the tie, the greater the confusion. Despite appearances to the contrary, we have to concede that mechanisms of relation always develop at the expense of transparency. The clarity of a sentence and the richness of its configuration are inversely proportional, and a syntax that guarantees the reign of order never takes over without threatening the clarity that it is supposed to serve. Syntax can also be compared to everything except a skeleton whose beauty resides in its invisible frame. As soon as links develop, however small, the reader will focus on their organisational principle rather than on meanings: at which point the reader will lose the thread of meaning and sink into the syntactic mass.
>
> *(Goux 1984:97–98)*[7]

He then illustrates this utterly surprising point of view:

> One reads, for example in the letters supposedly penned 'by the Portuguese nun': il est bien juste au moins que vous souffriez que je me plaigne des malheurs que j'avais bien prévus, quand je vous vis résolu à me quitter. Je connais bien que je me suis bien abusée, lorsqu'j'ay pensé, que vous auriez un procédé de meilleur foy, qu'on n'a accoustumé d'avoir, parce que l'excès de mon amour me mettait, ce semble, au-dessus de toutes sortes de soupçons, et qu'il méritait plus de fidélité qu'on n'en trouve d'ordinaire.
>
> *(ibid.)*[8]

One has to re-read this sentence several times to get its meaning. It presents a remarkable syntactic excess. Jean-Paul Goux cites an entire series of texts to demonstrate that where prose is concerned and more broadly the novel:

> syntax is what confuses the clarity of communication, the syntax no longer disappears behind the meaning that it is supposed to transmit, it acts as a screen, always interjecting its own material, its own texture between the reader and the object that it makes visible.
>
> *(ibid.:98)*[9]

The phenomenon that is denounced in translation – that literality suffocates meaning – is also a fundamental structure of the *original text*. In certain texts, and tendentially in all prose – and this is unconnected to translation – we find a form of syntactic literality of a pure sort, an enemy of meaning. It is obvious that when confronted with texts like these (and they possibly make up the greater part of all prose texts), translation has to choose between two possible paths: either dismantle the syntax, taking it apart to allow the meaning to shine, or reproduce it, thus placing meaning at a greater remove. What was already at a remove from meaning in the original text will be even further away. This is why, in the remainder of his text, Benjamin will say that translation has only the most fleeting relationship with meaning and he will requisition the image of the tangent. What has a tendency to be fleeting in the original text will be even more so in the translation.

When Benjamin writes:

> Wie sehr endlich Treue in der Wiedergabe der Form die des Sinnes erschwert, versteht sich vom selbst.
>
> *(p. 18. para 10)*

> In the end it is obvious that fidelity in the reproduction of form impedes fidelity in the reproduction of meaning.

> À quel point finalement la fidélité dans la restitution de la forme rend difficile la restitution du sens, c'est ce que s'entend de soi-même.
>
> *(Berman)*

[Literal translation of Berman's French translation:

> The extent to which finally fidelity in the restitution of form makes the restitution of meaning difficult is obvious.]

There is a rupture between the intention that concerns itself with the restitution of meaning and the intention that concerns itself with the restitution of the syntactic structure of the text. In so far as pure language is language where the letter dominates, translation accentuates this element, but it can also do the opposite, which is to say weaken the syntactic structure to the benefit of meaning.

Translation can push this process to its limit, something that no original can do. This is the great novelty of translation compared with the original text. One can take the process of avoiding meaning quite a long way. For Benjamin, thinking of Hölderlin, as far as madness.

We are just about to encounter another metaphor for translation, one that we have already talked about, that of the vessel. Benjamin takes the image of a vessel broken into a thousand pieces. In order to put it back together, the fragments have to be joined up wherever possible. This is the translational impulse.

anstatt dem Sinn des Originals sich ähnlich zu machen, die Übersetzung liebend vielmehr und bis ins Einzelne hinein dessen Art des Meinens in der eigenen Sprache sich anbilden, um so beide wie Scherben ein Bruchstück eines Gefäßes, als Bruchstück einer größeren Sprache erkennbar zu machen.

(p.19. para 10)

instead of making itself similar to the meaning of the original, the translation should rather lovingly adopt the way of meaning that the original has within its own language to the very last detail so as to make both broken pieces recognisable as fragments of a greater language, just as shards are fragments of a jug.

au lieu de se rendre semblable au sens de l'original, la traduction doit bien plutôt, dans un mouvement d'amour et jusque dans le détail, faire passer dans sa propre langue le mode de visée de l'original: ainsi, de même que les débris deviennent reconnaissables comme fragments d'une même amphore, original et traductions deviennent reconnaissables comme fragments d'une langue plus grande.

(Gandillac 1971:271–272)[10]

[Literal translation of Gandillac's French translation:

instead of making itself similar to the meaning of the original, the translation should rather, in an act of love and in detail, make the mode of intention of the original pass into its own language: thus, in the same way that the broken pieces become recognisable as fragments of the same amphora, the original and the translations become recognisable as fragments of a greater language.]

Joining up languages at the point where they both fracture and fit back together can only come about through literality. For Benjamin, far from producing a sort of informal mixture of two languages, this is how the two languages complete each other. What the detractors of literality see as a mishmash is, for the literal translator, the joining up of two languages point by point.

And Benjamin adds:

Eben darum muß sie von der Absicht, etwas mitzuteilen, vom Sinn in sehr hohem Maße absehen und das Original ist ihr in diesem nur insofern wesentlich, als es der Mühe und Ordnung des Mitzuteilenden den Übersetzer und sein Werk schon enthoben hat.

(p.18. para 10)

For this very reason translation has to quite radically turn away from the intention to communicate something, from meaning. The original text is essential to it only insofar as it has already released the translator and his work from the effort and order required by the message.

Et c'est bien pourquoi la traduction ne peut que renoncer au projet de rien communiquer, faire abstraction du sens dans une très large mesure, et l'original ne lui est, à cet égard, essentiel que pour autant qu'il a épargné au traducteur et à son œuvre la peine et l'ordonnance de ce qui est à communiquer.

(Gandillac 1971:272)

[Literal translation of Gandillac's French translation:

And this is clearly why the translation has to renounce the project of communicating something, has to make an abstraction of meaning to a very large extent, and the original is only, in this respect, essential to it to the extent that it has spared the translator and his work the trouble and the prescription of what is to be communicated.]

From Benjamin's perspective, if the purpose of translation is the creation of pure language, no matter how important the original, it is nonetheless not as important as the purpose of the fulfilment of language. If we attribute this Messianic aim to translation, then we have to say that for the translator, the original is just a pretext to give free flight to the language that it would like to create. This may look like exaggeration on Benjamin's part but it makes sense within the framework of his assertions.

This parallel can also be found in the status that Benjamin bestows on criticism vis-à-vis the text. There is always something about the trajectory of critical activity which means that it considers itself more important than the text itself. Benjamin states, for example, that criticism is the mortification of texts, which one can only interpret as meaning that criticism puts texts to death in a way that makes something more elevated spring forth: 'the fragment of a better world' (1991b:181).[11]

This can be found in a different guise in Blanchot, in his assertions about the process leading to the work counting more than the finished work itself.

This upsets the traditional perspective according to which the original text is always the fundament and translation always defaults.

Benjamin continues with a new citation that does not have quite the same status as the other two.

εν αρχη ην ο λογοσ[12]

im Anfang war das Wort

In the beginning was the word.

Dans le principe était le verbe.

(Gandillac 1971:272)

This citation from the Bible has such autonomy that it is barely a citation. It certainly cannot be treated in the same way as the Mallarmé and Pannwitz citations.

This is immediately followed by:

> Dagegen kann, ja muß dem Sinn gegenüber ihre Sprache sich gehen lassen, um nicht dessen intentio als Wiedergabe, sondern als Harmonie, als Ergänzung zur Sprache, in der diese sich mitteilt, ihre eigene Art der intentio ertönen zu lassen.
>
> *(p. 18. para 10)*

> Language can, indeed must, let itself go vis-à-vis meaning so that the note struck is not that of meaning's intentio as mere reproduction but as harmony, as a complement to the language through which meaning communicates itself – so that the note struck allows language's own intentio to be heard.

> En face du sens, c'est un droit et même une nécessité pour la langue du traducteur de se laisser aller, afin de ne pas faire résonner la visée intentionnelle du sens comme une simple restitution, mais plutôt son propre mode de visée comme une harmonique, comme un complément à la langue, dans laquelle se communique la visée du sens.
>
> *(Gandillac 1971:272)*

[Literal translation of Gandillac's translation:

> Faced with meaning, it is a right and even a necessity for the translator's language to let go, so as not to make the intentional aim of meaning resonate like simple restitution, but rather its own mode of intention like a harmony, like a complement to the language in which the intention of meaning is communicating.]

Abandoning the intention of restoring sense means that we attempt to make the two languages complete each other through literality. And thus we arrive at the following passage, which is fundamental for the practice and criticism of translations:

> Es ist daher, vor allem im Zeitalter ihrer Enstehung, das höchste Lob einer Übersetzung nicht, sie wie ein Original ihrer Sprache zu lesen.
>
> *(p. 18. para 10)*

> That is why, particularly in the era of its creation, the greatest praise bestowed on a translation cannot be that it reads as though it were originally written in that language.

> C'est pourquoi, surtout à l'époque où elle paraît, le plus grand éloge qu'on puisse faire à une traduction n'est pas qu'elle se lise comme une œuvre originale de sa propre langue.
>
> *(Gandillac 1971:272)*

[Literal translation of Gandillac's translation:

> This is why, especially in the epoch when it appears, the greatest praise that one can offer a translation is not that it reads like a work originally written in its own language.]

Translation theory's thesis, correlating to the restitution of meaning, is that a translation must never seem to be a translation, must never appear to be a translation. It should look as though it were naturally born into the translating language. Its translated nature should disappear. This obliteration of the translation – as I have already said – finds a corollary in the obliteration of the translator. Translation is presented as an original text that nobody has created.

And Benjamin continues:

> Vielmehr ist eben das die Bedeutung der Treue, welche durch Wörtlichkeit verbürgt wird, daß die große Sehnsucht nach Sprachergänzung aus dem Werke spreche.
>
> *(p. 18. para 10)*

> Rather the true meaning of the kind of fidelity guaranteed by literality is that the text communicates the great longing that languages might complete each other.

> Au contraire, ce que signifie la fidelité dont la caution est la littéralité, c'est que l'ouvrage puisse exprimer la grande nostalgie d'une complémentation de la langue.
>
> *(Gandillac 1971:272)*[13]

[Literal translation of Gandillac's French translation:

> On the contrary, what characterises fidelity whose guarantee is literality is that the work can express the great longing for a complementarity of language.]

Once again this completion never fully comes to be. The two languages never pass into each other. In translation, the inverse process is at work: a kind of suppression in which the translating language forcibly pushes away the translated language until it is no longer there. It can recall it to live in an echo but the translated language is not there. The translated language that might complete the translating language is there only in the modus of longing, of distance. Because the metaphor of the echo of language's mountain forest implies a true theory of distance. The translator in relation to the forest of language where the original resides is in a position where this forest is always distant. This notion of distance returns: the translation exists via a mode of distance in so far as the translator leaves the text in its mountain forest and keeps only its echo. The translation must leave the original text far away – and its language too. Translation is devoted to a deeply contradictory task: drawing infinitely close to the language of the original and, at the same time, placing the two languages at an infinite distance from one another.

This is what true translation is. This is how we can distinguish between true and false literality.

Then comes a sentence that is absolutely essential, almost historic, for translation, which is when Benjamin says:

> Die wahre Übersetzung ist durchscheinend
>
> *(p. 18. para 10)*

> True translation is translucent
>
> La vraie traduction est translucide (*durchscheinend*)
>
> *(Berman)*

[Literal translation of the French translation:

> True translation is translucent]

Translation is not 'transparente' [transparent] as Gandillac would have it (1971:272), rather it is like a translucent medium. It allows the light from the original to pass through, it does not place itself in between the original and language.

> sie verdeckt nicht das Original, steht ihm nicht im Licht, sondern läßt die reine Sprache, wie verstärkt durch ihr eigenes Medium, nur um so voller aufs Original fallen.
>
> *(p. 18. para 10)*

> translation does not cover the original text, does not block its light, but allows pure language to fall on the original all the more fully, as though strengthened by its own medium.

> elle ne cache pas l'original, elle ne se met pas devant sa lumière, mais c'est le pur langage que simplement, comme renforcé par son propre médium, elle fait tomber d'autant plus pleinement sur l'original.
>
> *(Gandillac 1971:272)*[14]

[Literal translation of Gandillac's translation:

> It doesn't hide the original, it doesn't place itself in front of its light, but it simply allows pure language to fall all the more fully on the original text, as though reinforced by its own medium.]

This sentence is not a contradiction of the fact that a translation practice that rejects the restitution of meaning – and consequently also the kind of translation that erases itself – gives us a translation that is translucent and looks like a translation. Benjamin keeps the two things together. The text of the translation has to look as though it has been translated and not resemble an original in the least. And a translation can only look like a translation if it introduces distortions into the translating language. If a translation wants to make itself felt in the texture of the text, it can only do this if one senses the foreign language behind and inside it, like a foreign element. It is not transparent, on the contrary. The theory of transparency in translation is the theory of meaning. But although translation is not transparent, it is nonetheless *durchscheinend*, translucent. On the other hand, translation which is directed entirely towards the restitution of meaning is not at all translucent: it places itself in front of the text, blocking it completely, because it makes the reader believe that the translation is an original text. There can be no greater denial of a text than making the reader believe that the translation is an original while asserting that it is not.

The translation exits this fallacious web when it looks like a translation but does not *break* the original in making itself felt, instead opening up to it in glorious fashion. Benjamin says that this comes about through literality and above all syntactic literality: 'but allows pure language to fall on the original all the more fully, as though strengthened by its own medium' (Benjamin 1991a:18).

To the extent that the letter becomes the dominant element in translation, the original text finds itself drawn towards pure language. This is what, above all else, literality in the transposition of syntax achieves, *Übertragung*.

The end of the paragraph is difficult to explain:

> Das vermag vor allem Wörtlichkeit in der Übertragung der Syntax und gerade sie erweist das Wort, nicht den Satz als das Urelement des Übersetzers.
>
> *(p. 18. para 10)*

> Above all this requires literality in the transposition of syntax and precisely this literality establishes the word, not the sentence, as the primordial unit of the translator.

> C'est ce que réussit avant tout la litteralité dans la transposition de la syntaxe, et précisément elle montre que le mot, non la proposition (*Satz*), est l'élément originaire du traducteur.
>
> *(Gandillac 1971:272)*

[Literal translation of Gandillac's translation:

> This is what above all literality achieves in the transposition of syntax, and precisely this shows that the word, not the sentence, is the originary element of the translator.]

At first sight this sentence appears incomprehensible because if the work – the task of the translator – consisted of transposing the order of syntax, of reproducing the system of relations in its richness, it is not obvious why the originary element of the translator would be the word; in other words, the opposite of syntax.

The sentence that follows is even more obscure:

> Denn der Satz ist die Mauer vor der Sprache des Originals, Wörtlichkeit die Arkade.
>
> *(p. 18. para 10)*

> For the sentence is the wall before the language of the original text, literality is the arcade.

> Car la proposition est le mur devant la langue de l'original, la littéralité est l'arcade.
>
> *(Gandillac 1971:272)*

[Literal translation of Gandillac's French translation:

> For the sentence is the wall in front of the language of the original, literality the arcade.]

I think that these two sentences can be parsed by connecting them to the Mallarmé citation on the one hand and on the other by paying attention to the German term that signifies literality, *Wörtlichkeit*.

In *Wörtlichkeit*, there is *Wort*, the word. Literality means word for word. Literality seems to be going in two (different) directions therefore: towards the restitution of the text's syntactic configuration, which according to Benjamin should be the main work of the translator, and towards the restitution of words which are supposed to be the originary elements of the translator.

We seem to be able to identify the originary element of the translator and the translator's task. But this doesn't get us very far.

On the other hand, if we go back to the Mallarmé citation and the thoughts that accompany it, Benjamin's utterance gradually becomes clear. In Mallarmé's text, we find neither phrases nor sentences – for philosophy, for the German school, the sentence is *der Satz*, a sentence with a subject, verb and predicate. Mallarmé's text is a text in which those elements are absent, to the benefit of a syntactic order that still exists but is more complex. When those elements that provide logical order are absent (the German word *der Satz* relates to these elements that provide logical order), one effectively resorts to words that will conduct themselves in relation to other words without any apparent ties, but this will still result in syntax.

Benjamin cannot be using the word 'syntax' in the sense of logical configuration or this passage would be incomprehensible. Syntax is the supra-logical order that we find in Mallarmé when the logical elements are absent. If there is a correlation between logical configurations and the units of meaning, there is also a correlation between the configurations of words and the syntactic torrent – these are made up of words, after all. From this perspective, there is no longer any contradiction in saying that the originary element of the translator is the word and, at the same time, that the translator's fundamental task is transposition, the transfer (*Übertragung*) of syntax. Because the word unfolds within the syntactical domain, not in the domain of the grammatical sentence.

If we look back, for example, at the text of *La Religieuse portugaise*, it is obvious that it would be simple to re-write this according to a clearer logical configuration. In leaving it as we find it, we are faced by words that are integrated according to modes of relation where all the grammatical categories have acquired a significant degree of irrationality.

I will quote another example given by Jean-Paul Goux that might explain the correlation between a syntax given over to itself and the way in which it plays with words – in a manner that has nothing to do with the logical configuration of sentences. The example is taken from *Au Château d'Argol* [At the Argol Chateau] (1938) by Julien Gracq, who was a great *provocateur* in this respect:

> Et cependant de quelque anormale urgence que témoignât la rectitude de cette tranchée ou comme si dans une planète habitée par des géomètres fous on eût considéré comme de première nécessité de peindre *d'abord* les méridiens sur le sol, le caractère de pure *direction* semblait sans la moindre idée de but se suffire à lui-même dans sa convaincante affirmation.
>
> (Goux 1984:100)[15]

When one reads this passage meaning escapes one. The construction is not logical, the syntax has gone to seed, developing its own capacities, through which the words appear very purely.

By the way, wouldn't it be correct to say that Mallarmé has suppressed the prepositional elements rather than the syntactic elements?

All this leads us to reflect on the fact that anything that has to do with the sentence will be an obstacle to literality. We can try to interpret Benjamin's statement in this way, thus illuminating his image: 'For the sentence is the wall before the language of the original text, literality is the arcade.'

If we translate expressions of this kind by remodelling them logically according to processes of rationalisation, embellishment, elucidation – processes that we analysed at the beginning of last year's seminar – then we would effortlessly produce chains of sentences. We might therefore say, with Benjamin, that these sentence chains essentially erect a wall in front of the language of the original text, a wall that prohibits access to this language. Translators who concern themselves only with meaning spend their time building walls in front of the language of the original. The French translator of Tolstoy's *War and Peace*, for example, said that all translation is *peignage* – grooming, tidying. We know what *peignage* means in a publishing context: arranging the text according to the order of sentences. The text therefore becomes a wall; its literality becomes the arcade, the opening. The text that produces literality isn't a finished text, it is a loose web.

Translating literally means translating word for word *and* reproducing syntactic structures – which is not exactly the same thing. In both cases, the 'letter' element is accentuated in the translation, whether this is in the word itself or in the configuration of words, the syntax. Mallarmé's text is enlightening in this regard. The sentence no longer constitutes it, a free syntactic structure emerges – the infamous *écriture mallarméenne*. An *écriture* that has its sources, that can be imitated but which cannot be said to be 'Mallarmé's style'. It is a style, as he said himself, that is characterised by erasure.

Erasing the verse, removing the conjunctions, making words collide, produces syntactic literality. We could go further: syntactic literality can exist in the abundance of prepositional structures and may end up destroying them.

Notes

1 [I have left these Mallarmé citations – the first is cited by Benjamin in 'The Task of the Translator' and the second, which is the continuation of the same passage, by Berman in his commentary – in French for two reasons. The first is that Benjamin himself does not offer a translation of this citation; the second is that Mallarmé's style will become the focus of Berman's discussion in this particular cahier.]

2 In another text Benjamin cites a remark by Claudel about Baudelaire's poetry. It is 'a mix of Racinian style and the journalistic style of the Second Empire' (Benjamin 1991c:603) ['Baudelaire [...] habe die Schreibweise von Racine mit der eines Journalisten des Second Empire verbunden'. Claudel's words in French are usually cited as follows: 'un extraordinaire mélange du style racinien et du style journaliste de son temps' (as cited in Rivière 1944:15)].

3 I have borrowed here from Lawrence Venuti, who uses the term 'self-same' to translate the French *propre* in his translation (2000) of Berman's essay 'Traduction comme épreuve de l'étranger' (1985).

4 ['gehört [...] in die innerste Bewegung der Geschichte'] The complete statement is: ['Der gedachte Zug besteht darin, daß die Übersetzung in solchen Fällen nicht nur Auslegung, sondern Überlieferung ist. Als Überlieferung gehört sie in die innerste Bewegung der Geschichte.']

5 I would remind you of what was said at the beginning of the seminar on the *Aufgabe/ Auflösung* correlation.

6 In this passage translated by Maurice de Gandillac, Antoine Berman replaces 'accomplissement' with 'solution' and 'pur langage' with 'pure langue'.]

7 ['[...] ce qui semble être une loi essentielle, évidente et pourtant jamais clairement exprimée, qui concerne les rapports de la syntaxe et de la signification; la formule abrupte en serait celle-ci: plus on lie, plus on brouille. Contre toute apparence, il faut admettre que les mécanismes de relation se développent toujours aux dépens de la transparence. La limpidité d'une phrase et la richesse de ses agencements sont inversement proportionnelles et ce qui doit assurer le règne de l'ordre, la syntaxe, ne prend jamais le pouvoir sans menacer la clarté qu'il devait servir. Aussi peut-elle être comparée à tout hornis à un squelette dont l'invisible armature ferait la beauté. Dès que les liaisons se

developpent si peu que ce soit, il faut que le lecteur s'attache plutôt qu'aux significations, au principe de leur organisation: dès lors il perd le fil su sens, et s'enfonce dans la pâte de la syntaxe.']

8 ['Lorsqu'on lit dans ces lettres dites «de la religieuse portugaise»'] ['it is at least just that you should put up with my complaints of the unhappiness that I predicted, when I see you resolved to leave me. I well know that I deceived myself when I thought you would proceed in the best faith that could be expected because my excess of love put me, it seems, above all kinds of suspicions and deserved more fidelity than one would ordinarily find […]']

9 ['[…] la syntaxe est ce qui vient brouiller la limpidité de la communication, elle ne disparaît plus derrière le sens qu'elle devrait transmettre, elle fait écran, interpose toujours sa propre matière, sa propre consistance entre le lecteur et l'objet qu'elle donne à voir']

10 Translation by Maurice de Gandillac, but at the end of the citation Antoine Berman has replaced 'langage' with 'langue'.

11 ['zum Fragmente einer wahren Welt']

12 [This should read ἐν ἀρχῇ ἦν ὁ λόγος. Gandillac omits the Greek from his translation.]

13 [Gandillac's translation actually reads 'un complement apporté à son langage'. The change was presumably made by Berman.]

14 [I have replaced a missing comma before 'comme' in the commentary's rendition of Gandillac's translation.]

15 ['And yet to some abnormal urgency for which the rectitude of this entrenchment vouched or as if on a planet inhabited by mad geometrists one had considered as an immediate priority *first* painting meridians on the ground, the character of pure *direction* seemed without the slightest idea of an aim to itself suffice in its convincing affirmation.']

Bibliography

Alain, 1964. *Propos de littérature*. Parsis: Gonthier.

Benjamin, W., 1991a [1923]. Die Aufgabe des Übersetzers. In: R. Tiedemann and H. Schweppenhäuser, eds. 1991. *Gesammelte Schriften*. IV.I. Frankfurt am Main: Suhrkamp. pp.9–21.

Benjamin, W., 1991b [1924–1925]. Goethes Wahlverwandtschaften. In: R. Tiedemann and H. Schweppenhäuser, eds. 1991. *Gesammelte Schriften* I.I. Frankfurt am Main: Suhrkamp. pp.123–201.

Benjamin, W., 1991c. Charles Baudelaire. In: R. Tiedemann and H. Schweppenhäuser, eds. 1991. *Gesammelte Schriften*. I.II. Frankfurt am Main: Suhrkamp. pp.509–690.

Berman, A., 1985. La traduction comme épreuve de l'étranger. *Texte*, 4, pp.67–81.

Berman, A., 2000 [1985]. Translation and the Trials of the Foreign. Translated from French by L. Venuti. In: L. Venuti, ed. 2000. *The Translation Studies Reader*. 1st ed. New York: Routledge. pp.284–297.

Berman, A., 2008. *L'Âge de la traduction*. Paris: Presses Universitaires de Vincennes.

Boase-Beier, J., 2011. *A Critical Introduction to Translation Studies*. London: Continuum.

Derrida, J., 1985. Des tours de Babel. Translated from French by J.F. Graham. In: J.F. Graham, ed. 1985. *Difference in Translation*. Ithaca, NY: Cornell University Press. pp.165–207.

Gandillac, M. de, trans. 1971. La tâche du traducteur. In: *Œuvres I, Mythe et violence*. Paris: Denoël/Les Lettres Nouvelles. pp.261–275.

Goux, J-P., 1984. Un peu faute de façon. In: R. Millet and J-M. Maulpoix, eds. *Recueil*. Paris: Éditions Qui Vive. pp.95–100.

Heidegger, M., 1978 [1957]. *Der Satz vom Grund*. Pfullingen: Verlag Günther Neske.

Hynd, J. and Valk, E.M., trans. 2006 [1968]. The Task of the Translator. In: D. Weissbort and A. Eysteinsson, eds. 2006. *Translation – Theory and Practice*. Oxford: Oxford University Press. pp.298–307.

Mallarmé, S., 1945. Variations sur un sujet. In: S. Mallarmé, *Œuvres complètes*. Paris: Gallimard. pp.353–420.

Pannwitz, R., 1917. *Die Krisis der europäischen Kultur*. Nürnberg: Verlag Hans Carl.

Rivière, J. 1944. *Études*. Paris: Gallimard.

Sayers Peden, M., 1989. Building a Translation, the Reconstruction Business: Poem 145 of Sor Juana Inés de la Cruz. In: J. Biguenet and R. Schulte, eds. *The Craft of Translation*. Chicago: University of Chicago Press. pp.13–27.

Venuti, L., 2008 [1995]. *The Translator's Invisibility*. London and New York: Routledge.

Venuti, L., 2012. *Translation Changes Everything*. London and New York: Routledge.

CAHIER 10

Benjamin's Messianic framework makes Berman uncomfortable. For Benjamin, natural languages are moving, Messianically, towards 'pure language', but Berman argues that we do not have to approach pure language from this eschatological perspective and that Benjamin's framework can be appropriated (or translated) into a more secular form. To this end he repositions pure language as the 'dialectal essence of language' (2008:181), which Berman locates in orality.

There is indeed something uncomfortable about Benjamin's Messianism. As noted by Steven Rendall (2000:24), Harry Zohn omitted the word 'Messianic' from his 1968 translation, and it is tempting to read this omission psychoanalytically, and to ask why Berman feels the same discomfort and why, for that matter, we do too. Is such a 'secularisation' of the text truly necessary for it to enter twenty-first-century thought on translation more properly? Nor is Berman's solution of locating 'dialectal essence' in orality immediately obvious: just as there is an irony in the translator's desperate attempts to impose meaning on 'The Task of the Translator', a text that celebrates the letter, so too is there an irony in the thought that Benjamin's translator might set 'free the spark of orality' (2008:180) within what is profoundly a *written* text, that is, a text that is guarded and deliberately unidiomatic in its mode of expression.

Cahier 10 as a whole is rushed to the point of being a fragment. Berman literally ran out of time. What it provides is a mere gesture towards a reinterpretation of Benjamin. Perhaps this gesture might have led to Berman's version of a New Task of the Translator. As things stand, such an essay remains to be written.

This session of our seminar will be the final one although initially a further session was planned. This will inevitably affect the rhythm of my commentary since there are still two paragraphs remaining. But this is unfortunately the way things are.

Structurally, the penultimate paragraph picks up where the paragraph that ends in the Mallarmé citation finishes. It too finishes on a citation – taken from Pannwitz – and its content is the same: the relationship between pure language and translation, but on a level that interrogates and exposes this relationship more intimately.

The preceding paragraph pronounced that translation has to make the greatest possible abstraction of meaning. This abstraction operates through literality – primarily of the syntactic variety. This is because, as we have seen, the same phenomenon manifests itself in the syntactic letter of the original text when the letter strives to separate itself from meaning, acquiring a peculiar autonomy.

If this is the case then the two fundamental concepts that structure the ethos of the translator, *fidelity* and *freedom*, appear more dynamically opposed than ever. They both connect to the two irreconcilable *essences* of translation, and a gulf emerges between the restitution,[1] *Wiedergabe*, of meaning, and literal reproduction, between which there can be no hope of compromise.

However, this opposition – which is a *real* opposition, not merely a historical and ideological one – is unbalanced. Seeing translation as the restitution of meaning, in pursuit of which the translator's alleged freedom unfolds, obviously overlooks the entire problematic of literality. But seeing translation as the production – via this literality – of pure language, one is confronted with the fact that, in every language, in every text, *there is meaning*. As soon as one posits that the essential thing in translation is not the transmission of this meaning, one is faced with the question of whether the transmission of meaning is (or should be) eradicated within a literal translation, just as the letter is eradicated within a translation focused on meaning. Or rather, does whatever meaning there is in a text constitute, in relation to its letter, an autonomous layer that can be recovered? Or does meaning point us towards something other than itself, something to which it is nonetheless essentially related?

Benjamin writes:

> Allein wenn der Sinn eines Sprachgebildes identisch gesetzt werden darf mit dem seiner Mitteilung, so bleibt ihm ganz nah und doch unendlich fern, unter ihm verborgen oder deutlicher, durch ihn gebrochen oder machtvoller über alle Mitteilung hinaus ein Letztes, Entscheidendes. Es bleibt in aller Sprache und ihren Gebilden außer dem Mitteilbaren ein Nicht-Mitteilbares, ein, je nach dem Zusammenhang, in dem es angetroffen wird, Symbolisierendes oder Symbolisiertes. Symbolisierendes nur, in den endlichen Gebilden der Sprachen; Symbolisiertes aber im Werden der Sprachen selbst. Und was im Werden der Sprachen sich darzustellen, ja herzustellen sucht, das ist jener Kern der reinen Sprache selbst.

(p. 19. para 11)

Even if the meaning of a linguistic unit were to be considered identical with that which it communicates, something final, decisive remains – extremely close and yet endlessly distant, hidden beneath it or extremely clear, broken by it or quite potent – beyond all communication. Beyond the communicable there remains in all language and in all linguistic units something incommunicable; something that – depending on the context in which it is encountered – is symbolising or symbolised: it is symbolising only in the finite units of languages; but in the very becoming of languages it is symbolised. And that which strives for performance, production in this becoming of languages, is the kernel of pure language itself.

Mais si le sens d'une configuration de langue (*Sprachgebilde*) peut être posé comme identique à sa communication, il reste, tout proche de lui et pourtant infiniment éloigné, caché par lui ou montré plus clairement, brisé par lui or plus puissant que toute communication,[2] un élément dernier, décisif. Il demeure dans toute langue et dans des configurations, hors du communicable, un non-communicable, quelque chose selon le mode de co-relation dans lequel on le trouve, de symbolisant ou de symbolisé. De symbolisant seulement dans les configurations finies de la langue; de symbolisé, par contre, dans le devenir même des langues. Et ce qui cherche dans le devenir des langues à se présenter, voire à se produire, c'est ce noyau de la pure langue.

(Berman)

[Literal translation of Berman's French translation:

But if the meaning of a configuration of language (*Sprachgebilde*) can be posited as identical to its communication, there remains, very close to it and yet infinitely removed, hidden by it or more clearly demonstrated, broken by it or more powerful than any communication, a final, decisive element. There resides in every language and its configurations, beyond the communicable, a non-communicable, something symbolising or symbolised according to the mode of co-relation in which one finds it. Of the symbolising kind only in the finite configurations of language; of the symbolised kind, by contrast, in the very becoming of languages. And what tries to present itself, to produce itself even, in the becoming of languages, is this kernel of pure language.]

Here the text is composed of an almost unbearable density. Because what Benjamin wants to say is that pure language, *symbolised* in the becoming [*devenir*] of languages (which for him is the Messianic march towards pure language) is 'symbolising' in literary texts. What does this mean? And more immediately: to what extent is this becoming-of-languages distinguishable from what languages 'become' in literary texts?

The becoming of languages is an empirical matter, of course, but the development [*devenir*] studied by linguistics or philosophy is not the same becoming of which Benjamin speaks. What he has in mind is the becoming-pure-language of languages, not the empirically verifiable diachrony of the various natural languages. Or rather, within this diachrony, within this *being-in-movement of languages*, Benjamin discerns an intention, an *intentio*. In the historical-being of languages, he asserts the symbolisation of pure language.

In this context symbol means the manifestation, the (lacunary) performance of pure language. Philology and linguistics study the being-in-movement of languages without, of course, enquiring into its basis. Speculative philosophy perceives within this movement the manifestation of pure language – without being able to verify it. More precisely: without this fundamental *intentio*, there would be no revelatory being-in-movement of languages. Symbol also implies a lacunary, fragmentary performance. The symbol is where the fragment reigns. Pure language is symbolised, which means that it arrives at a broken performance of its being in the becoming of languages. But this becoming is, as it were, passive, rather like the flow of a river.

In literary texts, by contrast, language converges and is concentrated. Pure language is not (passively) symbolised there but (actively) symbolises. This does not mean, however, that the active presence of pure language in literary texts is superior to its passive presence in the becoming of languages. Because in the literary text, pure language – the performance thereof – is connected to the element that is most alien to it – *meaning*.

> ist sie in den Gebilden behaftet mit dem schweren und fremden Sinn.
>
> *(p. 19. para 11)*

> it [*pure language*] is encumbered by meaning, which is heavy and strange.
>
> elle est lestée dans les configurations par le sens lourd et étranger.
>
> *(Berman)*

[Literal translation of Berman's French translation:

> it is weighed down in [*linguistic*] configurations by heavy and strange meaning.]

An expression worthy of note. The literary text is – also – communication. It transmits meaning. This meaning is 'heavy' (*schwer*) and 'strange' (*fremd*) with respect to the intention of the pure language that resides – in symbolising fashion – in the text. And it is from this that the unique task of translation is derived: delivering the text and its language from the heavy and strange meaning that inhabits it.

> Von diesem sie zu entbinden, das Symbolisierende zum Symbolisierten selbst zu machen, die reine Sprache gestaltet der Sprachbewegung zurückzugewinnen, ist das gewaltige und einzige Vermögen der Übersetzung.
>
> *(p. 19. para 11)*

To deliver it [*pure language*] from this, to turn that which symbolises into that which is symbolised, to win back pure language from the movement of languages, is the awesome and singular power of translation.

La détacher de ce sens, faire du symbolisant le symbolisé même, retrouver la pure langue structurée dans le mouvement langagier, tel est le pouvoir unique et violent de la traduction.

(Berman)

[Literal translation of Berman's French translation:

Detaching it from this meaning, making the symbolised from the symbolising, rediscovering structured pure language in the movement of languages, such is the unique and violent power of translation.]

This sentence is *the* pivotal sentence of 'The Task of the Translator'. Everything that Benjamin is saying and has said comes together here. It is this sentence that he commends, historically speaking, to our reflection. Any meditation on translation must contend with it. And this sentence confronts centuries of translation 'theory'. It renders 'theories' of translation obsolete because there is not a single theory of translation that does not concern itself with the restitution of meaning.

This discussion pertains to the sphere of *texts*. Because only in literary texts are letter and meaning magnified to a degree that goes beyond the ordinary capacity of language. Meaning has *weight* in literary texts, infinite weight. And the letter reigns. But the text is the very centre of a conflict between infinitised meaning and the infinitised letter. By communicating a text written in one language within another language, translation *frees* the text (and therefore its language) from the *weight* of meaning. This must be its most hidden power. For as soon as translation has the intention of literality, it liberates, albeit fragmentarily, pure language. What this means for us, moving away from the Messianic connotations that are historically peculiar to Benjamin, is language itself, in its existence-as-letter. Language's *existence-as-letter* is most likely what Benjamin means by:

In dieser reinen Sprache, die nichts mehr meint und nichts mehr ausdrückt, sondern als ausdrucksloses und schöpferisches Wort das in allen Sprachen Gemeinte ist

(p. 19. para 11)

In this pure language, which no longer means anything and no longer expresses anything, but which as a meaningless and creative word is that which is meant by all languages

Cette pure langue qui ne vise plus rien et n'exprime plus rien, mais qui est ce qui est visé, en tant que parole sans expression et créatrice, dans toutes les langues

(Berman)

[Literal translation of Berman's French translation:

> This pure language that no longer intends anything and no longer expresses anything, but which is that which is intended, as a creative word without expression, in all languages]

This is what is manifest – chaotically – in the becoming of languages; this is what translation liberates in the literary text. Everything that the original text might intend, whatever it is that it communicates, whatever it expresses (and a text is *also* nothing without this aim), is not translation's concern. Translation worries about *the pure letter of the text*. Or at least this is its most intimate *power* which is still hidden from it.

Benjamin's greatness, historically speaking, lies in having announced this pure power. I am less concerned with the Messianic framework of his reflection. It was by reflecting on Hölderlin's historic translations that Benjamin was able to expose this *second*, speculative rather than cultural, essence of translation. But in Hölderlin what matters is man's relationship to the letter, to the founding letter, and not the contingent Messianic constructions that spring up around this relationship.

Not only is this the case, but it is crucial that Benjamin's position not be interpreted as a choice between the two potentialities of translation – meaning *or* the letter. Because Benjamin does not think this way – rather *he considers the relationship between the meaning and the letter of translation speculatively*. This relationship is of the kind where meaning does not disappear but for the first time is re-ordered in relation to the letter, the letter being an ineluctable element. Moreover, translation is the only place where meaning appears as something that is, for man's residency-within-language, both secondary and real. The fact that translation has been viewed as both a liberation and expansion of meaning is a historical development that obscures its essence. Translation is scandalous because, while transmitting meaning, it relegates it to a lesser rank, like something which is, in the being of language, at best a consequence of a non-communicative, non-expressive, but 'creative' being.

Creative, *schöpferisch*, is a hackneyed and vague term. Benjamin does not go beyond it. He does not think the essence of pure language (he dreams it more than he thinks it).

This essence is that of *language itself*, as his great and only rival, Heidegger, thought it (or began to think it). Today Benjamin has to be read – and I will say this again – the Benjamin of 'The Task of the Translator' has to be read in the light of *On the Way to Language* [*Unterwegs zur Sprache*] (1959). Because there we find the essence of language thought as non-communicative and non-expressive, and it is not insignificant that Heidegger interrogates Humboldt and Hamann, whose work Benjamin knew well – Scholem thought he could well have become their successor. Pure language is language that is a non-signifying unfolding of the world. This is Heidegger's concept. From here one can begin to reflect upon translation in a way that Heidegger did not, or if so only in fragments.

For me, pure language is, in all its fullness, natural language. And this natural language is the language of *orality*.

'Creative', an under-defined term in Benjamin's writing, means: creative-of-the-world. That pure language which, anterior to any expression and communication, *establishes* a world. Translation, through its ability to render subtle meaning, more subtle than is the case in literary texts or in worldly communications, is one of the most powerful (and *violent*) means of performing – of giving a stage to – pure language – to language itself, in other words.

A new conceptualisation of the freedom of the translator, and of translation, stems from this, says Benjamin.

This freedom is confirmed and affirmed in literality, where the translator makes the syntax of the foreign language fall with all its might on her own language. This is the most 'violent' movement of all. Because what it produces is precisely a scintillating display of language itself. The language in a translation of this kind is not a bastard mixture – say – of Latin and French, it is, via the collision of the two languages, an affirmation of language itself in its existence-as-letter. Historically, of course, languages contaminate each other, mix, come into contact. But via translation, they succeed in releasing their existence-as-letter, their existence-as-language. In tearing the text and its language away from the sphere of communication, translation liberates the pure essence of language, which is the letter.

The image – the final image of this text – of translation only touching meaning in a *flüchtig*, fleeting manner, springs from here. The levity of the contact with what is 'heavy' and 'strange' (a stranger to the essential liberty of language) in the literary text is ironic – Benjamin himself says so – and it is the most intimate foundation of irony itself. Because the intention of irony is to lighten our load – the load of meaning, to the benefit of something more elevated than mere play, to the benefit of the supreme liberty of language. Any great translation *is* ironic.

And this is where the second citation, from Pannwitz, comes in. I have re-translated it from German, uneasily, orally.[3] Where Gandillac tries to 'comb' it nicely (see Gandillac 1971:274), I feel that it should be left unkempt. Strangely enough, this passage has also been cited as though these are Benjamin's words – notably by Meschonnic – and – it has to be said – who reads Pannwitz anyway? But these are also words of historical importance on the subject of translation.

> our transpositions even the best proceed from the wrong basis they want to germanify the indian greek english instead of indianing greekifying englishing the german. they have a much more significant respect for their own language customs than they do for the spirit of the foreign work
>
> *(Pannwitz 1917:240)*

> the fundamental mistake of the transposer is that he holds on to the coincidental status of his own language instead of allowing it to be violently moved by the foreign language. even when he is translating from a very distant language he has to push back to the final elements of language itself

where word image sound move into one he has to broaden and deepen his language through the foreign we have no concept of the extent to which this is possible the degree to which each language can be transformed a language differentiates itself from a language almost like a dialect from a dialect but this doesn't happen when one takes it far too lightly but when one takes it seriously enough.

(ibid.:242)[4]

This text is of interest in two ways: in the collision of languages that it is proposing – without grounding this in anything, as Benjamin points out – and in its push to the 'final elements' of language itself where word, image and sound come together – like one dialect and another.

This brings us to the *oral* essence of language itself, and the mention of dialect is no coincidence. All languages are *language* in the sense that they are *dialects*. There is no *le langage—les langues* (from genus to species), but *la langue*—dialects. The domain in which translation has the being-letter of language (*la langue*) as its intention is dialect. French and Chinese are two dialects of the same language. This is the vision that Pannwitz invites us to share and Benjamin sensed it, without, in turn, thinking it. It is of the utmost importance that we start to think languages as dialects and as things that fundamentally unfold in orality. This does not imply that we should shun 'the written' since of course there is no essential writing that does not maintain an essential link with orality. Translation, which is ostensibly restricted to the transmission of meaning from one written text to another – happens in the *accentuation* of the orality present in the original. The attention paid to the *letter* is therefore inseparable from the attention paid to *orality*.

Benjamin said that pure language was liberated from the written. This presupposes that the written is the sign of meaning and communication. We are not obliged to follow him on this point. What is truer, and decisive, is that liberating or redeeming the pure language enclosed in the foreign language means liberating – which is to say manifesting, *darstellen* – orality.

When translation comes to an understanding of its relationship with orality, it will have assimilated Benjamin's thought – and Pannwitz's. The translation of texts – whether poetry, theatre, children's books, novels, psychoanalysis, religious texts or law – is an encounter with orality. The element that has to be eradicated (unlike *meaning*) or accentuated. This does not undermine the written. The written is never heard so much as when orality is inscribed within it. Oral language is language itself. The ultimate definition of translation is that which frees the spark of orality within the original *written* text. The original itself cannot do this. The passage from one language to another *can* free the oral from the written. This is an unimaginably difficult impulse and it should be the translator's only desire.

That the orality of texts is only freed in and through translation requires further thought. This is the tremendous responsibility of today's translator.

This orality is linked to a problem that Benjamin knew well and that is the problem of tradition. *Traduttore traditore*: we might translate the Italian adage as 'translator, transmitter of tradition'. Tradition is oral. It is oral even when its pillars are written or stored on a computer. The mystery of translation is in fact that it is a vehicle of tradition – *the* vehicle of tradition. There is no tradition without translation. Translation preserves and activates this linguistic relationship to the world that we call tradition. For translation, everything is a dialect. The non-dialect becoming of languages is identical to their becoming. It is a system of signs and communication. Translation can act as a *dialectising* agent through which language returns to its oral origins. Through history, of course, the opposite trajectory seems to have held true. But all great translation is dialectical. This is true of Luther, of Hölderlin, of Klossowski, of Leyris with Hopkins.

In saying this, I am going beyond Benjamin. I am saying – quite boldly – and running the risk of all kinds of equivocations, that pure language is dialect. Or more precisely: the dialectal essence of language.

From this premise, we can (re-)read the final paragraph in an unconventional manner. The sacred text discussed there – the Bible – is both dialectal and oral, as Meschonnic taught us. And this text is simultaneously un-translatable (if only in the sense evoked here) and translatable. Which explains Gandillac's surprising *contre-sens*.[5] This textual *contre-sens* utters what goes unsaid in Benjamin's text – namely that the sacred text is untranslatable because it is oral and dialectal – and is always thus.

My commentary, as you can see, does not proceed line by line, it has come unstuck. I believe that as I finish – hastily, which is no excuse – I *have to* come unstuck. Benjamin's concept of pure language does not gain by *only* being approached from its Messianic purposefulness, because we cannot do anything with this (apart from inhabiting the same problematic as Benjamin, which is impossible). If we approach it with Benjamin himself and, subsequently, as the dialectal essence of language, *then* it becomes possible to appropriate it, because I would argue that the task of the translator, today, in all spheres, is linked to this constellation:

dialect   orality

———————

tradition

The central figure in this constellation is *tradition*. All the more so because today translation is caught up in an antagonistic constellation – translation as the transformability and infinite commutability of the written. This is the case in both the literary and technical spheres. This is why – and I have said this before – I deliberately chose the form of the *commentary* for my analysis of Benjamin. Commentary is a traditional form of approaching a text. But because commentary has established a tradition over many centuries, translation has to battle its *traditionalism*. Strangely, this has happened through a rejection of its historical *artisanality*, which has focused on meaning. Today, translation has to call upon all the instruments of modern technology to conquer its traditionalism – its own non-methodological *esprit-de-système*. These are not things that Benjamin ever said but I am sure that he would have thought them since we know that the link between tradition and technology – in the broadest sense – had become the centre of his thought.

Notes

1 [Berman translates *Wiedergabe* as *la restitution* [restitution]. I have followed Berman's translation throughout this cahier, even if I consider the English 'rendition/rendering' to be more neutral and closer to the German term.]

2 [Benjamin's 'über alle Mitteilung hinaus' [beyond all communication] functions as a separate clause in the first sentence of this citation. In modern German one would normally expect to see a clause like this offset with commas. Grammatically it is not connected with the two sets of contrasting adjective/participles – 'verborgen oder deutlicher, durch ihn gebrochen oder machtvoller' – that precede it, even if the absence of commas and the presence of the comparative forms means that one is tempted to read it that way. Berman, however, has made this separate clause part of a comparison, 'plus puissant que toute communication' [more powerful than any communication]. Arguably Benjamin's use of the comparative form of the adjectives *deutlich* and *machtvoll* is a rhetorical device and does not imply an actual comparison; hence I have opted for the translations 'extremely clear' and 'quite potent'. Semantically, there may not be much difference between Berman's translation and my own, but the emphasis is slightly different, probably because of how Berman has interpreted the (admittedly confusing) comparative forms.]

3 ['nos traductions même les meilleures partent d'un faux principe elles veulent germaniser l'indien le grec l'anglais au lieu d'indianiser de gréciser d'angliciser l'allemand. Elles ont bien plus de respect face aux usages propres de la langue que devant l'esprit de l'œuvre étrangère. […] L'erreur fondamentale du traduisant est qu'il maintient l'état fortuit de sa propre langue au lieu de se laisser puissamment mouvoir par la langue étrangère. (Berman) Surtout lorsqu'il traduit d'une langue très éloignée, il lui faut remonter aux éléments ultimes du langage même, là où se rejoignent mot, image, son; il lui faut élargir et approfondir sa propre langue grâce à la langue étrangère; on n'imagine pas à quel point la chose est possible; jusqu'à quel degré une langue peut se transformer; de langue à langue il n'y a guère plus de distance que de dialecte à dialecte, mais cela non point quand on le prend trop à la légère, bien plutôt quand on les prend assez au sérieux' (Gandillac 1971:274).] The orthography and the absence of capital letters replicate Pannwitz's German text.

4 ['Unsre übertragungen auch die besten gehn von einem falschen grundsatz aus sie wollen das indische griechische englische verdeutschen anstatt das deutsche zu verindischen vergriechischen verenglischen. sie haben eine viel bedeutendere ehrfurcht vor den eigenen sprachgebräuchen als vor dem geiste des fremden werks […] Der grundsätzliche irrtum des übertragenden ist dass er den zufälligen stand der eignen sprache festhält anstatt sie durch die fremde sprache gewaltig bewegen zu lassen. er muss zumal wenn er aus einer sehr fernen sprache überträgt auf die letzten elemente der sprache selbst wo wort bild ton in eins geht zurück dringen er muss seine sprache durch die fremde erweitern und vertiefen man hat keinen begriff in welchem masze das möglich ist bis zu welchem grade jede sprache sich verwandeln kann sprache von sprache fast nur wie mundart von mundart sich unterscheidet dieses aber nicht wenn man sie allzu leicht sondern gerade wenn man sie schwer genug nimmt.']

5   The *contre-sens* in Gandillac's translation that Berman refers to is a mistranslation of the word 'übersetzbar' [translatable] (Benjamin 1991:21) as 'intraduisible' [untranslatable] (Gandillac 1971:275) in the final paragraph of Benjamin's text.

Bibliography

Benjamin, W., 1991 [1923]. Die Aufgabe des Übersetzers. In: R. Tiedemann and H. Schweppenhäuser, eds. 1991. *Gesammelte Schriften*. IV.I. Frankfurt am Main: Suhrkamp. pp.9–21.

Berman, A., 2008. *L'Âge de la traduction*. Paris: Presses Universitaires de Vincennes.

Gandillac, M. de, trans. 1971. La tâche du traducteur. In: *Œuvres I, Mythe et violence*. Paris: Denoël/Les Lettres Nouvelles. pp.261–275.

Heidegger, M., 1959. *Unterwegs zur Sprache*. Pfullingen: Verlag Günter Neske.

Pannwitz, R., 1917. *Die Krisis der europäischen Kultur*. Nürnberg: Verlag Hans Carl.

Rendall, S., 2000. A Note on Harry Zohn's Translation. In: L. Venuti, ed. 2000. *The Translation Studies Reader*. 1st ed. New York: Routledge. pp.9–11.

INDEX

For Product Safety Concerns and Information please contact our EU
representative GPSR@taylorandfrancis.com
Taylor & Francis Verlag GmbH, Kaufingerstraße 24, 80331 München, Germany

www.ingramcontent.com/pod-product-compliance
Lightning Source LLC
Chambersburg PA
CBHW071105100726
47908CB00008B/2269